Praise for *Toward a Public Theology in Myanmar*

This collection of essays is a bright example of an ecumenical and transnational discussion of sociopolitical and religious issues in a theological perspective. It is illuminating and is a valuable resource for teaching and encouraging future ministers to reflect on a biblical basis on the public dimension of their ministries in the Myanmar context.

Rev. Michael Biehl
Evangelische Mission Weltweit—Association
of Protestant Churches and Missions in Germany

Very few theological reflections have come out of the Myanmar soil, but *Toward a Public Theology in Myanmar*, like a breath of fresh air, brings new theological exploration. This is a valuable book for theological students, pastors, and theologians who have a passion for harmonious relations and peaceful coexistence. The book proposes diverse theological elements for peacebuilding from the perspective of the suffering people. Violence, the result of injustice, increases suffering to the people of Myanmar, but loving peace with justice can reduce suffering (*dukkha* in Pali). This book is a great source for finding theological elements and methods for a public theology in Myanmar to promote peace through justice.

Rev. Si Khaw, PhD
Associate General Secretary
Mara Evangelical Church in Myanmar

Even a cursory glance into this book establishes the deep connect that Myanmar, also called Burma, has with India. The countries share a common history of the spread of Christianity and therefore a common development of theological education. Several Indian liberation theologians ventured into the theological world of Burma and contributed significantly to the strengthening of the voices of young Burmese theologians. Dr. Dyanchand Carr, from India, stands out among them, and as this volume demonstrates, he among others took a firm decision to venture into the politically troubled, land-locked country of Burma and supported the development of a theology that is unique to that context.

What makes this book special is the commitment of theologians from Myanmar and India to support each other in the birth of a theology that matters to the people in their context of imposed military rule. This work offers a breath of fresh air as solidarity among these Asian theologies and theologians flourishes. It certainly sets the tone for a vibrant and creative future of solidarity and cooperation.

Dr. Aruna Gnanadason
Author of *With Courage and Compassion:*
Women and the Ecumenical Movement

This collection of essays is rare and exceptional as it attempts public theology informed by incisive analysis and insightful reflection on a range of complex and critical issues that characterize today's Myanmar. These essays give expression to the deeply cherished yearnings of people for the dawn of a polity of justice, peace, and freedom. Accompanied by deeply committed partners in some parts of the world, *Toward a Public Theology in Myanmar* testifies that partnership is an expression of mission that lives out God's intentions for a world of interconnected and interdependent relationships.

Rev. Dr. Deenabandhu Manchala
Former Southern Asia Area Executive of Global Ministries, United Church of Christ & Christian Church (Disciples of Christ), USA

Toward a Public Theology in Myanmar

Toward a Public Theology in Myanmar

Lal Tin Hre and David Selvaraj

editors

FORTRESS PRESS
MINNEAPOLIS

TOWARD A PUBLIC THEOLOGY IN MYANMAR

Library of Congress Control Number: 2023933043 (print)

Cover design: Savanah N. Landerholm
Cover image: Htun Teza on Unsplash

Print ISBN: 978-1-5064-9159-2
eBook ISBN: 978-1-5064-9160-8

This book is dedicated to Rev. Dr. Dhyanchand Carr, pastor, theologian, educator, and activist. His indomitable spirit, scholarship, and compassion have made this volume a reality.

CONTENTS

PART I

INTRODUCTION

1

THE JOURNEY LEADING TO THIS BOOK

David Selvaraj and Mar Lar Myint

This publication has been in the making for nearly three decades. While no one person can be credited for the volume, the Rev. Dr. Dhyanchand Carr should be singled out for his unwavering commitment to the study of reading and teaching the Bible "with new eyes." By his own admission, this process was triggered by his journeying with and learning to be in solidarity with suffering people for five decades and more. It is this perspective that has led other theologians in Asia, especially in Myanmar, to reflect on their situation and arrive at a way of doing theology in their context. A cursory glance at the contents of this volume will make it abundantly clear that it is primarily, and largely, an intellectual contribution of Burmese theologians, teachers in seminaries, and ecumenical leaders from Myanmar.

While the book, in its present form, was not envisaged in 1985, Rev. Dr. Albert Emmanuel of the World Association for Christian Communication (WACC) sowed the seeds for it. As the executive secretary of WACC, he devoted significant time and attention to the project of reading the Bible with new eyes, with Dr. Carr as a key resource person. In tracing the history of this book, we prepared a timeline with the history of the country as a backdrop. As will be clear to the reader, the content and intent are rooted in an understanding of Christian hope and transformation. In tracing the history of the country, we draw extensively from Rev. Pau Lian Mang,[1] who made a good contribution to the process leading up to this book. Dr. Pau Lian Mang has drawn from and extensively quoted the work of Topich and Leitich[2] in tracing the sociopolitical history of Myanmar from the early sixties to the earlier part of the century. Significant for our telling of the history of this book is that the timeline reveals that the work initiated by Emmanuel and Carr in 1985 ("reading the Bible with new eyes") is set against the sociopolitical "events" in Myanmar. Though a considerable amount of work can be recorded leading up to the book, the *idea* of the book itself was almost an accident. After a long day of teaching in Yangon and in humid conditions, during an evening of "fellowship," the question was posed to Carr, "What do you have to show for all these years of teaching the Bible and in challenging conditions? The evening passed. The seed was planted, germinated, and began to grow.

A brief dip into the history of Myanmar over the last four decades, as interpreted by Dr. Pau Lian Mang, sets the context and tone for the chapters presented here and lends gravitas to the history-telling of this book. Starting with a coup d'état spearheaded by General Ne Win in 1962, for half a century the country was "a country in the dark." In the guise of protecting "the nation" and saving it from being split, General Ne Win imposed a military dictatorship. The general's promise to return power to the people did happen in 1974. However, it did not happen in the manner that the people expected. During his twelve-year rule as a leader of

---

1   Pau Lian Mang, *Telic Eschatology: A Quest for Myanmar Theology of Hope* (Yangon: Association for Theological Education in Myanmar, 2019).

2   William Topich and Keith Leitich, *The History of Myanmar* (Santa Barbara: Greenwood Histories of the Modern Nation, 2013).

the coup, the general and his colleagues founded a political party, the Burma Socialist Programme Party (BSPP). This done, the generals switched from holding military positions to holding power as elected representatives, with Ne Win as president for the next fourteen years. Pau Lian Mang describes this period[3] up to 1988 vividly: "During all this time, Ne Win attempted various means to maintain his power: first, brutal crushing; second, imposing long-term curfew and banning public gatherings (affecting public transportation and food distribution); third, changing three presidents within a period of two months (Ne Win, Maung, Sein Lwin); and fueling the chaos in various ways so that military intervention would become a necessity and could be legitimized. Finally, on September 18, 1988, the Army Chief General Saw Maung staged a coup (though Ne Win was still behind the scenes). The alleged reason was exactly the same as before; the current situation compelled the army to save the nation from the impending total destruction." The author alludes to subsequent years, right up to the present, as a "self-perpetuating group dictatorship." While the spectacular electoral win by the National League for Democracy (NLD) and its leader and democracy idol, Aung San Suu Kyi, kindled hope within the country and across the world, the restrictions imposed on her by manipulative constitutional interpretation and rigged parliamentary processes diminished her tone and passion. Aung San Suu Kyi, who took a bold stand in 2011 against the government's increasing repression of ethnic minorities, has currently gone silent on the issue. Her silence on the atrocious crimes against the Rohingyas (Bengalis) on the western coast of Myanmar is baffling.

It is in such a context that reading the Bible with new eyes was preserved and passed on, literally from one generation to the next. Over the last seven years, Rev. Dr. Lal Tin Hre took the helm of the project, through the Association of Theological Education

3   Mang, *Telic Eschatology*, 159.

in Myanmar (ATEM). However, the role of his predecessor, Peter Joseph, must be highlighted. He was key in promoting and sustaining the process, guided and encouraged by the indomitable spirit and vision of Dr. Anna Say Pa of the Myanmar Institute of Theology. As a leader of the church, Bishop Tsan Say Tae (of the Anglican Church in Myanmar) stood tall and ensured "the project" had ecclesial support. As a key contributor to this book, Dr. Carr never tired of remembering the colleagues mentioned above with profound gratitude to God for their lives and theological commitment toward the reign of God and the reading of the Bible with new eyes. At this juncture of remembering and giving thanks, mention must be made of Dr. James Vijaykumar of the erstwhile Common Global Ministries and his successor, Dr. Deenabhandhu Manchala. The "silent" but significant support from the Global Ministries and the intellectual contribution of Vijaykumar and Manchala have brought the project to its final stage of completion. ATEM is duty-bound to acknowledge these generous gifts.

As in the case of the Apostle Paul, Dr. Carr was accompanied by younger friends and colleagues from India, a team that included Rev. Dr. John Jayaharan (former professor at Tamil Nadu Theological Seminary and currently senior minister in the Church of South India), Rev. Dr. Daniel Premkumar (former director of Dalit and Adivasi Concerns—CSI Synod and currently a leader of the Anawim Satsang), Prof. Lourdu Nathan (currently teaching philosophy at the Jawaharlal Nehru University, Delhi), Dr. Lalrindiki Ralte (dean, SCEPTRE, Kolkata), the late Rev. E. Deenadayalan (pastor and social activist), and Rev. D. Selvaraj (former director of diaconal ministry, CSI, and currently a leader of the Anawim Satsang). Rev. Dr. D. Manchala joined the team contributing to the workshops. The team worked closely and under the direction of Dr. Lal Tin Hre, executive secretary of ATEM.

The process over the last seven years leading up to the book included:

1. Workshops in Mandalay, Yangon, and Kutkai. Each workshop, with twenty-five participants on average, included seminarians, teachers, and pastors, all of whom were potential contributors to this volume. The content of the workshops included Bible study and theological reflection, social analysis, and methodology of doing social analysis.

2. Even while the workshops were being conducted, ATEM republished the book *Reading the Bible with New Eyes* by Dr. Dyanchand Carr, in Myanmar. The book was used as a text during the workshops and widely disseminated.

3. The workshops led to a writers' workshop at which time drafts of papers were presented and discussed.

4. Receiving articles and initial edits at Bangalore and subsequently in Myanmar.

5. Though it did not materialize, ATEM had considered plans for an intensive field visit/exposure for potential writers and teachers on the subject, to India. This is now being considered as a follow-up to this publication.

It is appropriate to observe that the methodology applied throughout the training period was participatory. More specifically, the facilitators applied a problem-posing pedagogy (Freire) and a praxis of action-reflection. This is clearly reflected in excerpts from the report of a workshop by Dr. Mar Lar Myint. A typical workshop included biblical reflections led by one of the facilitators or participants. This was followed by a detailed recap of the previous day's discussion, which led to spontaneous seeking of clarifications on the subject and related areas. Subsequent time was divided into three slots. First, reading the Bible from the socioeconomic/political context of Myanmar and the challenges within the church to such a process. This is reflected in the chapter by Dr. Lal Tin Hre. Second, a detailed social analysis, and third, methodologies to facilitate social analysis in varied contexts. The methodology provided an opportunity for participants representing different ethnic groups to share stories and experience the solidarity of others. The workshops applied simulation exercises and theater to ensure effective participation and to elicit grounded knowledge. The last two workshops focused on writing, with each potential contributor presenting his or her outline and inviting feedback. The participants selected were then invited to prepare a draft of their paper and receive feedback for a second time. The challenges, as expected, were largely due to writing in English. Subsequently, this was a challenge to the process of editing. That said, despite the challenges, participants emboldened by the spirit of God and encouragement of their peers have made significant contributions.

The chapters included in this volume vary in size and depth of theological acumen. This reflects the journey of a team from Myanmar and India, listening and learning from each other. The intention is for theologians, pastors, and public intellectuals from Southeast Asia, starting from the Association of Theological Education in South East Asia (ATESEA), to initiate or strengthen a discussion on the theme of public witness. In situations where the discussion has begun, we hope this contribution will add to the process. At a fundamental level, we hope this volume will trigger a rethink on mission in Myanmar in the context of reimposed military rule.

The volume is divided into three parts. The first includes this introduction, detailing the journey leading to the creation of this book and to the Association of Theological Education in Myanmar (ATEM); the second is a section on the theology of public witness and broad theoretical formulations; the third contains examinations of a wide array of contemporary issues on the ground. The articles resulted from the five workshops held for professional theologians from seminaries, social activists from a Christian faith background, and pastors.

We dedicate this book to the Rev. Dr. Carr for his unstinting labor of love and unflinching courage to speak truth to authority. ATEM express their gratitude to Global Ministry USA and Rev. Dr. Manchala in particular for his support and presence during the workshops. Finally, our thanks go to Koshy Mathew for his timely and efficient support in copyediting, and Fortress Press, particularly acquisitions editor Dr. Jesudas Athyal, for tolerating our tardiness and offering encouragement every step of the way.

In conclusion, we record lines from the Kairos Palestine document. Since it has already been published in the *Myanmar Journal of Theology*[4] it should serve as a reminder to readers. It is a document that spells out the theological imagination and hope of Christians and suffering people valiantly dealing with a punitive state and military power. Most significantly, this was brought out in the context of Advent even as we put the final touches to our book in Advent 2022:

> This document is Christian Palestine's word to the world about what is happening in Palestine. It is written at this time when we wanted to see the glory of the grace of God in this land and in the suffering of the people. In this historic document, we Palestinian Christians declare that the military occupation of our land is a sin against God and humanity and that any theology that legitimises the occupation is far from Christian teaching because true Christian theology is a theology of love and solidarity

---

4   *Myanmar Journal of Theology* 10 (April 2015), drafted in December 2009, accessed February 9, 2023, https://www.kairospalestine.ps/.

with the oppressed, a call to justice and equality among peoples. As Palestinian Christians, we hope that this document will provide the turning point to focus the efforts of the peace-loving peoples in the world, especially our Christian sisters and brothers.

With prayers for discernment, the conviction of Christian hope, and thanks to God who is Emmanuel, we invite readers to come on this journey of exploring a theology of public witness for Myanmar. Our hope is that the reflections by the people of Burma for the church and seminaries in Burma are that God will raise up *spirit-inspired facilitators of transformation.*

2

ASSOCIATION FOR THEOLOGICAL EDUCATION IN MYANMAR (ATEM)

Lal Tin Hre

INTRODUCTION

The Association for Theological Education in Myanmar (ATEM) has its roots in the deeply felt need for national leadership back in the 1960s, when, in 1964, missionaries were ordered to leave the country. This unexpected turn of events placed the management and responsibility of both churches and seminaries upon the shoulders of the then unprepared national leadership. If for Christians everything that happens, happens for the glory of God, we believe that what took place in Burma (Myanmar)—the military coups and the self-imposed moratorium—all point to God and His working grace.

In 1962, the military staged a coup, established a Revolutionary Council, and imposed a self-moratorium, severing ties with the world at large. But we have to admit our failures and lack of courage, our trust in God to lead us, for we (the church) retreated into our own shell or compound, shying away from the world during that period. It took more than two decades to prepare ourselves and gather the courage to emerge. By then the country had—in 1979—opened its doors to the world outside, which brought back the hope of having missionaries again.

But that was not to be. The whole exercise, as we look back, is that the church in Burma was led into contextualizing the gospel and shedding its foreignness. Since then the question of leadership has become central to the life and witness of the church in Burma (especially members of the Burma (Myanmar) Council of Churches (BCC) and those historical churches that received missionaries). But then, it was so wonderful to witness the hand of God weaving the current programs of the day into preparing national leadership.

ARCHITECTS FOR BURMA PROGRAM

In 1959, the two architects and pioneers of the Burma Program met again at Rev. Dr. Chit Maung's residence. Rev. Dr. Chit Maung silently welcomed and gave his full support, and Rev. Dr. Kosuke Koyama actively promoted the Burma program.

As early as the late 1960s the Burma Program started under the deanship of Dr. Kosuke Koyama, when the urgent need for theological leadership was deeply felt. God opened the way through the South East Asia Graduate School of Theology (SEAGST), which launched its correspondence course leading to the master's in theology program. Dean Koyama took great pains to promote the advancement of the newly established SEAGST, according to Dr. Yeow Choo Lak.

The Council of Churches shared this opportunity with other members. Because of the difficulties of the situation, the so-called "Burma Section" of the Burma, Malaysia, Singapore, and Thailand Area was established to overlook the program in Burma. At 11 a.m. on March 9, 1977, at the Burma Baptist Convention Guest House,

Dr. Emerito Nacpil bestowed Master's of Theology degrees on the first six graduates of the Burma Program.

Rev. Werner Luoma from Indonesia, who has experience in this work, was invited and had discussions for two days, after which the Theological Education by Extension (TEE) concept was presented to the trustees of the theological schools. The TEE program was developed to meet the growing need in the area for theologically equipped and mission-oriented personnel through using nonformal educational methods. The TEE program was managed by the Study and Education Committee and appointed a full-time coordinator, Peter Joseph, in 1979, and subsequently the program gained momentum.[1]

COMMISSION FOR THE COOPERATION OF THE CHURCHES FOR HIGHER THEOLOGICAL EDUCATION

The commission included church leaders from the ten member churches, principals of the Burma Institute of Theology (BIT), the Myanmar Institute of Christian Theology (MICT), Holy Cross Theological College (HCTC), and Rev. U Ba Hmyin, Rev. Victor San Lone, Archbishop Ah Mya (Rtd), Rev. U Ba Ohn, Prof. U Khin Maung Din, Dr. U. Kyaw Than, Rev. U. Aung Khin, and Peter Joseph (later honorary secretary). After two years, on April 20, 1982, it became operational and submitted a report to the 68th AGM at Toungoo on May 6–9, outlining these suggestions: the pooling of faculty resources from member churches for the promotion of higher theological education; the promotion of a reference library for higher theological education; the standardization

---

1   1977/78 Study and Education Committee Annual Report to BCC, 68, 69.

of the curriculum in schools across Burma. To this the Toungoo AGM responded by suggesting that WCC Bossey types of training be promoted, and that a union of theological schools was formed, while aiming and working toward establishing a Union Theological Seminary.

On November 1–4, 1983, the first ecumenical workshop on curriculum and seminar on theological education were held at the Theological Institute in Mandalay. The seminar came up with the proposal to form the "Association for Upgrading of Theological Education in Burma," which was submitted to the commission. The commission agreed to the proposal and sent out consent letters asking for endorsements from the twelve member churches and major theological institutions (BCC-125/83) on two issues: the formation of the Union Theological Seminary and the formation of the Association for Theological Education in Burma.

The second Ecumenical Seminar on Theological Education was held on October 24–26, 1985, at the Theological Institute in Mandalay, where the following eight schools expressed their wish to join the association if formed. These schools were the founding institutions of ATEB:

Burma Institute of Theology, Rangon

Burma Institute of Christian Theology, Rangon

Holy Cross Theological College, Rangon

Kachin Theological Seminary, Myitkyina

Zomi Theological College, Falam

Emmanuel Divinity School, Mohgin

Tahan Theological Seminary, Kalaymyo

Theological Institute, Mandalay

FOUNDING OF THE ASSOCIATION FOR THEOLOGICAL EDUCATION IN BURMA (ATEB)

God has His plans and when the time became right He opened an avenue and ordained it for cooperation and coordination in building theological leadership for the church. With the blessing of the Burma Council of Churches, the "Association for Theological Education in Burma" (ATEB) was established on May 12, 1986, at a Special Theological Assembly held at the Burma Institute of Theology, Insein, Rangoon, with the following aims and objectives:[2] to pool faculty resources from member churches for the promotion of higher theological education; to promote a reference library for higher theological education; to standardize the curriculum in the schools across Burma. To this the Toungoo AGM responded by suggesting that WCC Bossey types of training be promoted, and that a union of theological schools be formed while aiming and working toward establishing a Union Theological Seminary.

PhD PROGRAM IN MYANMAR, IMGS

A PhD program under the Institute of Myanmar Graduate Studies (IMGS) was created by ATEM. The Higher Theological Education (HTE) Committee of ATEM discussed the need for and importance of initiating a PhD program in Myanmar in April 2019 and agreed to recommend this to the triennial meeting on May 3, 2019.[3] It was decided to explore ways to run the program in line with the procedure of ATESEA.[4] Dr. H. S. Wilson (FTESEA executive director) and Dr. Limuel Equina (ATESEA, executive director),

---

2   "A History of Association for Theological Education in Myanmar," unpublished manuscript.

3   HTE Meeting Minutes.

4   ATEM Board of Management Meeting Minutes No. 10.

great friends of Myanmar, were invited to help us and we sought their advice on the vision.

They reaffirmed that this venture would serve the long-overdue need for advanced theological research in Myanmar and agreed to support this noble work. In the light of their advice, ATEM organized a number of meetings and seminars/consultations and, on June 20, 2019, established a consortium named the Institute of Myanmar Graduate Studies (IMGS), with three seminaries—Karen Baptist Theological Seminary, Myanmar Institute of Theology, and Kachin Theological College & Seminary—as founding members. ATEM records its deepest appreciation to the three founding schools for their pioneering hard work amidst the overloaded schedules in their respective seminaries. Currently, these schools are the only schools that offer a Master's degree and we hope other schools will be able to join the IMGS when they upgrade to a Master's degree program.

Since this is a new program, we did not have much experience and we needed expertise in the field, especially to develop a "Consortium administrative structure of IMGS," including "the relationship between IMGS and ATEM." Dr. Wati Longchar was invited to present a draft proposal on an Ecumenical Consortium Administrative Structure for ATEM on July 15, 2019, at Patrick Seminar Hall. The paper and discussions paved the way for the adoption of the structures. Based on a strong endorsement from ATEM, ATESEA has accepted IMGS as one of its doctoral centers. We thank ATESEA for its support and encouragement.

The formation of IMGS (meetings, seminars, consultations, and a block grant to IMGS) was mainly supported by Barnabas Fund and FTESEA.

IMGS was envisaged to train leaders not only in Myanmar but also in the Mekong regions. With an understanding that we can achieve our goal only when we work together and stand together in solidarity, we decided to work together with ecumenical national bodies, including the Mekong region (Laos, Cambodia, Thailand, Vietnam, etc.).

ATEM BUILDINGS: ES QUARTERS AND ADMINISTRATIVE OFFICE

Administrative Office

The ATEM office officially began in a small room on January 1, 1997, with Rev. Peter Joseph as the first executive secretary. The Myanmar Council of Churches shared its storage room no. 209 (10' x 10'), which was used for general purposes and was turned into the office. During Rev. Smith Ngulh Za Thawng's time as general secretary of the MCC, at the end of 2001 the ATEM office gave way to the MCC library extension. It moved to a much smaller room (8' x 15'), room 401 on the top floor, and it was operated as the command center until 2015. Rev. Peter Joseph, who served for twenty-three years and retired from ATEM in 2009, was located in that office.

ATEM Office

As mandated by the board of management meeting in 2015,[5] the office bearers in Yangon worked very hard to acquire a new space for ATEM's administrative office. With the contributions from member schools and a grant of 20,000 Euros from Evangelische Missio Weltweit (EMW), a new location for the ATEM administrative office (15' x 60') was purchased in March 2015 at no. 157, Blk.- 2, Thiri 3rd Street, Hlaing Township, Yangon.

The dedication service of the space was held on March 16, 2015. Wati Longchar, the invited facilitator for the Second Research and Teaching Methodology Workshop (March 16–18, 2015), delivered the dedication message. The office was moved

---

5   Ref. ATEM Board of Management Meeting Minute, No. 17/2015.

from MESC (MCC) to a new office in April 2015. ATEM records its endless thanks to the MCC for renting the room for over twenty-three years. This building/office has now been converted as housing for the executive secretary.

ATEM Research and Administrative Center Building (ARAC)

One of the main projects of ATEM, the Myanmar Ecumenical Research Center (MERC), formerly the Myanmar Theological Research Center (MTERC),[6] was begun on November 27, 2002. The Myanmar Baptist Churches Union (MBCU) donated a small piece of land. However, due to the financial situation and other unknown reasons, the building could not be completed and the land was taken back by the owner.

At the board of management meeting in 2018 it was decided to establish a guest house project, because participants in training programs and delegates for the meeting had been facing difficulty finding lodgings, especially those who came from outside Yangon city.[7] ATEM worked out the project and shared the idea with ATEM partners far and near.

Unexpectedly, the Oxford Center in England came forward to support the PhD program in Myanmar under the supervision of ATEM. The center was also willing to provide a research building to implement the program. ATEM carefully discussed the matter at its second board of management meeting on May 2, 2019. Based on ATEM's unfinished project, MERC and the guest house, the meeting unanimously accepted the initiative of the Oxford Center and entrusted executive committee members in Yangon to search for a suitable building.

After several meetings, the building project was confirmed in a suitable building and the search committee agreed to inform

6   ATEM Triennial Meeting, dated May 5–6, 2011.
7   ATEM Board of Management Meeting Minutes, No. 010: 2018.

the Barnabas Fund. With full support from the Barnabas Fund in Oxford, two flats were purchased in July 2019. The ground floor flat is designated for administrative offices, a meeting room, publication office space, and guest rooms, and the fifth floor houses a seminar room called "Patrick Seminar Hall," a guest room, and a kitchen. The building is called the ATEM Research and Administrative Center (ARAC), and the office in Hlaing Township was moved to the new building in September 2020. The building is owned by ATEM.

What a wonderful blessing! Praise the Lord! ATEM records its sincere thanks to the Barnabas Fund for its generous and loving gift.

The dedication/inauguration service was successfully held on August 8, 2019, attended by presidents/delegates from a member school, national leaders—including Dr. Simon Pau Khan En, the former president of ATEM; Dr. Jabu, vice president of MBC; and Rev. Palmerston, MCC, GS—and international guests. ATEM president Dr. Aye Aye Maw led the service; Prof. Patrick Sookhdeo, international director of the Barnabas Fund delivered a message; the Right Rev. Archbishop Michael Jackson offered a dedication prayer; and Rev. Zothanmawia, emeritus bishop, pronounced the benediction.

ATEM is now equipped with a building with modern facilities and two guest rooms with air-conditioning, and the building is capable of accommodating up to fifteen persons.

ATEM'S MAIN CONCERNS

Currently, ATEM engages in the following activities:

Workshops/Seminars/Consultations

ATEM has been organizing workshops, seminars, and consultations with financial support from friends and organizations from outside the country. At least seven or eight different programs have been conducted every year in various locations and on different topics depending on the availability of individuals with the appropriate skills and background. The workshops aimed to promote faculty who are teaching particular subjects. ATEM continues to organize a series of workshops on various issues depending on the funds available.

Faculty Development Program

The faculty development program is one of the main missions of ATEM and has three main categories:

1. Sending our faculty members abroad for higher theological education (for MA in librarianship, MTh, and ThD).

2. Conducting the master's in theology program in the country (formerly called South East Asia Graduate School of Theology–Myanmar Area, SEAGST–MM). The SEAGST program was replaced by the Asia Theological Union (ATU) in 2012. Trinity Theological College in Singapore, Chung Chi College, and Lutheran Theological Seminary in Hong Kong are our partner seminaries. About seventy-five faculty members have graduated with doctoral and master's degrees, both in Myanmar and in other parts of West Asia. The Association of Protestant Churches and Missions in Germany (EMW) and the Anglican Church in Canada are also deeply involved in our faculty development program. A faculty exchange program among ATEM member schools was also successfully rearranged.

3. Seminars, workshops, and consultations among the faculty members within the seminary itself. Only a few seminaries under ATEM have been able to arrange this type of program to date.

Librarianship Training

Library science is one of the most important areas in developing theological education. ATEM tries to find possible ways for a one-year (or more) MDiv in library science course for member institutions, and is grateful for the kind assistance of the Mekong Mission Forum, based in the Lutheran Theological Seminary, to arrange a one-year librarianship course (MA in librarianship) from LTS, for those who were engaged as full-time librarians in their respective schools. Some seminaries do not have professional librarians and face problems in arranging or classifying books.

Ministers' Institute

ATEM felt that theological training should not be confined to theological institutions, but should also extend to Christian ministers and pastors who are serving in their respective churches and denominations. With the support of Mekong Mission Forum, based in the Lutheran Theological Seminary, ATEM has conducted fifteen conferences called "Ministers' Institutes" on various topics in different locations across the country. The main aims and objectives of the Ministers' Institutes are:

- to share new insights and new knowledge in the theological field with ministers who are serving in their respective parishes;

- to strengthen the ministers and their ministry through lectures and discussions;

- to provide mutual support between theological educators and ministers;

- to look for a mutual understanding and a better partnership among the ministers from various denominations.

Publications

Knowing the difficulties of bringing books into Myanmar from outside the country, ATEM tries to reproduce some useful books for students and faculty at a cheaper rate. Several books have been published with the support of international partners, including *The Westminster Dictionary of Theological Terms (in Myanmar)*. We thank Danmission, Langham Partnership (UK), and ETE/WCC for journeying with us on these publication projects. An annual journal, *Myanmar Journal of Theology*, is also published and distributed by ATEM.

Feminist Theology

ATEM encourages its member schools to offer feminist theology and has conducted occasional workshops and seminars for faculty who are teaching the subject. The time is ripe to recruit those faculty members to strengthen their knowledge and uplift their teaching capacity. With the financial support of Danmission, a feminist theology workshop was held in 2012 and resulted in a book, entitled *Rice Salad Table: Myanmar Women Doing Theology Together*, published in the same year with a print run of 500 copies, with another 500 copies reprinted in 2013, and 1,000 copies in 2019. The book was well received both by teachers and by students.

PART II

THEOLOGICAL
PERSPECTIVES
AND THEORETICAL
FORMULATIONS

3

THE THEOLOGICAL BASIS FOR PUBLIC THEOLOGY

Dhyanchand Carr

PREAMBLE

"Public Witness" is used here in the sense of Christian obligation to witness with accompanying involvement to the proclamation of Jesus about the emergence of the Just Reign of God to the whole world of human affairs. The word "public" needs to be clarified. In the United Kingdom, for example, children of the very rich were educated by private tutors. When schools which were intended to educate a larger number of students emerged through private initiatives, these schools were called "public" schools. However, the children who went to these "public" schools were mostly from privileged rich families and the children from less affluent communities did not have access to these "public" schools. The word "public" here is used in the sense that "private" schools are meant for privileged people. Most people could not dream of sending their children to any of these "public" schools, then as now.

The meaning of the term "public" radically changed later when the democratization of politics began; it came to refer to the larger sections of people who form the unit of the "republic." The people of the nation are deemed public and, accordingly, government undertakings were bound to be opened to the public. And hence the use of the term "public" came to refer to public works undertaken by the ruling government for the welfare of the people. The term "public" in this sense is used in an inclusive manner, that is, something meant for everyone without deference to social status or political clout.

BEARING PUBLIC WITNESS

Bearing public witness implies being concerned about the well-being of all people in accordance with God's purposes for the whole world. Public witnessing, therefore, includes being involved in public affairs, namely, the approbation of justice for all people, and it is both a social and political commitment and involvement to uphold justice to work for a government of the people and for the people. Public witness to/of the Gospel of Jesus Christ is an inclusive term with a wide range of meanings—it is focused on the well-being of all, so that peace adjudicated by justice prevails. This is discerned as God's will, as Jesus taught us to pray that *God's Kingdom Come* and *God's Will Be Done on Earth as It Is in Heaven*. Jesus also said that his disciples should stop worrying about their daily needs and concentrate on God's Just Reign and God's Justice. Once this goal is achieved, worrying about where their next meal comes from or what to wear and similar things would become unnecessary. When peace with justice prevails everyone's needs would be taken care of; it is part and parcel of God's agenda to realize His Kingdom on earth. It is our faith that God has acted in Jesus to establish and maintain human societies of peace with justice for all.

The social and political milieu is such that injustice is widespread with millions suffering deprivation; even so-called democratic governance is perverted/diverted/forced to serve the interests of the rich and powerful or ethnic/religious majoritarian groups. Developed nations exploit undeveloped nations. This is not a new phenomenon and is not restricted to particular nations and societies. Unfortunately, such an illegitimate and unjust political and cultural situation(s) is understood/interpreted as natural and divinely ordered by the Almighty Sovereign Lord. This is a gross misunderstanding of the public witness of the message of the gospels. Such misunderstanding is as old as urbanization, when people began to live in communities developing culture and systems of governance, often called the beginnings of civilization.

In the Bible, in the days of Isaiah (eighth century BCE), the prophet observes that the rich were enlarging their ownership of property, adding house to house and land upon land so that ordinary people were left without space (Isa 5:8). But the prophet also challenged the rich people of Israel as those whose houses were filled with plunder and spoil from the poor (Isa 3:14b) and charged high interests on loans, which led to a wide gap between the rich and the poor. Such situations are true even today in most nations. Given that injustice exists in one form or another in every part of the world, the demands of the deprived people for justice are bound to be met with violence. The state or the government agencies unwittingly take the side of the rich and powerful and crush the aspirations of the poor, although they are supposed to be representing the people. This leads to a lack of peace because there is a denial of justice and a violation of human rights.

The reign of God desires peace with justice to prevail in all human communities and nations. Psalm 85:10 speaks of a dream of justice and peace for each other. This will happen when there is a faithful response from people to God's measures of inspiration and gracious empowerment in diverse ways (through prophetic voices of the challenge; through living examples of committed people who prioritize the values of justice and peace above their own aspirations; through the story of their life and through counter-cultural teachings), the people of God bearing witness to Jesus, God's Son, the anointed Messiah, there is the possibility of public witness, that is, to live the gospel in faith in the human community. This is the most important aspect of the Christian faith that Jesus came to initiate and execute—the process of justice and peace kissing each other by overcoming the powers of evil which were the root cause of injustice. Jesus began his ministry by announcing that the *Just Reign of God* was about to dawn. The days of the realm of the powers of evil would soon be over if only the people of God turned around, gave up their allegiance to the powers of evil, and started working together with God to make the world accept God as its ruler. But we need a clear understanding of how God facilitates the process. That would be the foundational task of the invitation to public witness to the Just Reign of God.

Jesus, the son of God, came as a human person and shared the life of the poor living as a carpenter. He was baptized by John the Baptist when he received the call to be the Servant and Messiah (the role of both is to establish justice), and was endowed by the Holy Spirit as had been prophesied by Isaiah (11:1-2). Soon after he was baptized and endowed by the Holy Spirit, Jesus began his ministry by proclaiming the nearness of God's Reign and calling people to turn around and follow the demands of the Kingdom of God, that is, to engage in the development of a counter-culture enshrining the values of God's Just Reign.

MISCONCEPTIONS IN THEOLOGICAL REFLECTIONS

In Jesus's understanding, the whole world was being ruled by the demonic realm. Even Jewish religion, usually called a religion of ethical monotheism based on God's Law, had been infiltrated by the forces of the devil. Such a situation must be resisted to bring about peace and justice. And, by extension, the lies and the deceptions that govern all religious beliefs are that:

- God is a benevolent despot to the respective chosen peoples; such convictions of exclusivity sow dissension and pave the way for lack of peace.

- It is God who appoints even tyrannical rulers and so all that happens is willed by God.

- Cultures of domination such as patriarchy, racial supremacist ways of oppressing vulnerable groups, the feudal and capitalist exploitative ways of rich landlords and industrialists, and all other hegemonies are in accordance with the will of God.

Jesus maintained that all these were in accordance with the strong demonic power which had usurped God's throne. These are but deceptions planted by the demonic forces and are internalized by most people, as they do not consider that God fundamentally respects human freedom and hence does not intrude to recreate a human world order.

Jesus envisaged his mission as that of a stronger force than the strong man in control over human affairs. He had come to oust the demonic by disarming and rendering it inactive and establishing God's reign. The fundamental requisite for this to happen was for people in control of human affairs to turn around and cooperate with God. For it was through the power structures of the world of human affairs that the demonic held sway. But people preferred the demonic realm that closed its eyes to their corrupt, exploitative, and extortionist ways of exercising power. God's reign would make it impossible for them to continue their arrogant ways of extortion and selfishness. The son of God chooses solely the poor and the oppressed in order that they experience peace and harmony. Because of this, the powers that be of religion or state colluded to eliminate Jesus. The death of Jesus was in fact a death blow to the demonic realm as God raised him from the dead and made him Messiah and Lord. However, even those who came to believe in his resurrection and accept him as Lord started interpreting his death and resurrection as an event of salvation to eternal life for believers. The proclamation of the Kingdom of God with which Jesus's ministry began fell by the wayside and so the demonic was back in the saddle. Awareness about the side-tracking of the gospel of the Kingdom to that of the gospel of personal salvation of the believers is beginning to dawn upon the church, especially in the ecumenical circles. The call of Jesus to seek God's reign and God's justice is beginning to be emphasized. There is also the awareness that the church alone cannot fulfil God's plan to bring the whole world under a reign of Peace with Justice. There would need to be a cumulative effort incorporating all those who have a commitment for justice irrespective of their faith affiliation and even if they are atheists with a commitment to work for justice. This means that, rather than create a large church membership, we need to enlarge the number of disciples who are willing to follow the way to oust powers of evil adopting a lifestyle in accordance with the counterculture of God's justice. We should so live and make the inclusive love of God known in real terms of actualization of hope. God desires peace with justice in all human affairs and relationships and in all the institutions that emerge to ensure fair distribution of resources and opportunities (see Mark 3:21 and Eph 2:2–4). It is important to notice that Paul in his later life came to understand a different soteriology to resonate with that of Jesus.

God respects human freedom and hence desists from being intrusive and dictatorial. But the demonic forces contrive to maintain the make-believe that the world is ruled by God and that God is in favor of all irrespective of their deceptions, and by extension, they falsely hold that God is in favor of capitalism, white racism, Brahmanical casteism (as in India), majoritarian dominance in countries such as Myanmar, majoritarian religious dominance over the minority religious communities (sometimes a combination of many dominant forces), and patriarchy in the whole world. The consequence of such make-believe is that God is seen as pro-rich, pro-white, colonialist and imperialist, pro-male, dominating and exploiting the ethnically/racially poor and disadvantaged peoples, even daring to enslave them. Majoritarian formations along with race, caste, and religious lines grab power and suppress the rights of the minorities in the name of democracy and in the "name of God." This is also because the poor and the oppressed, vulnerable as they are, fall into traps of loyalty of race, ethnicity, religion, and dominant nationalism.

All the above is well attested in the life story of Jesus as we shall see later. Powers, be they of religion or state or the privileged, colluded with the political bosses in a bid to eliminate him. The Jewish leaders openly said that they did not want Jesus as the Messiah because he was a dissenter and a controversialist who upset their comfortable control over religion. They claimed that they were happy with living under the Roman emperor as ruler because he did not interfere in their private and religious affairs, thus turning a blind eye to the corruption that was going on in the Temple precincts by way of commissions from the traders. So, the devil rules with human consensus under the pretext it is God Almighty who is in control of the affairs of the world. The realm of religion is filled with the lies of the devil, as Jesus said (John 8:44–56). Thus, the very image of God and God's ultimate purpose gets continuously distorted.

LIVING A LIFE OF WITNESS VERSUS FORCES OF EVIL

As Christians, we are called upon by the risen Lord to become disciples following what Jesus taught during his lifetime. Thus, we are living a life of witness in the pursuit of God's reign and God's justice, that is, living as people of a counterculture is our witness. Our witness should be such that it overcomes the realm of evil and establishes the Just Reign of God, a reign of peace with justice and mutual love and service, a reign free from divisive and oppressive hegemonies and cultures of domination and oppression. This means entering into struggles along with the risen Jesus. For this, we need to identify all those who are committed to peace with justice, even if they were not Christian believers, and work with them to reclaim the world for God. The economic order, cultures of domination such as patriarchy, supremacist claims of race and caste, the continuing plundering of creation, and the pollution of the atmosphere are some aspects that need constant attention. Whatever the real origins of different cultures of domination are, it is no exaggeration to say that all this evil is sustained by the rapacious capitalist economy. Capitalism co-opts the support of the powers that be in all the hegemonies. It promotes insatiable greed for profit and the accumulation of wealth in the hands of the very few. Millions of workers are exploited, they are being paid insufficient wages. Many are kept deliberately unemployed, supposedly to control inflation. These are the most important realms where struggles have to be mounted to bring the world under the Just Reign of God. The demonic rule renders innumerable people desperately poor. Many women suffer as victims of domestic violence, because their husbands suffer humiliation at workplaces where they are exploited as well as humiliated. Many other women suffer molestation and abuse, and a large number suffer the loss of human dignity and self-respect.

We shall address these issues one by one, after laying the theological foundation. The sphere of economics which includes the profit-seeking capitalists and exploited workers is the most important domain in which we need to seek God's rule and God's righteousness. This is no easy task. We should take care to redeem nature from being plundered for self-interested profit. We do need an economy, and we also need the resources of nature. The question, however, is how the economy can be ordered to bring about equitable distribution of wealth and opportunities, and how the used-up natural resources can be replenished, and how the environment can be kept clean from pollution. Irresponsible plundering of nature results in global warming and the dwindling of underground water. It hastens the rapid depletion of fossil fuels, all of which contribute to climate change and rises in sea level resulting in destructive tidal waves and occasional tsunamis when combined with earthquakes occurring under the ocean. All these issues need special attention. All Christians, beyond denominations united in the faith in the gospel, should be concerned about all these aspects of life in order to be good stewards and co-workers with God, which means working together with all those who are committed to the protection and care of creation, whether they are Christians or not.

THE "HOW" OF PUBLIC THEOLOGIZING

In order to be empowered by God to resist the forces of evil, we need first to spend considerable time in theological reflection as the very image of God in humans and God's purpose revealed in Christ have all been side-tracked and have suffered dilutions of truth in the very name of piety and spirituality and personal salvation. To this purpose, we shall work out the strategies of public witness in this volume as follows:

I. **Stories of struggles as images of public witness:** First, we need to take note of the several models of historical life stories of oppressed people's struggles against the forces of domination. We need to take note of those historical figures and their contribution to leading such struggles. This provides the foreground for our public theological reflection as to genuinely live our Christian faith. This is to seek a truer understanding of the vision of God, God's purpose for the world, and the creation as revealed in Jesus the Messiah, which would equip us with theological clarity.

2. **Reflection on economic exploitation:** Second, we reflect on economics but limit this to the way in which laborers (who are in fact the producers) are exploited and kept impoverished, whereas wealth accumulation keeps gathering momentum, with implications for the simultaneous pauperization of millions and the plundering of natural resources resulting in impending doom for nature and the climate. We also examine how capitalism thrives in the context of racist exploitation, and the oppression of women, and the imperialist designs of the white races who enlist the support of leaders in the Global South for their expansion.

3. **Eco-justice as God's just order:** Third, we need to reflect on eco-justice so that the good earth is properly taken care of with a sense of stewardship.

4. **Joining the voice of the vulnerable:** Finally, we reflect on how discrimination is perpetrated on the basis of race, ethnicity, and nationality. We need to strive and join hands with the vulnerable, who are but the chosen people with the aim of seeking harmony and unity among diversity.

Deem it otherwise, we are involved in a partnership with God in creating new heaven, new earth, and a new human community of peace with justice which will dwell therein with God being our companion. In fact, we are called upon to be involved in creating a home for God to dwell in. Admittedly, this is a combination of biblical theology and social analysis as ways and means of socio-spiritual action to bring about justice-in-faith, and only through such an exercise can we be faithful to the call to seek God's Just Reign and God's justice in all the affairs of the world. In doing public theology, we try to follow the framework outlined above.

LIFE STORIES OF STRUGGLE AS MODELS OF PUBLIC WITNESS

The purpose of the following model stories of struggles of different peoples for freedom and dignity is to show how oppressed people do not acquiesce in situations of oppression but keep on trying to struggle until their goals of dignity, freedom, and economic justice are achieved. In the cases of believing communities, we have also tried to identify how their faith in God has been vindicated in spite of the oppressors claiming that God was on their side. Thus, we are pointing to a different understanding of God, one other than that which prevails in popular and dominant thought.

To this end, we need to be able to identify the apparently silent protests pronounced through songs, poetry, nuanced dramas, and satirical and sarcastic storytelling(s). In the brief exercise below, we may not be able to do full justice to all these sources of inspiration that kept the desire for freedom alive and which led to organized struggles that led to freedom. These stories also demonstrate how the certain Christian understanding of God is distorted in the pursuit of power and exorbitant profit. The Parent God of Jesus, however, enables and empowers the oppressed people to struggle to gain their freedom and dignity. God's ways of walking along with the oppressed people, bearing their burden, and inwardly providing inspiration and courage will be seen to emerge.

THE STORY OF SLAVERY IN AMERICA AND THE STRUGGLE FOR FREEDOM

Christopher Columbus of Spain, a seafaring adventurist, landed in South America in 1493. Subsequently, he visited the two American continents five times. Each time he visited, he conquered many Native land-owning tribes with his unmatched gun power and made the conquered lands into Spanish colonies. He also compelled many to accept the Catholic faith. In the process of colonization, he killed, according to his own admission in his diary, several million Native American people who resisted his demand to surrender and become Catholics. He mistakenly labeled Native Americans as "Indians." As a result of Columbus discovering the transatlantic sea route during the sixteenth century, many Europeans settled in the Americas. According to their countries of origin, the lands in which they settled became colonies of European countries and of Britain. The colonizers gradually gained domination and control over the Native American communities through deceitful persuasion and coercive intimidation and pushed the Native Americans into colonial settlements, taking away fertile land which had good irrigation and land containing plentiful natural resources, including oil and gold reserves.

All this took place in the seventeenth century. Britain gained political control over the white settlers of the North American continent in thirteen states. Four hundred years ago, in 1619, the practice of bringing slaves from the colonies of Africa and trading them as human commodities began. The settlers in the south (of continental present-day USA) started growing cotton and employed slaves as workers. The slaves were beaten with whips and tortured into subjugation. The settlers assuaged their consciences, being nominally Christians, by saying that the Africans had thick skins and did not feel pain as much as the white-skinned settlers did. The settlers also falsely claimed that long hours of work benefited the slaves' shrunken lungs by expanding them to normal levels. The settlers were reminded of the biblical myth from the story of Noah's curse of his son Ham, who made fun of his nakedness after getting very drunk. Ham and his descendants were to serve the descendants of Japheth and Sem, the other two sons, who had covered their father's nakedness. The white settlers called themselves sons of Japheth and claimed that they had the right to demand slave labor from the Black people, who they claimed were the children of Ham. The cotton that was grown was sent to Britain to supply textile mills. Thus was born the so-called Industrial Revolution, which began the rise of capitalism. The quantity of cotton production increased by 400 percent within a few years by the imposition of a heavy workload. At the same time as being involved in such an atrocious exploitation of slave labor, the slave-owners were also spreading another myth: that had they employed daily wage-earners from among free people it would be cheaper for them and that their profits would therefore have been even greater.

The story of the struggle of the people begins during the mid-seventeenth century, about thirty years after the beginning of the slave trade and slave deployment in the cotton fields of the southern states of North America. Most slaves had been forcefully baptized and made Christians. They were taught the myth of Ham, their supposed ancestor, and told that they were under a divine mandate to provide obedient service to their white owners. They were also told the story of Jesus and his suffering to save believers for eternal life and that they should be very happy because by becoming slaves and Christians they had been assured of salvation. Their (mis)understanding of the Christian faith led them to believe that they were as human-made in the image of God as their masters were, and so there was no divine mandate or obligation to serve their masters. However, a prophetic critique of slavery emerged from among the slaves, and they expressed this in their many petitions to government authorities who, of course, chose to ignore them even as they sent more petitions. During their weekly day off the slaves used to sing and dance, which had innuendos against their white masters and mistresses. Those of a pietistic nature indulged in singing spiritual songs in which they identified their suffering with the sufferings of Jesus. When their masters came to know of this, they were enraged and punished them even more harshly and increased their workload; if any rebelled they were hanged and killed. There were no laws to protect the rights of the slaves.

Notwithstanding such cruel repressive measures, the word of God of the people, the gospel, continued to inspire Christian slaves to rebel against slavery. They were ready to ignore Paul's advice to slaves to be obedient to their masters and serve them as if they served Christ. For them, the tenor of the gospel was decidedly antislavery. Three major insurrections during 1800, 1822, and 1831 were attempted by leaders such as Gabriel Prosser, Denmark Vesey, and David Walker, all from among the slave community. Walker denounced slavery as an evil ten thousand times greater than all other evils put together and stated that God would visit them very soon with stringent punishment for the slave owners. He also wrote a letter asking all the colored people of the world to join hands with the struggles of the enslaved Black people of the Americas.

THE CHURCH THAT REBELS AND THE BIRTH OF CIVIL RIGHTS MOVEMENT

The insurrections ended in failure and their leaders were executed. But God, who had inspired these suffering people, had other means of bringing about conviction and change. At the beginning of the eighteenth century, the Great Awakening among protestant Christians occurred in the United States and in Britain. Preachers like John Wesley and Charles Finney and churches (except for the

Anglican Church), such as the Methodists, Baptists, and Congregationalists, all declared slavery to be one of the very great sins. Missionary societies accepted only people of abolitionist conviction into their membership. Some churches also insisted that their members support the abolitionist movement. The Quakers took the lead in this. In Britain, as a result of the efforts of the indefatigable William Wilberforce, Parliament outlawed slavery and the slave trade. In the United States, Abraham Lincoln, an abolitionist, became president in 1860, and in 1863 he enacted a law by a constitutional amendment to free slaves and made them citizens to the extent of granting male slave voting rights. Eventually, the Roman Catholic Church also followed suit and declared slavery evil. However, this (mere citizenship) did not mean that the liberated slaves found full freedom and that their dignity was restored. The liberation struggle by the slaves led to the Civil War between the North and the South. Eleven southern states (where all the cotton fields which were making huge profits through the chattel slavery of Black people were), calling themselves the "Confederacy of States," rebelled against Abraham Lincoln's declaration that slavery was an offence. The Civil War was won by the North and the law against slavery was not repealed. When Abraham Lincoln tried to sanction a compensatory grant and land to the freed slaves, a white fanatic assassinated him.

Soon after the assassination of Abraham Lincoln, a set of segregation laws was enacted to force liberated slaves to live apart from the rest of the population, restricting their freedom to enter entertainment facilities and public toilets, among other places. In addition, when on public buses they were required to sit only in seats in the back half of the buses and to surrender their seats if demanded to do so by a white passenger. In addition, any socializing or conversation between white and Black people was forbidden, even if it was the white person who initially tried to greet and express friendship with a Black person, especially if they were of the opposite sex; in these situations the Black person would be arrested and incarcerated. And even worse, the Ku Klux Klan would drag people out of custody while sheriffs, police officers, judges, and mayors looked the other way, taking them out to be lynched and killed. Sometimes the lynching would be announced in advance and schools were closed to facilitate white children watching them. No white Christian leader protested against or condemned this, and white churches also stayed silent. Protests from within the Black community began to increase. The famous Montgomery Bus Boycott was a nonviolent protest movement which took the simple step of boycotting the bus service after the arrest of Rosa Parks, a female passenger, for refusing to give up her seat to a white man. Women workers in a sewing factory who had to travel eight miles both ways took to walking to and from work, refusing to get onto the buses. The bus service, heavily dependent on these commuters, went broke and buses remained in their garages. The company's attempt to force the women to use the service for work failed. Then the practice of seating restrictions was canceled, and thus began the civil rights movement, which was eventually led by Rev. Martin Luther King Jr. He preached powerful sermons and organized marches and rallies, eventually wresting the much-denied civil liberties from the government. Tragically, a white fanatic shot and killed him in 1968 when he was just thirty-nine years old. This was the moment that gave rise to Black Theology. James Cone, who died in May 2018, wrote *Black Theology and Black Power* in 1969 as an initial attempt to identify liberation as the heart of the Christian gospel and Blackness as the primary mode of God's presence.

REFLECTIONS FROM THE STRUGGLE AGAINST SLAVERY

We need to learn from this story of continued struggle against slavery, how God accompanies and empowers oppressed people in their quest for justice. God did not abandon the resistance movements which had drawn their inspiration from the Bible, which is filled with instances of God fighting the battles of the people of Israel, specifically from the story of Samson. But given the brute gun power of the oppressor, it is inevitable that attempts to fight, believing that God who helped Samson and David to fight battles, single-handedly would, by and large, fail and not be miraculously vindicated.

We should also note that the insurrectionist uprisings were partial and did not include all the enslaved people. The bus boycott succeeded because everyone from the Black community of Montgomery stood solidly as one. In times of struggle, lack of consensus always besets attempts toward freedom and dignity for all people. Many are forced to internalize oppression and acquiesce in situations of oppression and develop cold feet, especially if reprisals have been ruthlessly cruel for even small offences. Masters, like lion tamers, always keep the oppressed under fear of severe reprisals. But God walks along with the people nevertheless, and he instilled repentance among many white Christians of nonconformist pale in a huge wave awakening, leading to the abolitionist movement.

THE CONVERSION OF JESUS AS BLACK: THE STORY OF DIETRICH BONHOEFFER

The struggle of the Black American people to gain freedom and dignity in the midst of continued suffering had a far-reaching effect on the life and witness of Dietrich Bonhoeffer, who in turn fought against Hitler's pogrom against the Jewish people and against white fascism. Hitler claimed that he was killing the Jews in order to fulfil their own death wish expressed to Pilate at the trial of Jesus saying, "Let his blood be upon us and upon our children, you now crucify Jesus."

Bonhoeffer completed his doctoral studies in theology when he was just twenty-four years old. The church in Germany did not ordain people until after the age of twenty-five and also preferred that they married prior to their ordination. So Bonhoeffer decided to spend time taking up postdoctoral studies at Union Seminary, New York. He was not especially happy in the dry academic environment that prevailed there. There were few sociopolitical discussions in the seminary, even as the lynching of thousands of Black people was taking place in the former Confederate states in the south, with no response from the authorities or population in the north. Providentially, a fellow student who was Black befriended Bonhoeffer and invited him to attend worship at Abyssinia Baptist Church, a Black church in East Harlem. The church was called Abyssinia Baptist Church because Abyssinia, the name for Ethiopia, was the first country in Africa to become Christian and it had a distinctive theology. It had also taken the name Abyssinia Baptist Church to indicate that its loyalties were for the Black people of America. The pastor of the church was Rev. Robert Powell. On the day of Bonhoeffer's first visit, Powell's sermon was based on Jesus's parable of the Last Judgment in Matthew 25:31–46. The point of the sermon was not on judgment, but on the affirmation that Jesus, the Son of God, as a human person identified himself with those who were thirsty and hungry, naked, and in prison. The pastor preached the Good News to the Black community who were wondering what God was doing when thousands of their brothers and sisters were being lynched and killed and several had been thrown into prison without any justifiable reason. As God was with them in their suffering, the sufferers were participating in God's work. Beyond the suffering, there is resistance because the God of resistance was with them. This was the message of Rev. Powell.

This *Good News* transformed Bonhoeffer, the would-be Christian pastor, to become an activist theologian with a profound conviction that Jesus was Black and all depictions of Jesus as a white man were fascist in nature. He held that affirming Jesus to be Black, and the Jewish people as the people of the Black Jesus, and organizing a struggle against Hitler was one of the witnessing ways of doing public theology. He said that the suffering Jewish people of Europe under persecution by Hitler should also be deemed as Black symbolically. He then boldly launched his opposition against Hitler when his own parent church decided to stay silent about the Holocaust. He founded a new church and also started an underground seminary and developed a theology of the "Cost of Discipleship."

Bonhoeffer was convinced that humankind had come of age and that it needed to grasp divine interventions as its own. Humanity, which had become mature, needed to act with courage against all forms of injustice. Bonhoeffer was convinced that it was essential to remove Hitler as this would save many thousands of Jews from annihilation. Bonhoeffer's conspiracy to eliminate Hitler was exposed, and he was arrested and was hanged in 1944, at the age of just thirty-nine.

REFLECTIONS FROM THE LIFE STORY OF BONHOEFFER

We might raise questions such as: Why did not God make him succeed in his conspiracy? Was God on the side of Hitler? It is a matter of intrigue to note that Hitler had survived fifteen attempts on his life. Who protected him? We should not try to answer this question on moralistic grounds that killing was forbidden in the Ten Commandments and Jesus deepened that command by saying even angry thoughts and words were as bad as actual murder. The words of Jesus were pertinent in the realm of personal relationships. God seemed to have condoned murders, even unjust murders committed by David and Solomon. David indeed was reprimanded by Nathan the prophet for the cunning elimination of Uriah. But Solomon eliminated even potential enemies with paranoid fear. He cunningly got Adonijah, his brother, who in fact was the title heir to the throne, eliminated, but was not reprimanded by God. Nathan, the prophet, also kept quiet. This does not mean that God approved of such acts by Solomon. It was, in fact, Nathan, who indicted David for scheming to get Uriah to get killed in the battlefield, who ought to have challenged Solomon. We might think that God could do little. In the penultimate realm, because of God's reticence to intervene, and due to several other reasons such as the continuation of human sin and contingencies like fatal accidents due to human errors, many wicked deeds go unchallenged. And God is nonintrusive, leaving human contingencies as well as acts of wickedness without interference. But we know that humankind has come of age in understanding the acts of God and transforming them as human acts to freedom in faith.

We need to remember that Jesus did not succeed in getting his own people converted but got killed by them, the political powers readily conniving. Interpreting that as a vicarious death to effect the forgiveness of all human sin is "legal fiction" indulged in by theologians who attribute everything and especially the power of domination to God. But this interpretation does not bring honor to our living God. Life and death seem to have been given autonomy in the penultimate of God's final acts of redemption. Stories of failures and tragedies in the realm of social action therefore should not deter us from acting in concert with God for the new humanity. Tragedies and failures in the penultimate are to be expected. One thing is sure—God walks with those who act on God's behalf. The power of God's love was demonstrated when Jesus broke the bonds of death. Satan was defeated. Never mind the consequences within the realm of history and time; we need to participate in the work for the new creation/God's Just Reign, assured of God walking together with us. Bonhoeffer's challenge to white fascism and its influence in theology remains as an unassailable witness for those who have eyes to see and ears to hear.

THE STORY OF DALIT LIBERATION STRUGGLES IN INDIA AND THE EMERGENCE OF DALIT THEOLOGY

Another example of public theology is the story of Dalit liberation struggles against the caste system that propelled the emergence of Dalit Theology as the faith-inspired way of doing public theology. The suffering experience of the Dalits invites us to rethink our theological expressions as to direct them toward the public or people of God. Due to the caste system, which inhibits graded inequality, the Dalits in India are historically deemed as "no people," unworthy of socialization with fellow human beings. In the caste system in India, Dalits are considered as low and untouchable and hence "not-belonging," not to be treated the same as other people. This low estate of theirs has been determined by the so-called principle of karma, that is, the imaginary law created by someone called Manu according to which the fate of every soul during a lifetime is decided as to what they shall be in their next incarnation in the world based on their caste. God raised Dr. Ambedkar from among the Dalits, and he became the father of the Constitution of the Republic of India. Dr. Ambedkar renounced Hinduism for it sanctified casteism and worked for the annihilation of the caste system and became a Buddhist. Even Gandhi was not willing to accept his conversion and the reasoning to annihilate casteism. Dr. Ambedkar's contribution to the liberation of Dalits and the emergence of Dalit theology is a classical instance of public witness that opens up Dalit public theological discussions.

Sri Lanka is predominantly populated by Sinhala-speaking Buddhists who make up over 70 percent of the population, while

Hindus (mostly Tamil-speaking) are about 13 percent of the population, and others professing Islam and Christianity, speaking either Sinhalese or Tamil, constitute about 10 and 7 percent, respectively. There has been a long-drawn-out ethnic conflict between the Sinhala and Tamil people. Therefore, a church with both Sinhalese and Tamil people has the unique chance to play the role of peacemaker and also to provide a challenge against violations of human rights of all kinds.

SOBITHA HIMI: THE SOCIAL IS THE SPIRITUAL

Bishop Duleep de Chickera, former Bishop of the Church of Lanka (Anglican), speaks of a Buddhist leader who took a stand for justice in a situation of majoritarian consciousness when most Buddhist leaders were of the opinion Sri Lanka is for Sinhala Buddhists as bequeathed by the Lord Buddha himself (based on a myth with no historical evidence). Bishop Chickera stated that Sobitha Himi[1] is the servant of the *Dhamma* and a gift to us all.

---

1   Sobitha Thero was an influential Sinhalese Buddhist Monk well known for his advocacy of nonviolence and was a revolutionary leader. He was the chief incumbent of Kotte Naga Vihara, a type of monastic center, and was a prominent social and political activist. He took a stand against centralized power and threats against freedom of expression and in favor of civil rights and the rule of law. He opposed Indian intervention led by Rajiv Gandhi by getting a treaty signed and sending a peacekeeping force to eliminate the Tamil Eelam militants. He initiated the National Movement for a Just Society—NMJS. When General Fonseka was arrested for his opposition to President Rajapaksa, he campaigned for his release. When a courageous journalist whistle-blower, Lasantha Wickremetunge, who exposed government human rights violations, was murdered by unidentified assassins, everyone knew who was behind the brutal act. And Sobitha Himi said then that Sri Lanka is no more a land of the *Dhamma*.

There was a time when Sobitha Himi did not appeal to the minorities the way he did at the time of his death. Some may still have some reservations about his past. The recurring challenges of civil governance that brought us together fifteen years ago developed into a close friendship and enabled me to understand, respect, and appreciate him as a courageous and timely gift to us all. Among Sobitha Himi's several contributions to the life of the nation, two outstanding thrusts speak clearly to religion and religious leaders in particular. Sobitha Himi reminded us that if religion dares to offer solutions to our complex human challenges, it is compelled to engage with the harsh realities of life. For him, human crises were far too crucial to be left to those whose main objective is capturing power. This is why for him, the role of sound religion was to expose and distance itself from the snares of power and work for a just and transparent society instead of empty rhetoric, the common good. In Sobitha Himi's worldview, there was no room for religion to either withdraw from social realities or turn into a weapon of hatred, violence, and division. In his engagement with social issues, Sobitha Himi demonstrated a spiritual rhythm that religious leaders are to take note of. He listened with sensitivity to the grievance and hardships of the people and applied the Dhamma to what he heard. In other words, he responded to the hypothetical but helpful question, *"what would the Buddha say and expect?"* if and when confronted with these contemporary challenges.

Cries of the People—Wisdom of the *Dhamma*

The first beat of this rhythm came spontaneously as he had his ear to the ground and was connected with people, and he exercised the second through his remarkable ability to translate the wisdom of the *Dhamma* into a language that embraced all, a skill all religions are to acquire. In other words, he preached the *Dhamma* and talked about politics at the same time. This is why he was understood not only by Buddhists but also by Hindus, Muslims, Christians, and the secular world as well.

Self-Denial for Community Well-Being

A spirituality that helped him to stay faithful within these thrusts was his disregard, almost contempt, for status and position. By rising above these enticements that obsess and destroy so many, he exposed the fallacy that political office is the pinnacle of life. He taught instead that losing oneself for the good of others is the noblest option available to humans. This is why his life was a source of encouragement to the countless unsung Sri Lankans content to live with dignity and integrity wherever they were placed.

A Prophet in Our Midst

In spite of several worrying setbacks in today's civil governance, we are now able to breathe, largely because of Sobitha Himi's pro-people influence. His visionary leadership certainly saved us as well as those in divisive politics from the extremes that divisive politics can take us to. For many Christians, he was truly a prophet in our midst. In biblical tradition, these were persons who took sides with the cause of the oppressed against unrighteous rulers. They were often contrasted with the false persons who instead sought favors and goodwill from deceitful regimes.

Model for Reconciliation

The prophetic model of leadership that inevitably brings change, respite, and fresh opportunities offers a lasting lesson. It teaches us that the way to national reconciliation (especially between the two warring ethnic groups, Tamils and Sinhalese) and integration after a substantial period of arbitrary violence and entrenched impunity is to be discerned in a collaborative and sustained response to social injustice. To stay on this path is to honor our common humanity as well as the man who brought honor to the yellow robe.

Sobitha Himi's early ten-point proposal for democratic change did not refer to the Tamil problem. When this was pointed out, he patiently explained that it would be addressed after some degree of political and social stability had been realized. He returned to this obligation after January 8, 2015, to influence a decision of the Congress of Religions to once again revisit this long-overdue grievance and also came up with a novel approach on how this could be done. Rather than meet political leaders or the media separately, as was the practice, he suggested that the ministers of justice and resettlement should be engaged together at an open media conference. At this conversation at the Ministry of Justice in April 2015, the Congress of Religions called for and queried the delay in justice for the Tamils of the land. Throughout the conversations, Sobitha Himi was his typically charismatic self, urging that judicial action against Tamil detainees be expedited, that those without charges be released, that land acquired from Tamil civilians be returned, and that details of missing persons be made public. His passion on that occasion was as strong as his passion to liberate the country from the powers of the executive presidency. May his memory lighten our darkness, convert us into disciples of the truth, and bring us peace.

Learnings

There are four important lessons in this for theological teachers in Myanmar, or for that matter in any Asian country that experiences conflicts between ethnoreligious groups:

1. We learn what it is to bear public witness to God's Just Reign from the way in which Bishop Chickera, a Christian leader, was able to appreciate a colleague from among the Buddhist leaders. A lesson which is important for Christians in Myanmar.

2. We also learn from the example set by the Buddhist leader who chose to go against the current majoritarianism of many compatriot leaders of his own faith.

3. Let us take the lesson from Bishop Chickera to appreciate the value of the *Dhamma* so that we can engage in meaningful conversation with Buddhist leaders of our own country.

4. As a strategy, seek the cooperation of influential committed leaders from the majority religious community to deal with issues of justice and human rights when the minority and powerless are affected in our different contexts.

THE ROHINGYA IN OUR MIDST

The Rohingya in our midst brought out the worst in some of us: How and why Bishop Chickera of Sri Lanka came to speak of the Rohingya crisis, some of us will wonder. Some of us with a nationalistic fervor may also be outraged that someone from Sri Lanka dared to challenge our leaders regarding the Rohingya issue. Did he know that they were not really citizens of Myanmar? Bishop Chickera is not speaking of Rohingya of Myanmar primarily. During the riots against those powerless communities, some thirty-one people of the Rohingya community sought refuge in Sri Lanka and this small group of refugees was ill-treated. The nexus of a handful of government officials and a small section of people of the Buddhist faith was responsible for the ill-treatment meted out to them. Bishop Chickera sought to challenge his own compatriots. In that attempt, he also outlined the reasons for them to flee from Myanmar. He said: "The aggression of a mob that sought to intimidate and deny these vulnerable humans of compassion and security, shockingly incited by some who carry religious responsibility in the community, will go down as a sad shameful moment in our national conscience. The swift interventions of senior government ministers, to clarify and affirm our stance, however welcome. By then the contempt with which these vulnerable humans had been treated had done its damage. Their desperate dependence on our compassion and goodwill had resulted in the humiliation and trauma instead, of an already humiliated and traumatized people." After fleeing the sectarian violence in Myanmar and a perilous journey by sea, this group of thirty-one Rohingya refugees was brought ashore by the navy to be held at the Mirihana Detention Center. It was only after the devastating rape of a Rohingya woman, allegedly by an officer whose job it was to protect people, that the UNHCR was permitted to carry out its real mission: to provide humanitarian care for refugees. Housed together for the first time, they were surrounded by Sri Lankan neighbors with a traditional reputation for hospitality. The children of school-going age were very rightly provided with opportunities for schooling, a gesture of some stability and the right and dream of every child and parent. This slow return to dignity was suddenly shattered by the violent reaction of a mob, and the Rohingya people were once again confined to a restricted space behind high walls in the south of the country.

The lesson here is that when governments ill-treat those dependent on a country's generosity and protection, and arbitrarily relegate these people out of sight and out of hearing, they fail in their humanitarian obligation and disseminate negative signals, and no amount of verbal intervention to the contrary can undo that. This creates a climate in which opportunists can easily endorse such a mentality to do by violent means what the government has done through structural violence. While both these types of behavior humiliate the helpless and the harassed, one difference stands out. The state is unconditionally accountable for its behavior. Under no circumstances can those who represent the people in pursuing national wholesomeness and integration inflict or permit any kind of violence, whether against their own or those who seek refuge on its soil.

The Rohingya in our midst highlight the severe exclusion of humans by humans. Critical as these conditions are, they are more than refugees or asylum seekers. They are a stateless people as well. In spite of living on Myanmar soil they are not considered Myanmar nationals. They are consequently disqualified from constitutionally entrenched rights, freedom, and the basic facilities enjoyed by other Myanmar citizens, and denied recognition as a legitimate ethnic group in a land where numerous and diverse ethnic identities are recognized. Despite some courageous exceptions, the majority Buddhists and minority Christians of Myanmar inaccurately portray and disown the Rohingya as "Bengalis": illegal immigrants from Bangladesh. This is the wall of prejudice that Aung San Suu Kyi refuses to contest or dismantle.

The immediate crisis of nationality for the Rohingya is for the government of Myanmar to resolve. Given the current political intransigence, as well as the systemic violence unleashed against them, however, it will require sensitive diplomatic pressure, especially from friendly countries in the region if the Rohingya are to eventually enjoy this universal human right. The wider crisis of nationality for the world's ten million stateless is to be addressed by the peoples and nations of the world. The scope of engagement if this is to happen should range from awareness at the level of schools worldwide to global support for the UN Convention on the Reduction of Statelessness. Whether it is for the handful of Rohingya in our midst or the stateless of the world, it is the sustained combination of compassion, justice, and diplomacy from people's movements and the nations of the world that will one day eliminate the horrific humiliation of excluded humans.

The Rohingya in our midst points to a simmering ethnoreligious tension. The Muslim identity of these stateless refugees more or less explains the lack of public solidarity with their plight and their humiliation on our soil. Perhaps unknown to them, it is their religious identity that has made their presence in a land of four world religions controversial. For some time now there has been a growing prejudice against the Muslim community in Sri Lanka. This is not a majority versus minority tension, as both the majority Sinhala Buddhists and the minority Sinhala and Tamil Christians are known to nurse negative feelings about Muslims.

TOGETHER TOWARD CHANGE

Our collective response to this challenge cannot continue to be superficial. If it does we foolishly postpone a more serious conflagration. All mechanisms of reconciliation should, without delay, initiate conversations that address the causes of social prejudice against our Muslims. Sensitivity to the grievance and the rights of each other is of paramount importance and there can be no room for supremacy and intransigence. The unaddressed accumulation of these latter attitudes seems to have spilt over into animosity.

TOGETHER TOWARD LIFE

If we are serious about living together with dignity and integrity, all of us, the religious as well as the secular, will be obliged to engage in the task of introspection. To discern the kind of people we have become and then correct our own shortcomings before we become intolerable and offensive to others is a sign of humility and maturity. It is also a demonstration of goodwill that we recognize the public space is meant to be shared as equals with each other.

TOGETHER ACROSS BORDERS

Another essential step toward building social trust is that our tendency to speak and act out of self-interest only has to stop. It is this communal preference that repeatedly sends distorted messages that the needs, benefits, and privileges of our own ethnoreligious community matter most. To tread the same soil and breathe the same air and remain neutral in or indifferent to the wider social realities that exclude and crush others is a recipe for social turmoil. A primary lesson that has evaded us at much cost for too long is that we cannot expect dignity and freedom for our own if we do not cross borders in solidarity with other grieved and violated communities.

THE OPTIONS

If we do not come to our senses and shift from our self-seeking ways, chances are that whatever vision and energy there is for life together will diminish and impoverish us slowly. Signs that this could already be happening are worrying. Far from upholding the highest human ideals and cooperating for common good, our secular pursuits and established religions, in particular, have acquired a reputation (speaking of Sri Lanka and also being conscious that the author belongs to the majority ethnic group although his religion as Christian makes him belong to the minority) for being unreasonable and obstructive of fresh expressions of advancement, healing, and liberation. We cannot have it both ways. Either we could stay with the self-centered and exclusive ways that polarize us and undermine social integration and stability, or we could break from this bondage to stand with each other in our common pursuit of a more safe, just, and integrated world for all. To imagine that the latter is a betrayal of our identity, national or ethnoreligious, is a myth. To rise above division and endorse the human race as the highest race as taught by the Buddha and generate just compassion for our neighbor among whom the vulnerable stranger takes precedence, as Jesus taught, is to the contrary a manifestation of our highest collective human values. It is those who seek to consolidate their power base—political, religious, or ethnic—by controlling our emotions and freedom who suggest otherwise.

OUR REFLECTIONS

- In a situation when a vulnerable minority is affected, the emphasis should be on giving priority to protecting them—overcoming the traditional ways of reacting from our self-preservation instincts, and thus inflicting more pain to an already hurt people who seek refuge—and our compassion and generosity are important.

- Our common humanity should be brought to the fore. We should draw from our spiritual resources of the *Dhamma* of the Buddha and the teachings of Jesus.

- Unfortunately, ethnoreligious identity consciousness has taken over and whole communities are more concerned about protecting their own interests, and hence feel threatened in the face of a stranger seemingly demanding our space and our privileges being shared with them.

- The stranger, even though weak and vulnerable, is seen as a threat. Both the *Dhamma* and the teachings of Jesus demand that the consciousness of our common humanity comes to the fore.

- The method followed by Bishop Chickera also is important. He formed a multi-religious group comprising people who had transcended their particular identity/nationality loyalties and issued statements such as the two examples mentioned above. Such a strategy makes the authorities wake up and take note.

- We need to take seriously the aspirations of the tribal people of Myanmar and their struggle for democracy in Myanmar—for example, the telling incidents of the student martyrs of 1988 and the participation of some activist monks in support of NLD, which was suppressed by the then military government. Stories of struggles by different tribal communities and the other epic stories of Burmese culture must also be taken into reckoning sources of inspiration for public theology.

4

A THEOLOGICAL RESPONSE TO THE *DUKKHA*-RIDDEN PEOPLE IN MYANMAR

K. M. Y. Khawsiama

INTRODUCTION

The situation in Myanmar challenges me to create a *"Ludu* theology"* as a Christian theological response to the suffering people. It aims to encourage, empower, and conscientize them. The Burmese word *Ludu* means "people or the masses."[1] Another Burmese word, *Pyi dhu ludu*, refers to "the mass; populace."[2] Sometimes we use *Pyi dhu* or *Pyi dhu pyi dha*, which literally means "daughters and sons of the country," instead of *Ludu*. In Myanmar, *Ludu* is a strong Burmese political term, which excludes the power-holders and those who support them. The *Ludu* are oppressed, alienated, marginalized, and exploited. Certainly, most of them are economically poor. Thus, it is a significant term and represents the common people of all classes who suffer under any form of oppression.

---

1   *Myanmar-English Dictionary* (Yangon: Department of the Myanmar Language Commission, Ministry of Education, 1993), s.v. "Lu du."

2   *Myanmar-English Dictionary* (Yangon: Department of the Myanmar Language Commission, Ministry of Education, 1993), s.v. "Pyi dhu ludu."

In order to understand the *Ludu*'s life reality in the country, social analysis is used as a methodology. Social analysis is "the study of the individuals, groups, and institutions that make up human society." Its field covers an "extremely broad range that includes every aspect of human social condition."[3] It is also indispensable to reread Myanmar history from the *Ludu*'s perspective. We have to consider: Why do the *Ludu* suffer in Myanmar? What is their real situation today? How do we theologically respond to their suffering? As a Burmese Buddhist-dominated country, we have to use some of their terms.

LUDU: THE *DUKKHA*-RIDDEN PEOPLE

The *Ludu* can be seen as a *dukkha*-ridden people in Myanmar. *Dukkha* is a Buddhist term, which is derived from a Pali word. It is rooted in the central teaching of Gautama Buddha, the Enlightened One. He taught the Four Noble Truths: (1) *Dukkha*; (2) *Samudaya*, the arising or origin of *dukkha*; (3) *Nirodha*, the cessation *dukkha*; and (4) *Magga*, the way leading to the cessation of *dukkha*.

Dukkha is generally described as "suffering." However, it has a deep meaning and broad sense. Ram Kumar Ratnam and Bhaskara Rao, who studied *dukkha* in early Buddhism, define it as follows:

> "Dukkha" in Pali or "dukkha" in Sanskrit is a compound of two words "du" and "kha." The prefix "du" is used in the sense of "vile" (kucchita). It signifies something "bad," "disagreeable," "uncomfortable," or "unfavorable." The suffix "kha" is used in the sense of "empty" (tuccha). It signifies "emptiness" or "unreality." Therefore, "dukkha" stands for

3   *The World Book Encyclopedia*, vol. 18 (Chicago: World Book, 1985), s.v. "Sociology."

something that is "vile" and "imaginary." Buddhaghosa is the option that is impermanent, harmful and devoid of substantiality is characterized otherwise by ignorant people and this leads to pain and misery. Hence, these are called "dukkha."[4]

For the people in Myanmar, *dukkha* is a common word to express their daily problems. Melford E. Spiro, an American cultural anthropologist, rightly observes and remarks:

> it is on everyone's lips. One hears it scores of times every day—at work, at school, in the house, on a trip. For the Burmese people, as for the rest of mankind, the notion that life involves suffering is not an article of faith; it is a datum of everyday experience. But it is one thing to agree that life involves suffering, and another to agree that life—every form of life—is suffering.[5]

The term *dukkha* is not strange to Christians in Myanmar. In his Burmese Bible translation, Adoniram Judson (1788–1850), a successful American Baptist missionary, employed it to refer to "affliction" in Job 30:27, "trouble/affliction" in Psalm 90:15; 138:7, "adversity" in Proverbs 17:17 (KJV), "persecution" (RSV) and "trouble" (NIV) in John 16:33, "hardships" (NIV) in Acts 14:22, "sufferings/suffering" (RSV and NIV) in Romans 5:3, "tribulation" (RSV) and "affliction" (NIV) in Romans 12:12, and "weaknesses" (NKJV) in Hebrews 4:15. At this point, Christians could understand the concept of *dukkha*.

---

4   M. V. Ram Kumar Ratnam and D. Bhaskara Rao, *Dukkha: Suffering in Early Buddhism* (New Delhi: Discovery Publishing House, 2003), 45.

5   Melford E. Spiro, *Buddhism and Society: A Great Tradition and Its Burmese Vicissitudes*, 2nd ed. (Los Angeles: University of California Press, 1982), 74.

I have observed two forms of *dukkha*: (1) individual/personal *dukkha* and (2) social *dukkha*. Individual *dukkha* can create social problems. Social problems can never be separated from personal *dukkha*. The *Ludu* suffer both. The root cause of their *dukkha* is a social evil, which was created by power-holders. Most of individual *dukkha* is the result of one's choice of evil or bad things. The *Ludu* individually suffer under oppression. That is not their choice, but the free will of oppressors. They choose knowingly to mistreat the *Ludu*. This becomes social evil. It is true to say that the *Ludu* suffer individually and collectively due to social evil. The *Ludu*'s suffering is not merely the result of their own *kamma*, which means "deeds," or sin.

THE *DUKKHA* OF *LUDU* IN MYANMAR

This section illustrates the reality of the *Ludu*'s life and the reason of their *dukkha*. They have suffered throughout different historical eras of Myanmar.

The *Ludu* under the Pyi-daung-su (Union) Party (1948–62)

Burma, the former name of Myanmar, gained independence from the British on January 4, 1948. General Aung San, the father of the Myanmar nation, was assassinated on July 19, 1947. In the early years of her independence, Burma followed the federal democratic path. U Nu (1907–95) became the first prime minister of Burma under the provisions of the 1947 Constitution of the Union of Burma. He was a strongly religious person. He practiced both Buddhism and *Nat* (spirit) worship. Later, he created a form of Buddhist socialism.[6]

---

6   E. Sarkisyanz, *Buddhist Backgrounds of the Burmese Revolution* (The Hague: M. Nijhoff, 1965), 210.

U Nu faced problems with ethnic groups shortly after attaining independence. Ethnic groups, especially the Karen people, demanded federal states. The Burma Communist Party also began its revolt on March 28, 1948. The journey of the newly born Union of Burma was, from the very beginning, overshadowed by internal confusion and instability. There were civil wars under U Nu's leadership. He also tried to make Buddhism a state religion in 1960. It challenged other religious groups, especially those ethnic groups with a Christian majority or Muslim majority. He failed to lead the country in the right direction, although he was seen as a charismatic leader. His final failure was largely psychological. He could no longer reconcile the requirements of political leadership with his desire to achieve Buddhist religious integration and face its consequences in public life.[7]

The *Ludu* under the First Military Regime (1962–88)

On March 2, 1962, claiming to prevent chaos and to serve the country, the Burmese army (*Tatmadaw*) took over the country and put it under the leadership of General Ne Win (1910–2002). In the beginning, *tatmadaw* was a "caretaker government." Then, General Ne Win formed the Revolutionary Council. He quickly rescinded U Nu's declaration of Buddhism as a state religion in Burma and created a Burmese way to socialism. Ignoring the federal democratic system, he adopted a centralized one-party system. He also held the role of chairman of the Socialist Programme Party and put the state under a socialist economic system until 1988.[8]

---

7   See Richard Butwell, *U Nu of Burma* (Stanford, CA: Stanford University Press, 1963).

8   F.S.V. Donnison, *Burma* (New York: Praeger Publishers, 1970), 163–82.

It was evident that Ne Win's *military autocracy* became a *party dictatorship*. The *Ludu* can be defined as the proletariat in this system. The Burmese way to socialism practiced a closed-door system, which advocated isolation from the international community. Consequently, the economic situation became worse. The state economy was ineffective because of the superficial ideology. This led to corruption and despotism, because the Socialist Party leader U Ne Win, a former general, was a right-winger wearing a socialist costume.[9] Under this first military regime, the *Ludu* lost their freedom and human rights; they became poor and the ethnic minorities were alienated and marginalized.

The *Ludu* under the Second Military Regime (1988–2011)

In August 1988, a massive democratic movement was initiated in Yangon and spread throughout the country. All classes of people joined on August 8, 1988, making it the largest rebellion in a series of peaceful student-led demonstrations to end single-party rule. Hundreds of protesters were killed when the army opened fire on demonstrators. This historical event is called the "8888 Uprising" (Four Eights Uprising) and is also known as the "People Power Uprising." Shortly after the uprising, taking the name of the State Law and Order Restoration Council (SLORC), the *tatmadaw* took power and controlled the *Ludu*. In 1989, the name of the country was changed from Burma to Myanmar by the military junta. For them "Myanmar" is the name of the union. However, the *Ludu* suffered harshly under the second military regime.

In September 2007, Buddhist monks demonstrated in Yangon and other towns in Myanmar in response to the economic crisis. The government announced a sudden increase in fuel

---

9   See Peter John Perry, *Myanmar (Burma) since 1962: The Failure of Development* (Hampshire: Ashgate, 2007).

prices in August 2007. This had a devastating effect on the population, especially in terms of obtaining food and other basic necessities, prices of which shot up drastically. The event was called the "Saffron Revolution" or "Golden Revolution" because of the color of the *thin-gan* (the robe) worn by Buddhist monks in Myanmar. U Gambira, a twenty-seven-year old monk, was the leader of this "revolution." The people were dismayed that the revolution ended without any positive results. The military government formed a State Peace and Development Council (SPDC), also known as the State Law and Order Restoration Council (SLORC), which oversaw the affairs of Myanmar from 1988 to 1997.

The *Ludu* in the Transitional Stage (2011 to 2016)

General elections were held on November 7, 2010, in accordance with the new constitution approved during the time of the military regime in May 2008. The Union Solidarity and Development Party (UDSP) won that election and led the country. U Thein Sein, a former military leader, became the president. In the national and provisional parliaments, 25 percent of the seats are reserved for serving soldiers, who are appointed by the commander-in-chief. Although Myanmar had not fully transformed, the country began its journey toward democracy. Since U Thein Sein took office in March 2011, many changes can be observed. Aung San Suu Kyi was released from house arrest and all political prisoners were released from jail. Censorship was lifted and private newspapers started to be published. Remarkably, Suu Kyi was persuaded to stand in the byelections in 2012. She won and became a member of parliament.

The National League for Democracy won a landslide victory in Myanmar after the general election on November 8, 2015, which is considered to be the most democratic general election ever held in the country. The *Ludu* expressed great hope when a new chapter in Myanmar's sorrowful history began to unfold on April 1, 2016. Leader of this government was the world's best-known living "icon of democracy," Aung San Suu Kyi. The people raised their heads out of the darkness of *dukkha* to breathe the fresh air of democracy and see the blue sky of a better future. However, today, some people among the *Ludu* are expressing their disappointment and criticizing the government because their dreams have *not* come true. They expected a better life from the NLD government, but the economic situation has not improved and is unstable. In addition, ethnoreligious tensions and civil wars still continue.

A THEOLOGICAL RESPONSE TO THE *DUKKHA* OF *LUDU* IN MYANMAR

The only similarity between the *Ludu* in Myanmar and the people of Israel in Egypt is their suffering under oppression. They experienced authoritarianism, and their captivity and their labor were used for the benefit of the rulers rather than for themselves. The means of their production and their land were held by those who held power. The fruits of their production were enjoyed by others. Thus, they were slaves. At this point, the *Ludu* share the same quandary as the Israelites in captivity in Egypt. The biblical account of the Exodus experience is rooted in their faith and hope, and it becomes the prophetic voice of the initiation of the Exodus experience among the people of Myanmar.

The Old Testament clearly illustrates that God is with the oppressed Israelites. In the Exodus event, God guided them by the pillar of cloud during the day and the pillar of fire at night. The pillars of cloud and fire can be seen as symbols/signs of God being with the Israelites (Exodus 13:20–22). God was revealed among them. The similarity between the Israelites and the *Ludu* in Myanmar is their suffering under oppression. We have seen that the *Ludu*'s *dukkha* is the offspring of its own people, by the dictatorship. Their suffering is comparable to the experience of Israelites under Pharaoh in Egypt. God is Immanuel who is always on the side of poor people.

The Hebrew words *'ani, dal, 'ebion, rash,* and *misken* refer to the poor. The connotation of "poor" is individuals who are inferior to the rich and the powerful. However, it is clear that in Christianity we can perceive that God is significantly concerned for the poor. In the Bible, there are over three hundred verses on God's deep concern for the poor and social justice.[10] We realize that God is the God of the poor who are most troubled by *dukkha*. The power-holders made them economically poor. The poor among the *Ludu* in Myanmar worry about survival every day. They are crying for their daily rice. In this situation, the Lord's prayer—" . . . Give us today our daily bread . . . "—is very meaningful for them (Matt 6:11). God is also the hope of the poor. He is the maker of hope for them.

We see poverty both in the material sense and in the spirituality of the *Ludu*'s lives. Christianity in Myanmar needs to identify itself with the people who are poor and marginalized in society. In its most important part, all the Scripture messages make sure that it is God's eternal wish to choose the poverty-*dukkha*-ridden people to be his agents. God himself was born in human form; the real human as a little poor boy, named Jesus. He had to flee to Egypt because of Herod's persecution (Matt 2:13–23). He became a *dukkha-dhe*, meaning "refugee." That is understood as "forced poverty." The *Ludu* share the oppressed and poor life of Jesus, and similarly, Jesus himself occupies the poor and suffering life of the *Ludu*. Jesus experienced both voluntary poverty and forced poverty. In the darkness of economic *dukkha*, the *Ludu* can see this biblical picture of God who is of the poor people.

10   Rabbi Reuven Chaim Klein, "The Poor and Unfortunate," https://ohr.edu/8366, accessed May 20, 2023.

In a long journey of socio-politico-economic *dukkha*, the *Ludu* can learn and experience God's discipline as a spiritual lesson. Scriptures speak about the characteristics of God who disciplines, rebukes, corrects, and injures God's people individually or otherwise.[11] The concept of God as a disciplinarian was derived from the parent–child relationship. God is the loving parent who desires children to experience fulfilment, but who knows that obedience to God's revealed will is the condition for realizing the goal.[12] The attitude and action of Yahweh as a parent were one of concern, love, pity, and patience, but also discipline and correction.[13] In the desert experience of *dukkha* in different ways for forty years, God provided food, that is "manna," and sometimes discipled the Israelites (Deut 32:19–20). Like the Israelites, the *Ludu* in Myanmar can learn their spiritual lesson in their *dukkha* journey.

The *Ludu* in Myanmar has a messianic hope as the Israelites had. The meaning of messianic hope is "the expectation throughout Judaism that a Messiah will arise in the nation. The hope evolved through the period of the Old Testament period."[14] According to Walter C. Kaiser, "'Messianic' usually is applied to everything in the Old Testament when it refers to the hope of a glorious future. This suggests that the central feature of the coming golden age is the expectation of the Saviour and King

---

11   See Proverbs 3:11–12; 15:5; 20:30; Job 5:17–18; 1 Corinthians 11:32; Revelation 3:19.

12   *The International Standard Bible Encyclopedia*, vol. 3, ed. Geoffrey William Bromiley (Grand Rapids, MI: W.B. Eerdmans, 1986), s.v. "Discipline."

13   *New International Dictionary of Old Testament Theology and Exegesis*, vol. 1, ed. Willem VanGemeren (Grand Rapids, MI: Zondervan Publishing House, 1997), s.v. "Discipline."

14   Donald McKim, *Westminster Dictionary of Theological Terms* (Louisville, KY: Westminster John Knox Press, 1996), s.v. "Messianic Hope."

Messiah."[15] The Messiah will inaugurate the messianic age when he comes and there will be peace among all nations (Isa 2:4; Mic 4:3). He will also suffer to heal the nation (Isa 53:1–9). The praxis of hope can be found among the *Ludu*. They practice hope in their life experience of expecting the messiah of the Myanmar nation. Their hope is a new leader who can liberate them from the *dukkha* of socio-politico-economic crises and who can establish a better society.

God sent God's begotten son, Jesus who is a savior, into the world to show God's concern for the *Ludu*. Jesus opens his mission among the poor, the sick, and the least of his fellow human beings. He preached the Good News to them. Christians believe that Jesus is the Messiah. In him, God is the hope for the poor and suffering people, their resurrection, enrichment of life, and change in physical and mental needs. Jesus himself was the son of poor parents. The poor people were called by God and their salvation brought glory to him.[16] Gnana Robinson suggests, "God, revealed in and through Jesus of Nazareth, is a servant God, weak and vulnerable, a suffering God, who opted to be the weak, the vulnerable, the poor and the suffering."[17] In Jesus, God is revealed among the *Ludu* in Myanmar. Christians can realize the suffering of Jesus for liberation in the Saffron Revolution event. Monks spoke up for the voiceless. Monk demonstrators suffered and some died. We can see self-denial in their lives. They prayed for all beings by chanting *Metta Sutta* and carried the cross of social *dukkha* in the event.

The church in Myanmar is a symbol of the body of Christ that suffered under the military dictatorship. The church also

---

15   Walter C. Kaiser, Jr., *The Messiah in the Old Testament* (Michigan: Zondervan Publishing House, 1995), 15.

16   D. R. W. Wood, I. Howard Marshall, *The New Bible Dictionary*, 3rd ed. (Leicester: InterVarsity Press, 1996), s.v. "Poverty."

17   Gnana Robinson, "Re-Orientation of Theological Education for a Relevant Ministry," *East Asia Journal of Theology* 4, no. 2 (1986): 47.

copes with the members who belong to the *dukkha*-ridden people. However, most Christians do not participate actively in political movements in Myanmar because they are a minority. Christina Fink rightly observes that "they have been reluctant to take an active role in politics in the heartland of Burma, although church leaders in predominantly Christian ethnic minority areas have in some cases been out-spoken."[18] In Myanmar, the church is always on the side of the *dukkha*-ridden people. The church has been encouraging them. Nevertheless, we do not see the involvement of the church in *Ludu* liberation movements. The church should not neglect the suffering of *Ludu* and has a responsibility to liberate them.

CONCLUSION

To sum up, the *Ludu* are *dukkha*-ridden people in Myanmar. They are tired of waiting to live a better life in their country. Needless to say, their social *dukkha*, which also affected their personal lives, is created by power-holders. In other words, their suffering is the consequence of social evil under authoritarianism. They also need to see themselves as the subjects of their own transformation and liberation from socio-politico-economic and ethnoreligious problems in the country. The present situation of the country strongly challenges theologians in Myanmar to encourage, empower, and conscientize the *Ludu* by doing public theology/contextual theology focusing on the people's *dukkha*. The argument of this chapter is that it is a God-given responsibility to theologians in Myanmar to create a *Ludu* theology from different points of view as a public witness through a loving yet prophetic engagement for liberation and transformation.

---

18   Christina Fink, *Living Silence: Living under Military Rule* (London: Zed Books, 2001), 224.

5

PUBLIC WITNESS TO THE JUST REIGN OF GOD
A South Asian Perspective

Korson Srisang

INTRODUCTION BY LAL TIN HRE

The reflections in this chapter were presented by Dr. Koson Srisang during a writers' workshop at Yangon in December 2019. In his inimitable style, the author pieced together his notes and articles which he had compiled over many years. He is a theologian from Thailand committed to the struggles of people in neighboring countries and has visited Myanmar several times. He earned his PhD in social ethics from the University of Chicago in 1973. As part of his illustrious career, he has developed his own methodology, which he calls hermeneutics of *Dhamma*. The following lines are from the author:

> Written 28 years ago, this paper was shared among friends and colleagues in the Asian Friendship Society (AFS). Due to a number of personal struggles, the author became inactive with AFS for some number of years, and only recently did he re-join. The real use of the paper, later on,

was shared with my PhD students at North-eastern University, Khon Kaen, between 2006–2017, Koson Srisang. (November 20, 2019)

THE HUMAN CONDITION TODAY

Deep down in the bottom of our hearts, all persons, all families, and all nations yearn for a humane life and harmonious relationships. This is the truth about humanity, the universe, and the cosmic order. Authentic reading of myths, folktales, history, literature, philosophy, religion, and science reveals this fundamental truth, in all places and at all times. This is "the vision of common humanity in the universe." It is the ultimate truth.

But what is true is not always real, and what is real is not always true. However, truth and reality are the two dimensions of being, like "yin" and "yang" in the Chinese tradition, "woman" and "man" in the human gender, "day" and "night" in natural phenomena, "freedom" and "compassion" in religion, "theory" and "practice" in science and technology, and "order" and "chaos" in the cosmos. At this level, truth and reality are quite similar, sometimes identical. This is the realm of human experience in time and space and in relation to all beings. We may call it the historical truth.

It is at this level of actual existence that we experience happiness and sadness, joy and sorrow, fulfilment and disappointment, poverty and abundance, marginalization and participation, despair and hope, evil and good, exploitation and sharing. In the historical experience, there have been moments when one dimension is more real, more prominent than the other. But the two dimensions are always there in some proportion, often mixed.

Ideally, human life and human relations should be characterized by happiness rather than sadness, joy rather than sorrow, fulfilment rather than disappointment, abundance rather than poverty, participation rather than marginalization, hope rather than despair, good rather than evil, and sharing rather than exploitation. But today, the real condition of our human existence is far, far from ideal. Most people, especially people in the rural and slum areas, are living in a condition of sadness, sorrow, disappointment, poverty, marginalization, despair, and even starvation. Besides, people who possess mere material wealth find life meaningless, alienated, and lonely. In short, a societal crisis exists everywhere today.

The intention is to follow up with another paper on "the human condition: the roots of poverty and the search for justice, peace and human dignity," yet to be written.

FOCUS ON ASIA: THE CHALLENGE

The biggest contrast between wealth and poverty is in Asia, within a country and within the region. It is universally clear that Japan stands out most prominently as the richest country in Asia. And most other Asian countries, except a few, are poor. This is the general perception of the condition in Asia today. Is this really true, however? Actually not: most countries in Asia are blessed with rich natural resources. But the majority of people are living in poverty. This is the biggest contradiction. That is the real truth; injustice is the other face of poverty.

The Challenge for Japan

Why has Japan become so rich? Are the Japanese more human because of their riches? What is the ethical responsibility of being rich? With her extreme economic power, how should Japan behave in order to prevent other people in their efforts to overcome material poverty?

The Challenge to All of Asia

With such natural wealth in each of our countries, why are our people so poor? Why are the various national development plans not working for the people at the bottom of society? Why has the official development assistance (ODA) led to more debt and a wider gap rather than overcoming poverty? In the final analysis, what has to be done? These are some of the basic questions for all Asians of goodwill. In this connection, a small but growing network of Asian peoples has come together in friendship and solidarity in order to accept the challenge and to take common action on these issues. We call ourselves the "Asian Friendship Society" (AFS). While not claiming to have the definitive answer, AFS is committed to the vision of true humanity in Asia (and in the world), seeking more justice, lasting peace, and greater unity among all peoples, thus moving toward realizing cosmic harmony. Admittedly, this is a dream—an impossible dream, some may say. We in AFS disagree with that; rather, we believe that this dream can and must be realized. Otherwise, all will perish together, eventually, both the poor and the rich.

THE ROOTS OF MODERN POVERTY

Poverty is, of course, not new; nor is it natural. In fact, poverty is created by the excessive greed of the ruling elite, those in control of wealth and power. In order to maintain their privileged position and in order to gain even more, the ruling elite does not hesitate to impose its will on the people, oppressing them in various ways, including violence and corruption. And in order to justify their action, the elite claim to be doing service to the people and to what they call the ultimate truth. But more often, such claims are mere clever propaganda if not all-out lies. Sadly, in all this, the poor who are oppressed believe in the words of their oppressors, tending to look down upon themselves and thus perpetuating their own poverty, a curious phenomenon in human history.

More concretely, here is the making of modern poverty:

1. Through colonialism and other forms of Western imposition, most of the Asian and other Global South nations have lost much of their cultural, historical, and religious roots. Over the past centuries, we have been gradually but effectively dominated by Western powers and ethos. Rarely have our people been able to maintain their own cultural integrity. Instead, we tend to look down upon our own roots, while trying to imitate the West, which has led us to more misery. In recent years, the power elite of most Asian nations has begun to look east, toward Japan and the lesser "tigers" of Hong Kong, Singapore, Taiwan, and South Korea— peoples of "chopstick culture." It is doubtful whether this "look east" policy will solve our problem; in fact, it may bring about the same result, or even worse, because this second round of imitation will further deteriorate the loss of our own cultural integrity and the breakdown of our spiritual foundations. History has revealed that it is such a loss of culture and spirituality that makes poverty. Citing Japan and the other "tigers" as examples, some may say that this is not true. But the Japanese friends themselves are saying that except for material wealth, they are otherwise very much lacking. In truth, colonization of whatever kind is the root cause of poverty in its many forms.

2. Having lost our cultural roots, society is wide open for the ascendancy of materialistic consumerism, which has become a new ethos and a new culture. Properly understood and managed, money and profit cannot do

too much harm. In fact, they could serve us well. But today, the love of money and what money can buy has widened the gap between people, internationally and within a nation. What is more, this love of money and profit has weakened the pursuit of excellence in matters of culture, the arts, music, literature, thoughts, and religion, especially among the power elite. When money and profit have become the new gods, poverty is the inevitable result, because the power elite will simply continue to accumulate increased wealth and power, while the poor are systemically forced to spend all their time and energy simply to survive. As a result, authentic intellectual, spiritual, and cultural leadership is sadly lacking among the power elite, who not only detest people with such quality but also seek to destroy them, especially those who refuse to be co-opted. This is the root cause of intellectual, spiritual, and cultural poverty.

3.   In the present world order, the notion of the "nation-state" itself has led to more poverty. The doctrine of national interest and the doctrine of national security, imposed upon us by the superpowers, have led to the drastic curtailment of freedom, the violation of human rights, the denial of human dignity, and the destruction of the environment and wars. With money having become a new god, people are led to trade everything and the poor are often forced by corrupt and powerful organizations and individuals to sell their land. People are expendable, it appears. Life is no longer respected. Force and violence prevail. The power elite is in control, for the time being. This is political poverty.

4. In most Asian countries, the power elite (including the new rich) invoke the welfare of the people as the cause of their actions, but in truth, most of them have nothing but contempt for the people. Furthermore, they join hands with transnational corporations to make sure that they lose nothing and gain everything. Therefore, in addition to the concentration of wealth and power in their hands, the power elite also serves as the conduit for the siphoning off (??) of human and material resources from the people to foreign countries. This is the epitome of material poverty.

5. To overcome poverty in all these forms is the greatest challenge for people who seek justice, peace, and true humanity. For, only when poverty is overcome can justice, peace, and human dignity become a reality. But why? In one sense, this is so because the modern world has been ordered in such a way that certain countries, certain families, or certain individuals are in control of most of the wealth and power. When there are only so many resources to go around, the "having more" of some automatically means the "having less" or even the "having not" (material poverty) of the others. In short, the love of power and money proves to be the root of all these problems.

6. Particularly, characteristic of the present world condition is the ambiguity of technology. Controlled by a few, it plays such a decisive role today that the gap between the "haves" and the "have-nots" has become so big that most of the "have-nots" are crying and dying in despair. The vicious circle seems endless; poverty begets more poverty, and material poverty begets other poverty as well.

This, then, is the basic human condition today.

WHAT CAN BE DONE

What can we do concretely in order to fulfil such a dream? Here AFS does not claim to have the definitive answer either. We have been searching, however. And we do have some experience and insights to share:

1. *Self-understanding as power:* Poverty in its many dimensions must be overcome once and for all. To accomplish this goal, political power is, no doubt, needed. But more basic and more urgently needed is the power of self-understanding. Through interpretive and creative dialogues our own conceptual and artistic genius can and must be recovered. We have found that the wisdom and insights recovered from people's own cultural roots constitute a more authentic basis for our actions. For, such wisdom is the only thing people still have. And what they still have is what it takes to redeem themselves and humankind.

2. *Focus on the rural poor:* Action to redeem and rebuild true humanity must take place at all levels. AFS has chosen to focus its activities on the rural poor, who are in the majority, who suffer the most, and who retain the most cultural wisdom. Working with the rural poor is a calling that, in our experience, has proven most liberating and celebrative, not only for the poor themselves but also for all who are in solidarity with them. Authentic solidarity with the rural poor is required of all people who seek the ultimate truth. In solidarity with them, and only so, can we find meaning and life in its fullness.

3. *Through friendship and solidarity:* The starting point of AFS action is the commitment to fundamental

unity and harmony of all beings. This is expressed, in actual work, in the friendship between individuals and the solidarity among communities. In friendship and solidarity, the AFS movement aims to build up grass-roots democracy. In friendship and solidarity, true humanity is possible.

AFS AT WORK

AFS provides opportunities for and shares material and human resources. Opportunities are also provided for people to share their cultures, insights, and practical wisdom with each other. Leadership development and technical training are also integral to AFS programs. Of special importance is the careful nurturing of "organic intellectuals," namely, persons who are rooted on the ground, committed to the people, vested with both conceptual and blessed spiritual profundity.

The AFS movement has chapters in different countries of Asia. Each chapter functions as an NGO and, in some cases, as a people's organization; in other words, not as part of the governmental structure nor of private business. In short, AFS is a voluntary organization committed to the public good of all by making it the fundamental option for the poor and the most oppressed.

AFS has neither economic nor political power of its own. Nor does AFS seek power. Rather, the authority of AFS depends on its resolute commitment to being in solidarity with the rural poor and on its faithfulness to that commitment.

Since AFS has neither economic nor political power of its own, AFS needs help from those who have it and those who are enlightened and compassionate enough to support the rural poor with or through AFS. Such support is seen as participating in the rebuilding of our common humanity. To be true, such support must be given in trust, and AFS must work with the utmost integrity.

Individuals and corporate entities who share a similar vision and commitment are cordially invited to join or otherwise support AFS. Their particular gifts and talents, offered in commitment to the ultimate truth, will make true humanity closer to being realized.

6

UNITY AND DIVISIONS AMONG THE TRIBES IN MYANMAR
Intertribal Hermeneutics for Doing Public Theology in Myanmar

La Rip Marip

INTRODUCTION

This chapter presents intertribal hermeneutics as a method for doing public theology—theology for the public—in Myanmar. Public theology may be defined as relating contextual public issues to the biblical text to discern the well-being of all and support the common good of the society. Since the unity among and divisions between the tribes in Myanmar is one of the country's key public issues and since it affects the whole of society, it is necessary for us to do Myanmar public theology now.

This chapter will first present the unity and divisions among the tribes in Myanmar by exploring the official and unofficial tribes and their political struggles throughout recorded history so that readers may discern public issues and strive for the common good. To relate these public issues of unity and divisions among the tribes in Myanmar and the reading of the Bible, the chapter proposes seven steps of intertribal reading as a method for doing Myanmar public theology.[1]

OFFICIAL AND UNOFFICIAL TRIBES IN MYANMAR

Ethnically, Myanmar is an extremely diverse country. The Myanmar government officially recognizes 135 distinct ethnic groups, which are grouped into eight major national ethnicities—Kachin, Kayah, Kayin, Chin, Bamar, Mon, Rakhine, and Shan.[2] According to this list, Kachin comprises twelve different ethnic groups, Kayah comprises nine different ethnic groups, Kayin eleven, Chin fifty-three, Bamar nine, Mon one, Rakhine seven, and Shan thirty-three.[3]

However, this list is very controversial. For example, it counts clans as separate ethnic groups. For instance, in the Kachin group, it counts twelve different ethnic groups—Lhaovo, Lashi, Azi, Rawang, Lisu, Jinghpaw, Gauri, Hkahku, Duleng, Taron, Dalaung, and Kachin. It counts Gauri, Hkahku, and Duleng as separate ethnic groups, but in reality they are not separate ethnic groups but clans of Jinghpaw group. Similarly, it counts Taron and Dalaung as separate ethnic groups, but they are clans of Rawang group. More inappropriately, it counts Kachin as a separate ethnic group, but it is a term encompassing all the six groups of Kachin people—Lhaovo, Lashi, Azi, Rawang, Lisu, and Jinghpaw. Therefore, twelve

---

1   More information regarding Asian public theology can be found in Felix Wilfred, *Asian Public Theology: Critical Concerns in Challenging Times* (Delhi: ISPCK, 2010).

2   Than Tun Win, "Composition of the Different Ethnic Groups under the 8 Major National Ethnic Races in Myanmar," Embassy of the Union of Myanmar, Brussels, accessed February 17, 2023, https://tinyurl.com/yeyk5urf).

3   Than Tun Win, "Composition of the Different Ethnic Groups."

Kachin ethnic groups listed by the Myanmar government actually amount to six. The same cases have been made for other ethnic groups except Mon group.

In addition, some groups are excluded from this list of 135.[4] As Jane M. Ferguson writes, "A few of the groups not included in the list are: Panthay Chinese Muslims, Overseas Chinese (speakers of Hokkien and Cantonese), Anglo-Burmese (Eurasians of mixed Burmese and European background), Burmese Indians, Gurkha, Pakistanis, and Rohingyas."[5]

Why are 135 ethnic groups officially recognized and why not the rest? It is mysterious.[6] One of the arguments is that it is because of the Burmanization of General Ne Win who was deeply reliant on omens, numbers, and stars.[7] According to Richard Cockett, "Ne Win was famously fixated on the number nine."[8] The digits (1+3+5) added up to nine and that is the lucky number for General Ne Win. Another argument suggests that the Myanmar government adopted the number from the 1931 British census, which lists 135 languages.[9] In any case, one may conclude that spoken language is one of the root causes that unites and divides ethnic groups of people in Myanmar. This diversity of ethnic groups in terms of spoken language can even lead to killing each other—Taiwanese

---

4   Jane M. Ferguson, "Who's Counting? Ethnicity, Belonging, and the National Census in Burma/Myanmar," *Bijdragen tot de Taal-, Land- en Volkenkunde* 171, no. 1 (2015): 15–16, www.jstor.org/stable/43819166.

5   Ferguson, "Who's Counting?" 16.

6   Ferguson, 15.

7   Richard Cockett, "Burmanisation," *Blood, Dreams and Gold: The Changing Face of Burma* (New Haven, CT: Yale University Press, 2015), 67–68. Also see Ferguson, "Who's Counting?" 15.

8   Cockett, "Burmanisation," 67.

9   Ferguson, "Who's Counting?" 15. "People and Society," Myanmar National Portal, http://mnp.gov.mm/people-society, last accessed December 11, 2019.

theologian Choan-Seng Song has observed that in the Sino-Japanese War the five brothers of a leading Taiwanese family were shot dead by the Japanese because of different spoken languages.[10] There have been numerous wars and armed conflicts in Myanmar since it gained independence from the British in 1948. Currently, Myanmar is facing a lawsuit at the International Court of Justice (ICJ) as Gambia is accusing Myanmar security forces of committing genocide against Bengalis or Rohingya during the conflicts in northern Rakhine in 2016 and 2017.[11] The unending civil war in Myanmar is one of the longest civil wars in the twentieth and twenty-first centuries anywhere in the world.

POLITICAL STRUGGLES OF THE TRIBES IN MYANMAR

People of all tribes in Myanmar are struggling for their survival under various kinds of hardships, including unequal opportunities in the social, political, and economic spheres.

The British annexed King Thibaw's Burmese kingdom to the British Empire in 1885. However, some highland areas, such as Kachin land, were still independent, with their own chieftains ruling system. The Kachins resisted the British troops when they invaded their land. Therefore, it was only six years later, in 1891, that Kachin land was annexed to Britain's Burma colony. Due to the continued Kachin resistance in the Kachin Highlands, the

---

10   Choan-Seng Song, "Genesis 11:1–9 An Asian Perspective," *Return to Babel: Global Perspectives on the Bible* (Louisville: Westminster John Knox Press, 1999), 27–33.

11   Gambia submitted a forty-five-page application to ICJ on November 11, 2019. The ICJ held a public hearing on that request for three days, December 10–12, 2019. Also, see "Report of Independent International Fact-Finding Mission on Myanmar (27 August 2018)," accessed February 17, 2023, https://tinyurl.com/3eub88k6.

British did not manage to occupy the whole of Kachin land until 1930.

Kachin states, as well as Shan and Chin states, were separately administered by the British as "frontier areas." Throughout the British rule in Kachin land, Kachin chieftains had been demanding autonomy along with other ethnic groups like the Bamar in other parts of present-day Myanmar. The Kachin had dealings with governor Sir Spencer Harcourt Butler in 1925, governor Sir Hugh Lansdown Stephenson in 1935, governor Sir Dorman Smith in 1945, and director of the frontier areas administration Mr. H. N. C. Stevenson in 1946.[12] However, Kachin was only allowed to form three infantry battalions in 1925.

During the British colonial period, Kachin soldiers fought for the British and American allied forces as well as for their land within their own land, and in Asia and Europe. The Kachins' impressive skills in the fighting were evident in both World War I and World War II.[13]

In 1947, along with Shan, Chin, Kayah, and Burma, Kachin signed the historic Panglong Agreement, which guaranteed freedom and autonomy in the frontier areas and equality among the ethnic people of the Union of Myanmar, but this was never fully realized under successive Myanmar rulers. Sadly, after Myanmar gained its independence from the British Empire in 1948, the Myanmar government broke the historic Panglong Agreement.

Moreover, the Myanmar Parliament proclaimed Buddhism as the official state religion of the country on August 29, 1961.

---

12   Mahka Kam Htoi, "The History of Kachin State Day," unpublished lecture, Chapel, Myanmar Institute of Theology, January 10, 2009.

13   C. M. Enriquez, *In Quest of Greatness* (reprint, self-published, 2003); C. M. Enriquez, *Handbooks for the Indian Army: Races of Burma*, 2nd ed. (Delhi: Manager of Publications, 1933); Herman G. Tegenfeldt, *A Century of Growth: The Kachin Baptist Church of Burma* (South Pasadena, CA: William Carey Library, 1974).

Many ethnic armed resistance groups appeared after independence. At present, there are seventeen ceasefire groups and four northern alliance armed groups. The peace process in Myanmar is still a work in progress.

During the civil wars, hundreds of ethnic women were raped and killed. Hundreds of men were arrested, tortured, and persecuted. Hundreds of political leaders were arrested and incarcerated. Thousands of citizens fled.[14]

Recently, the Myanmar government changed the former military ruling system to one of a democratic parliamentary system, but many people have already been forced to leave their homeland because of many kinds of human rights violations of the successive governments. Thousands of internally displaced people can

---

14   Kachin Women's Association Thailand (KWAT), "Kachin Women Denouncing Offensive by the Burmese Army and Atrocities against Kachin People," www.kachinwomen.com, last accessed July 19, 2011; KWAT, "Kachin Women Demand Immediate End to Burmese Regime's Use of Rape as a Weapon of War in Northern Burma Offensive," www.kachinwomen.com, last accessed June 21, 2011; KWAT, "Justice Delayed, Justice Denied," www.kachinwomen.com, accessed January 21, 2018. This was published in January 2016. The subtitle of this publication is "Seeking Truth about Sexual Violence and War Crime Case in Burma (with a Special Focus on the Kawng Kha Case, in Kachin Land)," and it was collectively compiled by the Legal Aid Network (LAN) and KWAT; Earth Rights International, "Rape in Burma across Ethnic Lines," http://www.earthrights.org/news/nosafeplace.shtml, last accessed April 8, 2003; Burma Campaign UK, "Rape and Sexual Violence by the Burmese Army," April 16, 2014, Burma Briefing No. 34., https://tinyurl.com/9bz6jb9x; Shan Human Rights Foundation (SHRF) and Shan Women's Action Network (SWAN), "License to Rape: The Burmese Military Regime's Use of Sexual Violence in the Ongoing War in Shan State," May 2002, https://tinyurl.com/szhhkbae; SHRF, "Displacement in Shan State" (Thailand: Shan Human Rights Foundation, April 1999), 17.

be found these days in Kachin, Rakhaing, Shan, Karen, and Mon states and other parts of the country because of the social, political, and religious conflicts. Thousands of Burmese refugees can be found even in other countries.

RELATING CONTEXT AND TEXT: A HERMENEUTICAL METHOD FOR DOING PUBLIC THEOLOGY

The painful social and political situations have divided the unity of the tribes in Myanmar. What shall the people of Myanmar do in the light of the biblical teaching to promote unity amidst diversity? For instance, in the Old Testament, Psalms 133:1–3 says, "How very good and pleasant it is when kindred live together in unity! . . . For there the Lord ordained his blessing, life forevermore." In the New Testament too, 1 Corinthians 12:12 says: "For just as the body is one and has many members, and all the members of the body, though many, are one body, so it is with Christ." In fact, we are living in just such a diverse and multifaith society. How can we relate the life stories of the people of Myanmar to those of the people in the Bible in order to have the resilient power for social transformation? How do the insights of the Bible contribute to the well-being of all and support the common good of Myanmar society?

In order to do a Myanmar public theology, let me propose the intertribal reading of the Bible method as a hermeneutic.[15] The intertribal reading of the Bible is an adaptation of the intercultural

---

15   M. La Rip, "Intertribal Hermeneutics in the Context of Myanmar: A Study of Roles and Functions of Jeremianic Female Imagery" (PhD diss., Vrije Universiteit Amsterdam 2018); La Rip Marip, "Personal Application, Social Justice, and Social Transformation (A Dialogue between Myanmar and the Netherlands)," in *Bible and Transformation: The Promise of Intercultural Bible Reading*, ed. Hans de Wit and Janet Dyk (Atlanta: SBL Press, 2015), 159–66.

Bible reading model.[16] Intercultural reading of the Bible is a way of reading in which the same biblical text is read by different groups of people from different social-political-cultural backgrounds. The groups first read the text in their own context and then get involved in a dialogue about its significance with a partner group. This reading methodology can be found as new biblical empirical hermeneutics in contemporary biblical scholarship. This methodology was initially designed by scholars from the Netherlands, Africa, and Latin America in 1998, and the method has been tested by an international group of scholars within the framework of the worldwide project "Through the Eyes of Another," the result of which were documented as a book in 2004.[17] The intercultural reading of the Bible seeks to stimulate interaction, not to favor exotic (fantastic/romantic/marvelous) encounters, but to precisely enhance the social commitment of the participants. The purpose is to involve biblical stories with present-day readers in a discussion about the future of the earth.[18]

This method had been originally designed for groups of readers from different cultures, but I tested this method among the tribes of Myanmar people and proved how it worked. In my study of intertribal hermeneutics in the context of Myanmar, sixty-seven people took part from twelve different ethnic groups. In terms of gender, thirty-six were males and thirty-one were females. In terms of ethnicity, the participants came from Kachin, Kayin, Chin, Shan, Mon, Bamar, Lisu, Lahu, Akha, Wa, Naga, and Chinese backgrounds. In terms of a Christian denomination, the participants

16   Hans de Wit, Louis Jonker, Marleen Kool, and Daniel Schipani, eds., *Through the Eyes of Another* (Nappanee, IN: Evangel Press, 2004). To study "A Countercultural Reading of the Bible," see Dhyanchand Carr, *God with Us: A Bold Understanding of Suffering, Jesus Christ and Forgiveness* (Chennai: The Christian Literature Society, 2018), 169–218.

17   Carr, *God with Us*.

18   Carr.

were from Baptist, Methodist, Anglican, Assembly of God, Church of Christ, and Lisu Christian Church of Myanmar. The ages of the participants were between twenty and seventy years. Participants included the unemployed, disabled, day laborers, military pensioners, retirees, police officers, school teachers, music teachers, nurses, accountants, NGO workers, pastors, church ministers, seminary lecturers, church moderators, deacons, deaconesses, religious organization workers, evangelists, day-care workers, night-care workers, students, seminarians, and housewives. The main data were collected in Yangon city and slum areas of Yangon during 2011 and 2012, while the empirical data for my pilot project were collected in the Netherlands. In addition to the Christian Bible readers, this method also works among people from other faiths.[19]

In doing the intertribal reading of the Bible, the reading groups go through the following seven steps.[20]

Step 1: Form a group.

Step 2: Find a partner group.

Step 3: Read the text spontaneously.

Step 4: Re-read the text through the eyes of another.

Step 5: Interact/dialogue with the partner group.

Step 6: Change of perspectives.

Step 7: Rounding off and starting over

---

19   See HtetPaing YeMaung, "Interreligious Cultural Reading of Proverbs 4: 1–27" (term paper submitted to the class "Theories of Biblical Interpretations," Yangon, Myanmar, November 15, 2020).

20   Hans de Wit, *Through the Eyes of Another: Intercultural Reading of the Bible: Manual for Facilitators and Reporters* (VU University Amsterdam, August 2008). Also see Arie Moolenaar, "Listening with the Heart: The Reading Experience of the Dutch Groups," in *Through the Eyes of Another*, ed. de Wit et al., 90.

Step 1: Form a Group

First of all, a pair of small reading groups will be formed to engage in a dialogue with the partner group. In my research, a group with five to ten members is the best size to deal with the different perspectives and to exchange ideas. Among the Bible reading groups, the social situations of the readers are usually different from each other. Their pains, problems, and major concerns are not the same. For example, while one group is concerned about sociopolitical conflicts, the other group is concerned about education, healthcare, and the holistic development problems inside and outside the church.[21] Within the group, a group portrait will be drawn up so that the partner group will understand the social situation of the other partner group and will be able to read the text again through the eyes of that partner group. In order to produce the group portrait, the participants will talk about their respective social, religious, economic, and political backgrounds. During this stage, we have the opportunity to listen to the voices of the Myanmar people who are facing various issues, such as diversity, war, and disharmony, to name only a few. We may pay attention to personal issues, but it is important for us to focus on the issues related to the public.

It is observed that the people's voices can be a resilient power that can empower people to people.[22] For example, an ordained

---

21   La Rip, "Intertribal Hermeneutics in the Context of Myanmar," 150.

22   Hlaing Bwa, *Contextual Theology: Resilience Power* (Yangon: Myanmar Institute of Theology, 2020). In this collection of voices and reflections from the people, the research collected people's voices regarding interrelated community issues, such as armed conflicts, natural resources crisis, human trafficking, drug abuse, poverty, voices of women, voices of youths, voices of leaders, relationships between tribes, and relationship between interfaith groups. The methodological development for contextual theology formation is as follows:

deaconess participant in the Kachin group said that her family had been moving from one place to another due to the political instability in her region. She was born and brought up in Shan state, but the endless armed conflicts between the ethnic armed groups and the Myanmar army in her village forced her family to move from Shan state to Kachin state and finally to Yangon. When she was two years old, her mother died. She could not attend school, hence she had no access to a good education. She was a born animist as her father had been a priest of animism, but later she became a Christian when her father converted to Christianity. In this situation, the church became her haven. She expressed pleasure with the religious services at the churches she attended.[23] In the interaction of the Kachin and Mon groups, the Mon group noticed that the Kachin never detached from their social ties, hence they saw that as a Kachin social structure; even the Kachin group living in the comfort zone strongly identified with the Kachin living in the war zone. Therefore, the Mon group said, "Kachin people are proud of their nationality, race, culture, tradition, heredity, and natural resources. They dared to raise their voice against injustice." Through the interaction with the partner's profile, the Mon group agreed to preserve their Mon culture.[24]

Within the group, a facilitator and a reporter for the individual reading group are selected; the meeting schedules and venue of both groups are set up so that this intertribal reading practice can exchange its reading reports with its partner reading group.

Step 1. Emphatic listening as a tool for collecting voices of the people.

Step 2. Portraying in the form of true story as documentation.

Step 3. Experience sharing and theological reflection for positive energy.

Step 4. Engaging key leaders for ownership, confirmation, publication, and effective implementation.

23   La Rip, "Intertribal Hermeneutics in the Context of Myanmar," 155.
24   La Rip, 172.

Step 2: Find a Partner Group

Groups are free to choose a partner group. They might decide on a specific Bible text or choose a particular topic. For instance, a Myanmar Christian group chose a non-Christian group and they decided to read Proverbs 4:1–27.[25] In my research of intertribal hermeneutics in the context of Myanmar, all the paired groups are Christians, but they are from different tribes, ethnicity, denominations, gender, and social status.

Step 3: Read the Text Spontaneously

At this stage, the group will start reading the text without outside inputs, and this stage is called the spontaneous reading of the Bible. Since the text is semantically autonomous and it opens up to anyone who can read, participants will read it with their hearts and from their own situations and experiences. According to De Wit, who wrote a manual for the facilitators and reporters of intercultural reading of the Bible, "the main focus is not so much on the historical background of the text, but on the 'foreground' of the text: the effect the text has on new readers, the way it affects you, what it evokes. What strikes you? What touches you? What makes you angry, what do you recognize?"[26] In any case, it does not

---

25   HtetPaing YeMaung, "Interreligious Cultural Reading of Proverbs 4: 1–27."

26   de Wit, *Through the Eyes of Another, Intercultural Bible Reading: Manual for Facilitators and Reporters.* In this handbook, Hans de Wit says, "These questions show three ways in which one can deal with (biblical) texts. In this context, the terms 'behind the text,' 'in the text' and 'before the text' are used. Looking 'behind the text' implies that one looks at the historical context in which the biblical text was created. Looking 'in' the text implies that one primarily focuses on what the text expresses, as a collection of words and phrases. Looking 'before' the text, or looking at its 'foreground' implies that one especially focuses on what new readers do with

totally reject the importance of the historical context of the text. Any professional exegete from the group can contribute historical background information to the text. Some guiding questions for spontaneous reading in intertribal Bible reading are as follows:[27]

- Does the text refer to certain conflicts? (Behind the text.)

- What traces of culture do you discover in the text? (In the text.)

- Do you understand everything in the text? (In the text.)

- What is the central message of the text in your opinion? (In the text.)

- "With whom" do you read the text, meaning by that: What person in the story do you identify with and why? What role do you think you would have played if you had been part of the story? (The foreground of the text.)

- What aspects of the story especially touch you? What thoughts, memories, and experiences from your own life does the text you read evoke? Why? (The foreground of the text.)

- How would the text be able to play a role in your life? (The foreground of the text.)

---

the old text and what the old text does to new readers. If participants want to consult scientific commentaries, they are of course entirely free to do so. It is important that the voice of professional readers (exegetes) does not become dominant in the discussion (exegesis is only one way to deal with biblical texts!) and that the group also learns to assess the value of its own insights."

27   de Wit, *Through the Eyes of Another, Intercultural Bible Reading: Manual for Facilitators and Reporters.*

In my analysis of the heuristic keys and focalization of the groups, I have discovered that the readers' life experiences in their sociocultural context are important in their spontaneous readings.[28] The readers can explain the text not only by using exegetical methods but also by relating one's own life experience or feelings to the components presented in the story, which is a form of appropriation. The hermeneutical process of appropriation works when the readers read the text and the readers focus on either character or action in the text and they connect the text with their life experiences to encounter injustice in their social context or to grow their spirituality. It was found that all reading groups are able to unlock the meaning of the text by using their heuristic keys, such as gender inequality, a wrongful death case, church discipline, civil war, new year festivals, problems of exploitation of natural resources, socioeconomic issues, political problems, poverty, education, drugs, and natural disasters. For instance, when a group of Myanmar people read Jeremiah 4:29–31, their life experience helps the group members understand why and how the inhabitants of Jerusalem fled to the thickets and to the rocks because all the ethnic people have been suffering from the civil war. Karen people said that during the civil war in the Karen state, many Karen people had to flee to Thai–Myanmar border areas for their survival. Many villages had been quiet and there was no one in such villages. If they do not flee to the border areas they may be tortured by government troops. Many similar indications of the relationship between Myanmar people's life experiences and the biblical texts were discovered in my research of intertribal hermeneutics in the context of Myanmar.

---

28   La Rip, "Intertribal Hermeneutics in the Context of Myanmar," 222–28.

Research has shown that Myanmar readers appropriate the text by means of allegory, typology, and parallelism of terms so that the crying of the biblical character Rachel becomes the crying of the people of Myanmar.[29] Rachel's crying even empowered the readers for social transformation. In this perspective, Rachel (in Jer 31:15–22) is compared with Myanmar so that Rachel is to be comforted by the readers themselves—they are to participate in the nation-building of Myanmar. For example, the Myanmar diaspora male youth group living in the Netherlands had read with Rachel and her sons so that the weeping mother Rachel gradually became the crying mother Myanmar, who is crying for the loss of her diasporic sons. Rachel/Myanmar is crying for her diasporic sons in terms of the political, economic, and ecological situation. This understanding and interpretation of the text had empowered the Myanmar diaspora to return to Myanmar and to comfort their crying mother Myanmar by means of participating in nation-building. This personal commitment was discovered as a social transformation in front of the text.[30]

Step 4: Reread the Text through the Eyes of Another

At this stage, the partner reading groups will exchange their reading reports and interact with each other. The interaction will be to observe the similarities and differences between the partner groups. It is the moment to reread the text "through the eyes of another." The group's observation of the divergences will enable it to figure out where the differences come from.

---

29   La Rip, "Intertribal Hermeneutics in the Context of Myanmar."

30   Also see La Rip, "Personal Application, Social Justice, and Social Transformation," 159–66.

Then the reading groups will carefully examine the group portrait and read the report of the partner group to see the partner group's faces, feel their experiences, and get a clearer idea about them. Some questions for this step are as follows:[31]

- What is the partner group's profile? What problems do they wrestle with? What pains do they suffer?

- How did they deal with the biblical text? Were there any conflicts in the group, any disagreements? Was there a consensus as to the meaning of the biblical text? Does the group use scholarly commentaries? Does the group address the entire text or do they concentrate on a part of it? What part? What components in the text, defined by culture, attracted the partner group's attention? How does the group view the central message of the text? To whom do they identify in the story and why?

- Do the group members appropriate/actualize the text? Do they apply the text to their own lives?

In the paired reading groups of Christian and non-Christian readers, both groups look carefully at the group portraits and reading reports of either group. They saw their differences not only in ethnicity and religious backgrounds but also in reading the biblical text. The members of the Christian group were a Chin Christian, two Karen Christians, a Chinese Christian, a Kayan Christian, and a Paoh-Karen Christian. In the non-Christian group, the participants were two Burmese Buddhists, an Arakanese Buddhist, a Nepali Hindu Buddhist, and a Muslim. Each group rereads the text through the eyes of another and sees the

---

31   de Wit, *Through the Eyes of Another, Intercultural Bible Reading: Manual for Facilitators and Reporters*, 27–29.

similarities and dissimilarities. Both groups see the text as ethical or moral teaching. In their reading of Proverbs 4:1–27, both groups could pay attention to the human rights issue too. This is to be found as a good starting point for public theology.[32]

Similarly, in the study of the intertribal interaction between the paired groups, it was discovered that groups developed their hermeneutical process by dealing with similarities and differences between them. For instance, drug trafficking, language extinction, and culture are key issues for a group that can redirect them to see and judge their own local situations. Their partner group also pays attention to new knowledge. They have acquired perseverance and diligence as keys to a successful mission and evangelism.[33]

Step 5: Interact/Dialogue with the Partner Group

After one has looked at the text "through the eyes of another," there will be interaction/dialogue with the partner group with the following questions: What heuristic keys, focalization, and exegetical methods does the partner group use? Do certain issues of the partner group stand out? Does the reading become a place to practice developing a new praxis?

In the interaction between two groups of theological students, it was discovered that the reading served as an occasion to practice developing a new praxis. To illustrate this, a reader said that the text (Jer 13:20–27) directly taught him to avoid all evil and to cultivate good because he understood that God could judge all people, not just those people of Jerusalem who committed sin. This reader reads the text with the original audience of the text. Since the text empowers him to work for social transformation,

---

32   HtetPaing YeMaung, "Interreligious Cultural Reading of Proverbs 4:1–27."

33   La Rip, "Intertribal Hermeneutics in the Context of Myanmar," 238.

this reading becomes a session to practice a new praxis. For instance, women in his culture have to work more than men. This is culturally defined in his context, wherein men do not gather firewood for cooking, but it is the women who have to do this, because the gender construct defines the role of males and females that way. If a man gathers firewood, he is considered to be abnormal. In addition to this work of gathering firewood, women also have to cook for the family and wash clothes, and also feed their babies if they are mothers. Furthermore, women have to work together with men in the field, since their main occupation is hillside cultivation. When these farmers return home, women will carry the firewood while men do not carry any heavy things. The reader considers this culturally defined gender inequality as a sin, a sin against the will of God who could judge those people who would commit sin. The culturally defined gender inequality will receive God's judgment. Therefore, the reader makes a vow to educate his people to abolish gender inequality, to change the unequal gender construct in his context, and to practice gender equality.[34]

Step 6: Change of Perspective

In this step, the groups are to focus on three important issues: (1) How did the partner group deal with the group's reading report and interpretation of the Bible story? What did the partner group notice in particular? Were they amazed, pleased, irritated, or angry about this? (2) What happened to them; how did they deal with the similarities and with the differences? (3) How did they subsequently address the other group, with admiration and empathy or critical and condemning? In this last phase, the group will rethink whether they will change their perspective and follow

---

34   La Rip, 199.

their partner group's understanding or whether they have reached saturation point.[35]

In the paired reading groups of Christians and non-Christian readers, a Buddhist reader said that the reading of the biblical text (Prov 4:1–27) gave a lot of new insights to the non-Christians.[36]

Personally, she accepted and agreed with the ethical teachings from the text. What she also learned from her partner group, who were Christians, was that Christians read the text with their lives, interpreted it critically, and asked questions about it. She believed the Christian friends from her partner group were not extreme or one-sided believers but were progressive. Even though her partners might not accept the other group's point of view, the responses were not aggressive to them, she felt. She was also happy to know that her friends from her partner group were very flexible; they did not judge the views of non-Christian readers and were not offended by the non-Christian response to the text.[37]

In the paired reading groups of theological students, a change of perspectives was discovered. Group A observed the partner's identification patterns so that they found some similarities and differences between the two groups. The group maintained the similarities between them and adopted different identification and said "identification with the land is new to us. We did not notice this identification pattern as a fruitful method. Now it is possible through the partner's contextual situation." This is a direct expression of admiration. Group B also paid attention to the partner's focalization—judgment of God—and to the rhetorical reading. Then, the group reread the text through the focalization that the partner group had used so that

35   de Wit, *Through the Eyes of Another, Intercultural Bible Reading: Manual for Facilitators and Reporters*, 29–32.

36   HtetPaing YeMaung, "Interreligious Cultural Reading of Proverbs 4:1–27."

37   HtetPaing YeMaung.

Group B could unlock the new meaning of the text—punishment of God. Then, the group analyzed the identification patterns and reread the text. As a result, the group acquired new insights of recontextualization from the partner group. In this intertribal interaction, Group B expressed direct admiration of the partner group, saying, "We gain such new insights of the need of care and counselling method. Through discussing our group partner's perspective, we come to realize the importance of interpreting, preaching, and reading biblical passages with new eyes or with the eyes of another." In sum, both groups developed their hermeneutical process by exchanging perspectives. Group A acquired reading perspectives, such as liberation, spiritual, mission, and evangelism perspectives, from Group B. Likewise, Group B enriched their hermeneutical process by adopting the partner's focalization and rhetorical reading.[38]

Step 7: Rounding Off and Starting Over

After the dialogue with the partner group, some time is allotted for the group to look back at the whole process for a last reaction to the partner group. The groups may ask themselves: Was the process worth the investment? What did the group members learn? Does the group want to do something with the experience in the local community of faith or local context?

A beautiful illustration may be found in the Kachin–Mon paired groups. By reviewing the whole process, the Kachin group members, who were deeply rooted in their Kachin culture, realized that all ethnic people were the children of God. For instance, the Kachin group focused on a Kachin participant in the Mon group who married a Mon. This Kachin woman was working among Mon and other ethnic groups, both Christians

---

38   La Rip, "Intertribal Hermeneutics in the Context of Myanmar," 239.

and Buddhists. Therefore, the Kachin group was convinced that service was more important than race preservation. In addition, they also learned the benefits of collaborative group discussion that enabled the Mon group to deal with difficult texts. However, the Kachin group agreed to continue to appeal to God to pardon their sins and restore their people and land to a state of peace. They saw the current situation as God's judgment over their earlier sins. They saw repentance and prayer (with fasting) as what they urgently needed in their context. They also committed to hope in God, like Rachel who was weeping for her children (Jer 31:15–22).

In the case of the Mon group, they were impressed by the Kachin's humble confession, repentance, and hope in God. Through this Kachin group's reading, the Mon group members reminded themselves to reconsider their spiritual journey. The Mon group admitted that Mon Christians also had to have a public confession for their sins of the past and the present. For instance, some Mon people in the missionary period in Myanmar had killed missionaries or driven them to insanity. As part of social transformation, the Mon group agreed to renew their spiritual journey. Moreover, the Mon group imitated the humbleness and unity of their partner group. The Mon group encouraged each other to greet group members wherever and whenever they ran into each other. They would confess their shortcomings and return to God. They committed themselves to helping Kachin internally displaced persons and refugees in any possible manner. Finally, the group stood up and prayed for the Kachin refugees and those who were internally displaced, in solidarity with the victims.[39]

---

39   The Mon Church has been making charitable donations to Kachin refugees since the Kachin war broke out in 2011. These donations are channeled through the Mon Baptist Convention and Myanmar Baptist Convention headquarters. The donations include money, medicine, and clothes.

CONCLUSION

In the midst of divisions among the tribes in Myanmar, intertribal hermeneutics were proposed to restore the unity of the community. The reading practice outlined above aims to relate public issues to biblical text so that participants will engage not only with people but also with theology for the people. This proposed intertribal hermeneutics is comprised of seven steps for doing public theology, each step allowing people to raise their voices of pain, suffering, fear, and hope. God does not stay away from the people whom God created. God always uses people as God's agents. Therefore, people will stand in solidarity with the people who have pain, suffering, fear, and hope. The well-being of all and the common good of Myanmar society will be achieved by the people, the agents of God.

7

INTERFAITH DIALOGUE AS THE RELEVANT CHARACTERISTIC FOR MAKING PEACE AMONG CHRISTIANS AND BUDDHISTS IN MYANMAR

Ram Lian Thang

What is peace-making? According to Robert Guelich, to make peace is to engage actively in bringing God's reconciling love to all of the broken society.[1] It is to build a bridge to reconcile alienated parties and maintain peace. Peace is the product of human effort. Peace does not come where it does not feel invited or stay where it does not feel welcomed.[2] Who are the peacemakers? The peacemakers are "those who experience the peace of God, and become God's agents establishing peace in the world."[3] Peacemakers are

---

1   Robert A. Guelich, *The Sermon on the Mount: A Foundation for Understanding* (Waco: Word Books, 1982), 107.

2   Erik Kolbell, *What Jesus Meant: The Beatitudes and a Meaningful Life* (London: Westminster John Knox Press, 2003), 116.

3   Guelich, *The Sermon on the Mount*, 92.

those who bring peace between two conflicting parties and are actively involved in the work of making peace, bringing about wholeness and well-being among the alienated.[4] Peacemakers do not have a passive attitude, but rather render positive actions for reconciliation.

Peacemakers are concerned about the destruction caused by war and are committed to transforming hateful minds to prevent the outbreak of war between nations. Peacemakers exhort governments to spend more funds on humanitarian works and less on military services. Peacemakers are concerned about the safety of the whole of humanity. They are moved by love and concern for the well-being of all humanity. This act of love is nothing less than the redeeming love exhibited and demanded in Jesus's ministry.[5] Peacemakers are actively committed to working for reconciliation and wholeness where there is conflict and estrangement. Their commitment involves a readiness to engage in conflict when it is necessary for reconciliation and is related to the respect for neighbors that precludes behavior that leads to alienation. It involves a struggle to reorder and renew relationships when they are broken and marked by hostilities.

Peacemakers shall be called "sons of God." The phrase "they shall be called" implies "they shall be recognized as." This means those who help establish God's peace by means of preventing war, providing care to those in need, putting two neighbors back on speaking terms, and restoring unity within a society are recognized as assisting in God's activity in our world.[6] The phrase "son of" reflects a Palestinian idiom, which is used to designate a person when their action is different from their origin. This means

---

4   Guelich, *The Sermon on the Mount*, 107.

5   Guelich, *The Sermon on the Mount*, 92.

6   Jim Forest, *The Ladder of the Beatitudes* (Maryknoll, NY: Orbis Books, 1999), 132.

people are called "son of" when they imitate something that they do not have normally. God is the author of peace, and peace-makers are imitators of God.[7] Therefore, peacemakers are "sons of God" because they share in God's peacemaking mission in the world with true commitment for the prevalence of peace. Peace is therefore always related to the flourishing of reconciliation between enemies, the development of social stability and pros-perity in the midst of chaotic situations, and the overwhelming harmonious unity and transparent social relationship prevailing over any kind of hatred, misunderstanding, and estrangement. It is when we commit ourselves to the mission of peace-making that we are recognized as "sons of God."

In Myanmar, there is a misunderstanding among many religions, and this leads to conflict between the ethnic groups in Myanmar. So, it is necessary to discern which method will resolve religious conflict in Myanmar. There is only one way to build a peaceful society in this country, and that is through "dialogue." As mentioned, a peacemaker brings peace between two parties that are in conflict with each other. In Myanmar, the Christians see Buddhists as their enemy, while the Buddhists regard Christianity as an alien religion. This is because of a misunderstanding.

THE NATION AND THE PEOPLE OF MYANMAR

Myanmar is the largest country in Southeast Asia and lies between Thailand and India. It has a total area of 261,228 square miles with a population of 59 million belonging to 135 ethnic groups (as per 2012 figures). Total life expectancy is 63.4 years—65.7 for females

---

7   David S. Dockery, and David E. Garland, *Seeking the Kingdom: The Sermon on the Mount Made Practical for Today* (Wheaton, IL: Harold Shaw Publishers, 1992), 32.

and 61.2 for males. In terms of demographic distribution, Yangon has a population of between three and four million, and Mandalay (the second-largest city in the country) has a population of about one million.[8]

Myanmar is a pluralistic country. Ethnically, Myanmar has several nationalities, of which the eight major groups are Kachin, Kaya (Karenni), Kayin (Karen), Chin, Mon, Bamar (Burmese), Rakhine (Arakan), and Shan. Linguistically, Myanmar has more than one hundred languages and dialects. Religiously, 89.3 percent of the people practice Buddhism, while 5.6 percent follow Christianity, and 3.8 percent follow Islam. Those practicing Hinduism and Animism account for less than 1 percent of the population. Politically, Myanmar has experienced monarchy, colonialism, parliamentary democracy, socialism, and militarism.[9]

POLITICAL BACKGROUND

In the realm of political history, Burma was all about the rise and fall of numerous kingdoms in south and central Burma until the mid-seventeenth century, with the Mons, Burmese, and Shans struggling for dominance. Britain invaded Burma in 1852, and from 1885 to 1937 the entire country was a province of British India. Burma regained independence on January 4, 1948, under the leadership of General Aung San and joined the United Nations in the same year. General Aung San was assassinated shortly thereafter, and U Nu led the country under military rule.[10]

---

8   Michael Aung Thwin and Maitrii Aung Thwin, *A History of Myanmar since Ancient Times* (London: Reaktion Books, 2012), 49.

9   Aung Thwin and Aung Thwin, *A History of Myanmar since Ancient Times*, 51.

10   Donald E. Smith, *Religion and Politics in Burma* (Princeton, NJ: Princeton University Press, 1965), 39–40.

POLITICAL CLIMATE IN MYANMAR

When we study the political climate of Myanmar, there are five stages of political change. First, Myanmar had monarchical rule from the early eleventh century to the late nineteenth century. There were three Anglo-Burmese wars in colonial times—in 1824, 1852, and 1885. The last Burmese king, Thibaw, was arrested in 1885, at which point the whole country became a province of the British Indian Empire until 1937.[11] This was the first political change in Burma (Myanmar).

Second, Myanmar experienced a 124-year period of colonial rule under the British Indian Empire, that is, from 1824 to 1948. In 1824–26, the first Anglo-Burmese War led to the British take-over of Pegu. In 1886, the British abolished the Konbaun court and annexed Burma, placing it under the control of the Government of India. A brief rebellion against the British took place in which monks participated; the *sangha* accepted British rule in the hope that the British would take on royal duties (strong anti-Thibaw sentiments existed among the *sangha*[12]).

Third, a parliamentary democratic system was experimented with in Myanmar for a very short period of fourteen years, from 1948 to 1962. This could not be continued, because Prime Minister U Nu declared Buddhism to be the state's religion, to which declaration ethnic minority groups offered resistance, and opposition groups were also opposed to this act by the national government.[13]

Fourth, in 1962, a military regime led by General Ne Win took power and ruled the country for almost three decades under

---

11   Samuel Ngun Ling, "Indigenous Theology Amidst Multi-Faith Context: Myanmar Experience" in *Doing Indigenous Theology in Asia*, eds. Hrangthan Chhung i, M.M. Ekka and Wati Longchar (Nagpur, India: NCC/SCEPTRE/GTC, 2012), 135.

12   Juliane Schober, *Modern Buddhist Conjunctures in Myanmar: Cultural Narratives, Colonial Legacies, and Civil Society* (Honolulu: University of Hawai'i Press, 2011), 155.

13   Ngun Ling, *Indigenous Theology*, 135.

the "Burmese way of socialism" until 1988. Throughout this period, the mismanagement and corruption of the military prevailed in the country, and it became one of the poorest countries in the world.

Fifth, as a result of mass demonstrations in favor of democracy in the late 1980s, the military regime took power for the second time in 1988 and introduced free enterprise carefully monitored by the military. This system prevails until the present day. The first general election was held in 1991, at which Aung San Suu Kyi, a daughter of General Aung San, won a landslide victory. The military regime refused to hand over power to Aung San Suu Kyi and kept her father under house arrest for twenty years.[14] This military regime uses power to deal with ethnic groups such as the Chin, Kachin, and Kayin. People in Myanmar live under the shadow of the military in fear.

RELIGIOUS BACKGROUND

Relatively little is known about religion in Myanmar before the eleventh century. Indigenous animism coexisted and combined with the religions of India, including several Hindu sects. Both Theravada and Mahayana Buddhism, during the eleventh century, were introduced in Myanmar. It was still a divided state of several small kingdoms, each with its own distinctive ruler or king. According to oral tradition, it is believed that Theravada Buddhism was introduced to central Myanmar after Aniruddha had conquered Thaton, the hometown of Mon, in 1057.[15] Burmese historian Than Tun maintained that Buddhism had existed in Pagan, the ancient capital of Myanmar, in the ninth century.[16] It is undeniable that the state of Myanmar declares Buddhism as the

---

14   Ngun Ling, 136.
15   Than Tun, *Essays on the History and Buddhism of Burma* (Whiting Bay, Scotland: Kiscadale Publications, 1988), 23.
16   Tun, *Essays on the History and Buddhism of Burma*, 24.

nation's religion. When General Ne Win took power through a military coup on March 2, 1962, he dissolved parliament and abrogated the constitution. And so ended the declaration of Buddhism as the state religion as well. Non-Buddhists heaved a sigh of relief. But twenty years later, history repeated itself. "Buddhism as state religion," which was one of the ostensible reasons for the military coup, was reaffirmed once again as the favored religion in 1982.

CHRISTIAN–BUDDHIST RELATIONS IN MYANMAR

One of the obstacles that creates a sharp division among Buddhists and Christians in Myanmar is misunderstanding and misconception. There is no respect for each other's religion in their respective faiths. Buddhism is known as the "favored religion" in Myanmar. This "favored religion" concept claims to embrace all religions in the country so that they flourish together peacefully and harmoniously while minimizing the freedom of the "un-favored religions." This means that no real encounter between the favored religion (Buddhism) and unfavored religion such as Christianity can occur as long as special attention is given to one major religion. The net result is that the concept of "favored religion" implicitly condones the idea of "favored adherents" set against the adherents of other unfavored religions so that this concept brings about discrimination between people of different faiths, at least at the individual or ethnic level. This is the ground against which the minority ethnic Christians (unfavored adherents) and the majority Burmese Buddhists (favored adherents) confronted each other in a conflict leading to a breach of communication between them.[17] This conflict leads the country to being an "unpeaceful" society.

---

17   Samuel Ngun Ling, *Communicating Christ in Myanmar: Issues, Interactions and Perspectives* (Yangon: Association for Theological Education in Myanmar, 2010), 12–13.

THE BURMESE BUDDHIST VIEW OF CHRISTIANITY

Dr. Simon Pau Khan En has rightly pointed out that "to many people in Myanmar, Christianity is an alien religion, and some people identify Christians with anti-nationalist or pro-westerners."[18] He further comments:

> The suspicion from Buddhists, which eventually caused the alienation of Christianity, actually was not without reasons since there were some factors leading to these suspicions. First, Christianity came to the country in the same package as colonialism, and therefore some Buddhists assumed that the Christian Mission had the same "mission" as colonialism and that both desired the same end, namely the speedy conquest of the Burmese Kingdom by the British.[19]

Another negative view may be caused by the mission of Christians to the public. The soul-winning-oriented Christian mission seeks to increase church membership, to win the souls of the Buddhists. Such actions reinforce the suspicions of Buddhists that Christianity is a colonial religion.

It is said that Burmese culture is deeply embedded in the form of the Theravada Buddhist tradition. Theravada Buddhism is the only foundation of the creativity, philosophical thinking, and way of life of the Burmese people. Theravada Buddhist Abhidhamma philosophy shadowed the Burmese worldview, the conception of human existence, meaning, and destiny, and also

---

18   Simon Pau Khan En, *Nat Worship: A Paradigm for Doing Contextual Theology in Myanmar* (Yangon: Judson Research Center of the Myanmar Institute of Theology, 2012), 8.

19   Pau Khan En, *Nat Worship*, 8.

the idea of the Ultimate or God. Religion and culture, for them, are just two sides of the same coin. This means that the religious life of the Burmese cannot be separated from their sociocultural identity. Understanding Burmese culture means understanding the Burmese Buddhist way of life.[20]

Therefore, it is clear that the Buddhist attitude toward Christians is negative. Since Christianity was seen as colonial religion in history, a negative image of all that is Christian remains even today. That is one of the reasons why Myanmar Christians need to refocus on interreligious dialogue to encourage a better understanding, which is relevant to the present existential context.

THE BURMESE CHRISTIAN VIEW OF BUDDHISM

The Christian understanding of Buddhism also tends to be negative. A traditional view is that Buddhists in Myanmar were influenced by an "exclusivist" view where non-Christians were seen as the ones who will not inherit heaven and as those who worship idols.

I feel that Christians in Myanmar usually do not try to learn from other faiths. In the present context, most Christians consider people of other faiths as nonbelievers and idolatrous and even claim that they will never attain salvation because they do not believe Jesus Christ as their savior, and they are not converts. Moreover, they claim that their way is the best way to lead to liberation. Some Christians see Buddhists negatively as just worshippers of an idol: the idol of Buddha. Some Christian preachers blindly attack Buddhism in their sermons without knowing what the essence of Buddhism is. It is not only the preachers but also many ordinary Christians in Myanmar who believe in the exclusivist view that

---

20   Pau Khan En, 45.

Buddhism is a hell-bound religion. This belief leads the Christians in Myanmar to consider Buddhists as their enemies.

BUILDING PEACE IN SOCIETY THROUGH INTERFAITH DIALOGUE

As the world we live in today is religiously pluralistic, interreligious dialogue is, therefore, urgent and imperative for world peace, justice, and love. The prioritized responsibility of Christians should be to initiate Christian engagement in interreligious dialogue since Christianity is a religion of self-giving love and peacemaking.[21] In the present situation of Myanmar, we have faced conflicts between Buddhism and other faiths such as Islam and Christianity. So, interfaith dialogue is a prerequisite for making peace and building peace in the nation.

THE MEANING OF DIALOGUE

The word "dialogue" comes from the Greek word *dia-logos* (*dior*, *dia*, two; *logos*, words) which means "to converse" or "a conversation between two or more persons, and also an exchange of ideas and opinions." The word "inter" comes from the Greek word *enteron* meaning "between, among, in the midst and reciprocal," so that the word "interreligious" bears the meaning of what happens between persons of different religious faiths. Interreligious dialogue in general is, therefore, reciprocal yet convincing communication between two persons of different faiths. The interreligious dialogue is not merely an outer communication between the two persons but the inner communication with what they believe in terms of God or in the Mystery and the sharing of such inner convictions with one another at the deepest level.[22]

---

21   Ngun Ling, *Communicating Christ in Myanmar*, 131.
22   Ngun Ling, 199–200.

It is said that there are three goals of interreligious dialogue. These are:

1. To know oneself ever more profoundly and enrich and round out one's appreciation of one's own faith tradition.

2. To know the other ever more authentically and gain a friendly understanding of others as they are not seen as a caricature.

3. To live ever more fully accordingly and to establish a more solid foundation for a community of life and action among persons of various traditions.[23]

Paul Knitter says that, normally speaking, dialogue is just a human-to-human conversation. But in practical reality, it is not merely a human-to-human conversation, but it includes mutual learning and transformation. Therefore, dialogue is an open relationship where the participants mutually recognize and respect the authentic existence of each other and agree not only to coexist with all their differences and peculiarities but also to build together a common future.[24]

For Hlaing Bwa,[25] in the context of religious plurality, dialogue means "mutual enrichment and mutual cooperation" with individuals and communities of other faiths in obedience to truth and respect for freedom. To him, dialogue can be interchanged with "relations." This indicates something much wider than verbal exchange. Not only formal exchanges are intended, but also

---

23 Interfaith Dialogue Association, *Principles and Guidelines for Interfaith Dialogue* (Cairo, October 2008), 9.

24 Ngun Ling, *Communicating Christ in Myanmar*, 200.

25 Saw Hlaing Bwa is professor and head of the Department of Theology and director of the Judson Research Center of Myanmar Institute of Theology, Yangon, Myanmar.

gestures of solidarity, action together, and even silent presence. The importance of nonverbal communication should not be underestimated.[26]

The goal of dialogue is first of all mutual understanding, trying to understand the other as that other wants to be understood, but is not learning to misunderstand. A second goal is a mutual enrichment, and the final goal is mutual cooperation.[27]

Saw Hlaing Bwa holds that mutual enrichment on a spiritual level can lead to common action. Once we get out of our own enclosures, we can experience the beauty, the value, and the truth of the other. Our mutual enrichment comes only in and through our relationship, and this relationship is the outcome of our will to relate to each other. The will to relate is the outcome of the ability to love and love is the core of all religious spirituality. Love is never to be seen as an abstract phenomenon but visible in the mutuality of our relations and developed into action where people can experience the fruit of love in society. Interreligious dialogue is, therefore, a "must" today that brings our heads, our hearts, and our hands together to be responsible in our society. In order to be religiously responsible, we must be interreligious both in person and in action.[28]

For Ngun Ling,[29] interfaith dialogue is not merely an outer communication between two persons but the inner communication with what they believe in God or in the Mystery and the sharing of such inner convictions with one another at the deepest level. Dialogue is actually a human-to-human conversation. But

26   Saw Hlaing, "Inter-Religious Dialogue," *Engagement: Bulletin of the Judson Research Center for Interfaith Studies, Dialogue and Current Issues* 2012: 97–98.

27   Saw Hlaing, 98.

28   Saw Hlaing, 99.

29   Samuel Ngun Ling is a professor of the Department of Theology and president of the Myanmar Institute of Theology, Insein, Yangon, Myanmar.

in a practical way, it is not merely a human-to-human conversation; rather, it is a human-to-human through God or, by God, conversation. Dialogue is God's delighted action of communication with humans. It originates with God. God created man and said it is not good for man to live alone and created woman—Eve for Adam—and with both of whom God can communicate. Hence, by nature dialogue means God's initiated relational and communication process with humankind and Creation. This is how the process of dialogue began in this world. In interfaith dialogue, we are seeking reconciliation not only between humankind but also with God.

APPLYING RELIGIOUS DIALOGUE IN THE DAILY LIFE OF CHRISTIANS IN MYANMAR

In the churches of Myanmar, interreligious dialogue is necessary, and not optional for the time being. However, the challenge we, as Myanmar Christians, are facing is that interreligious dialogue is still strange and foreign for most of us. It is incumbent on us to give an orientation or special training in interreligious dialogue for volunteers who submit themselves to be ministers. Interreligious dialogue should not end in discussions and presentations. What we need today is not merely a sound doctrine of religious dialogue but actual or practical dialogue; in other words, dialogue in action. Christians in Myanmar should be encouraged to actualize religious dialogue in their daily life. In fact, about 97 percent of all the Christians in Myanmar are lay Christians who encounter adherents of non-Christian religions in their daily activity. This tells us that religious dialogue can be taking place at work, in the park, and in conversation with friends who are non-Christians. Therefore, grassroots religious dialogue or interreligious dialogue should be promoted and encouraged for Christians to undertake without hesitation because the dialogue is not a win–lose situation but a win–win situation.

To sum up, religious dialogue is necessary for Christians today. Religious dialogue should not be seen as a hindrance to traditional beliefs, because it accomplishes the mission of Jesus in a new and fresh way. As mentioned, dialogue is part of a way of life that we should live. Sermons, preaching, conversation, and our daily life should be dialogue-centered so much so that Jesus's mission, preaching, and teaching to build the kingdom of God (peace society) will be fully actualized on the earth.

8

EXPLORING PROPHETIC DIAKONIA IN MYANMAR

David Selvaraj

INTRODUCTION

In this chapter, I suggest that the work of prophetic Diakonia, in essence, is public witness. It also reflects my trajectory of "doing theology." This book is the culmination of a "project" spanning four years. It can, and hopefully will, serve as a resource for seminaries in Asia and missional congregations in Asia and Africa.

The project was put on hold, due to the COVID-19 pandemic. However, not even the pandemic could dampen the zeal of the primary movers. It is anchored by the Rev. Dr. Lal Tin Hre, the general secretary of the Association of Theological Education in Myanmar (ATEM) in active partnership with the Global Ministry, USA. Initially, this was facilitated by Dr. James Vijayakumar and subsequently by the Rev. Dr. Deenabandhu Manchala. The latter distinguished himself with his active participation in the project. On behalf of the members of the team in India and the editors, I extend our gratitude to Global Ministries, USA, for their unstinting support even when the project was floundering.

That said, the very committed ministry of Rev. Dr. Dhyanchand Carr remained the glue that kept the team together and the inspiration to think and respond beyond conventional theological frameworks. His ministry of *presence* and theological education in Myanmar spans more than three decades, starting with the seminars on rereading the Bible. He sustained the process, visiting the country many times, like the present, in the context of military rule and ethnic conflicts. Generations of pastors, bishops, theologians, and seminarians have participated in these seminars. The project took on the focus of *public witness* with the inclusion of this writer. While the rereading of the Bible remained the primary and central focus, systematic social analysis was included as part of the curriculum. The sessions on social analysis were anchored on a theology of the cross: suffering and solidarity with all who groan and birth alternative communities of peace with justice. This chapter is an "offering" from a *neighbor* and *co-worker* in ministry. It is offered in the spirit of mutual learning by sharing the pedagogical experiences and engagement of prophetic diakonia. While the publication is primarily for seminaries in Myanmar, the nature of the chapters lends itself to a wider audience.

This chapter will situate the ministry of prophetic diakonia in the context of military rule, civil war, the negative impact of the current paradigm of development, the pandemic of COVID-19, which is far from over, and ethnic prejudices. It is precisely this context that leads to authentic movements of dissent, toward freedom and dignity. In the midst of the chaos, destruction, and mayhem, voices heralding a counterculture were heard in various parts of the world—the voices of "the *anawim*" yearning for and shaping *new heaven and new earth*. This is a theme I will return to later in this chapter.

Respectful of the rich contributions from theologians in Myanmar, this chapter will limit itself to a brief historical overview of the country, an introduction to the theme of prophetic diakonia, an introduction to the theme of *anawim*, and very briefly a section on forebears in public witness.

MYANMAR–PEARL OF THE EAST

This section attempts to offer a very brief overview of the historical context of Myanmar and the ground for exploring prophetic diakonia. The branding of the country as "the pearl of the east" by the tourist industry is not altogether a misnomer. It is indeed a land of precious gems, rich in biodiversity, breathtaking landscapes, and an unimaginable diversity of communities of people.

What is equally true is that Myanmar, a neighbor to India, has been in pain, with sections of its population who live in torment. Myanmar has the dubious distinction of having waged several civil wars over the last seven decades, between ethnic communities and the Burmese army, chiefly comprising the majority of Burmese. In the recent past, Myanmar has been in the news for its government's treatment of the Rohingya Muslims and the military takeover of a democratically elected government. However, for hundreds of years, stories from Myanmar include land mines, bandits, and the opium trade. According to the United Nations, based on the gross domestic product or intermediate consumption, Myanmar is the poorest country in Southeast Asia. Historically this can be traced back to the Anglo-Burmese wars of the nineteenth century. Three such wars have been documented spanning over six decades: 1824–26, 1852–53, and 1885. Scholars studying the economy of war place the cost at over one billion British pounds sterling as of 2019.[1] Subsequently, the policy of "scorched earth" applied by the retreating British Army during the Japanese occupation left the agricultural economy in chaos. The icing on the cake of external interventions was the process of globalization in the guise of the free market and the continued presence of British and European corporate interests, which have led to a beleaguered

---

1   Data from a seminar based on the book *The Making of Modern Burma* (New York: Cambridge University Press, 2012), by Thant Myint-U, an American-born Burmese historian.

and resource-strapped government opening up the country and its resources, with one hand tied behind their backs.

Fast forward to 2021, and in the midst of the pandemic, Myanmar experienced a reimposition of military rule. The democratically elected National League for Democracy (NLD) was deposed by the *tatmadaw* (armed forces/military). February 2021 marked the most recent *coup d'état* in Myanmar. The general election was declared invalid and President Win Myint and State Counsellor Aung San Suu Kyi were detained, along with twenty-four ministers and deputies. This act of military terror led to protests, including the anti-junta rally in Yangon, which came to be known as the Spring Revolution. Though short-lived, the Spring Revolution included demonstrations, strikes, acts of civil disobedience, and protest art. In May 2021, the might and brutality of the military were on display when 818 protestors and bystanders, including forty-four children, were killed, both by the military and by police, and 4296 were detained. The state of emergency was extended, and the military has postponed elections to 2023.[2] At the time of completing this chapter, Aung San Suu Kyi and deposed president Win Myint face charges of corruption, carrying a maximum of fifteen years in prison.[3]

The context for prophetic diakonia is embodied in the social and political life of Myanmar. For the church to take prophetic diakonia seriously is a daunting task. According to "Christianity in Myanmar," an article published by Religion and Public Life at Harvard Divinity School,[4] Christians in Myanmar comprise 8.2 percent of the population across denominations, with the majority hailing

2   "Fighting Surges in Myanmar Growing Anti-Junta Conflict," Reuters Asia Pacific, May 2, 2021, https://tinyurl.com/2728rjrz.

3   *The Economic Times*, January 14, 2022.

4   "Christianity in Myanmar," Religion and Public Life, Harvard Divinity School, accessed February 20, 2023, https://tinyurl.com/yeyj8n7b.

from the Karen, Kachin, Chin, Karenai, Luhu, and Nagas—all ethnic minorities. Several of these groups have been in conflict with the Burmese. Historically, ethnic groups had benefited during the colonial era. The article suggests an increase in literacy, with the spread of education through Christian missions. This also led to the formation of a religious (Christian) identity, which in turn contributed to consciousness and unwillingness to accept Burmese Buddhist rule. Each ethnic group brought with them a specific brand and rationale to the protest against mainstream imposition. Dr. Lal Tin Hre challenges this argument. In his chapter in this volume,[5] he argues that the Christian education of missionaries has stilled voices of dissent. Dr. Khawsiama in his *Ludu* Theology,[6] also included in this volume, pleads for Christian participation with "fellow pilgrims" in a common cause, a struggle against oppression. He draws attention to the refusal of Christian leaders in participating alongside their Buddhist counterparts (monks) during the Saffron Revolution of 2007, a series of protests and demonstrations led by the religious against the national military. To circle back, the concluding statement of the Harvard Divinity School article "Christianity in Myanmar" sums up the plight of the community. "Christian ethnic minorities have faced significant discrimination in Myanmar. Christians have reported campaigns of forcible conversion to Buddhism, restrictions on church buildings and religious organizing, forced labor conscription and killings, torture, rape abductions and other acts of violence against Christians by the Burman military."[7]

PROPHETIC DIAKONIA

This section will serve as an introduction to some and a reminder to others that diakonia is a key discipline of Christian study and

5   See chapter 9.
6   See chapter 4.
7   "Christianity in Myanmar."

formation. It is the conviction of the author that diakonia must be made integral to the mission, as understood as the *missio Dei*, the mission of God.

Young's Analytical Concordance to the Bible has one hundred references to diakonia in the New Testament. A study of the verses would suggest that, for Jesus, caring for persons in need was not an incidental act but core to his mission as recorded in Mark 10:45: "For the son of man came not to be served but to serve, and to give his life a ransom for many." In the Acts of the Apostles, Luke writes of the "empowered Peter" at the home of Cornelius: "Jesus Christ is Lord of all . . . . God anointed Jesus of Nazareth with the Holy Spirit and with power; how he went about doing good and healing all who were oppressed by the devil" (Acts 10:36, 38). In the Gospel text (Matt 11:4–6 and 9), the evangelist records Jesus, responding to the disciples of John the Baptist, pointing to "actions": "Go back and report what you hear and see, the blind receive sight, the lame walk, the deaf hear," actions that reflect a bias and a reminder that the good news to the poor could also be offensive to those who have forced them into a state of chronic dependency. In verse 9 Jesus reminds his listeners that this is a prophetic act.

Prophetic diakonia is the public witness of the church. Drawing from statements from the World Council of Churches (WCC) and Lutheran World Federation (LWF), this section will lay a foundation for deeper study. "The ministry of prophetic diakonia seeks to confront the powers of this world that lead to violence, exclusion, death and destruction, and calls for the transformation of unjust structures and practices into God's kingdom of justice with the fullness of life for all and for creation."[8] Professor Reinerio Arce, the Cuban theologian, who anchored the consultation, argues that diakonia is an essential ministry of the ecumenical

---

8   From the Statement of the Global Consultation, led by the World Council of Churches, on Prophetic Diakonia, at Utrecht, The Netherlands, December 13–15, 2010.

movement. The conference in Utrecht, The Netherlands, was the second in a series that came out of the Ninth Assembly of the World Council of Churches in Porto Alegre, Brazil. The WCC has a long history of calling member churches to recognize and affirm diakonia as integral to the *missio Dei*. Statements coming out of conferences bear testimony to this. To list a few: Roadmap for Congregations, Communities and Churches for an Economy of Life and Ecological Justice (March 2019), Communities Make the Difference, a Liturgical Text in the Context of Solidarity with People Living with HIV and Aids (November 2019), Creative Solidarity in Common Fragility (July 2020).

Earlier, and in keeping with their mission goals, the WCC initiated and encouraged a movement on Ecumenical Diakonia (ED). WCC defined ED as *faith and rights-based action*, based on the biblical concept of justice: "prophetic heritage of unmasking systemic injustice and defending the rights of the poor."[9] The ED could best be described as a "common platform for acting and reflecting together," clearly highlighting a dimension of praxis. The ED was established on theological and practical perspectives. The former confirms the position that diakonia is an integral dimension of the nature and mission of the church. This was based on two motifs. The first is that all humans are made *in the image of God* and the second is a *vocation to compassion and justice*. In this lies the relationship between what the churches "do" and "are." The latter, which is the practical perspective, reflects the engagement of churches across denominational and geographical lines. Within the WCC this was made manifest through the facilitative body of the Inter-Church Service to Refugees, established in 1949. The *Dictionary of the Ecumenical Movement* defines diakonia as "the responsible service of the Gospel by deeds and by words performed by Christians in response to the needs of people." Speaking at a conference jointly hosted by the WCC and the

---

9   Ecumenical Diakonia document of WCC (2017).

Christian Conference of Asia (CCA), General Secretary Mathews George Chunakara stated, "the challenge of diakonia as emphasized by the ecumenical movement through WCC's facilitation has always been to encourage diakonia to move from charity model approach to justice and leap over national and ecumenical frontiers to respond to local and global issues; to partner in God's mission, and be prophetic, transformative and justice-seeking."[10] Critiquing the "lost vision" of the ecumenical movement in the realm of equipping churches in fulfilling the mission and vision of diakonia, Chunakara made reference to the widening gap between rich and poor and the fragility of the ecological balance.

Kjell Nordstokke, professor at Diakonhjemmet University College, Oslo, Norway, in his "Reflections on the Theology of Diakonia" calls for renewed ways of understanding diakonia and participating in the mission of God. The author argues that diakonia does not stand alone. It is sustained by the Word and sacraments. He offers a threefold typology—contextual, ecclesiological, and praxeological. He argues for diakonia to be a ministry of the church, speaking to the context as "a ministry of prophecy and transformation." As a core component of the gospel, diakonia is not an option. "While diakonia begins as unconditional service to the neighbor in need, it leads inevitably to social change that restores, reforms, and transforms." For Nordstokke the cross of Jesus Christ is central to his theology: "We should be shaped by a theology of the cross which compels us to identify with and for the suffering rather than the successful, even when this threatens the established order."[11] It is striking that Nordstokke's picture of the context more than a decade ago is relevant today, perhaps in a far more intense and chronic manner.

Reflections, conferences, and statements on diakonia are not restricted to ecumenical organizations alone. The World

---

10   CCA News and Views posted on December 9, 2019.

11   Carlos E Ham, *The Ecumenical Review* 63, no. 4, book review.

Evangelical Fellowship (WEF), using the nomenclature of *transformation*, refers to similar motifs and perspectives. The key theological articulation is the emphasis on biblical faith-inspired social engagement. Historically, the origin could be traced back to the international conference on world evangelization at Lausanne, Switzerland, and the Lausanne Movement as a significant outcome. Fifteen years later in Manila, The Philippines, in 1989, the second conference, which resulted in the Manila Manifesto, took place. Preceding the Lausanne conference was the Congress on the World Mission of the Church, held in Wheaton in 1966, bringing together evangelicals from seventy-one countries. An extract from the document of the congress is significant: "We (evangelicals) are guilty of an unscriptural isolation from the world that too often keeps us from honestly facing and coping with its concerns . . . the failure (of the church) to apply scriptural principles to such problems as racism, war, population explosion, poverty and communism."[12] A key theological debate reflected in the "Lausanne Covenant" is the relationship between evangelism and social responsibility. The more traditional view, championed by the evangelist Billy Graham (at the Berlin conference), leaves little doubt as to the hesitancy to bridge the gap between faith and public engagement: "If the church went back to the main task of proclaiming the gospel and people converted to Christ, it would have a far greater impact in the social, moral and psychological needs of man." The second view was championed by participants from India and the less affluent countries of Latin America. These voices challenged the forced dichotomy between evangelism and social involvement. These articulate voices were championed by Vinay Samuel from India, Rene Padilla from Ecuador, and Samuel Escoba from Peru, among others. The theologians argued that an understanding of the Christian mission included expressing

---

12   Wheaton Declaration in *International Review of Mission* 55, issue 220.

the love of God and neighborly love. This was not only rooted in Christian Scripture but also exemplified in the ministry of Jesus. The impetus for this shift in focus (inclusion of social responsibility alongside evangelism) came largely from "the 2/3rd world," specifically from the Latin American Theological Fellowship (1970s) which brought "integral (wholeness) mission" to center stage.

The International Consultation on Relationship of Evangelism and Social Responsibility (ICRESR, 1982) and the Consultation on the Church in Response to Human Need (Wheaton, Illinois, 1983) are part of the third track to a WEF conference titled "I Will Build Ny Church." These debates are compiled in *The Church in Response to Human Need*.[13] The editors, in a succinct manner, introduce readers to the subject of holistic mission and transformation. In their introduction, replete with biblical references, the authors spell out the core themes, which include: (1) Christian social movement; (2) not only development but transformation; (3) stewardship; (4) culture and transformation; (5) social justice and mercy; (6) local church and transformation; (7) Christian aid agencies and transformation; and (8) the coming of the kingdom and the church's mission. This very comprehensive coverage takes the dimension of "sin" seriously. Emphasis is placed not only on personal but societal sin. Evil is not only in the human heart but also in structures. The basis for their understanding of transformation comes from the reading of the "reign" of God and reflects a focus on change: "condition of human existence contrary to God's purpose, to one in which people are able to enjoy the fullness of life in harmony to God." Transformation entails "not conforming" and a "process of the renewal of the mind" (Rom 12). Responding to the situation of chronic poverty in the world, the text emphasizes the motif of belonging to *one body* (2 Cor

---

13   Vinay Samuel and Chris Sugden, eds., *The Church in Response to Human Need* (Grand Rapids: Wm. B. Eerdmans, 1987).

8:14–15) and proposes a reexamination of the early church model (Acts 2:42–47), which could contribute significantly to eliminating global poverty and a considerable reduction in the gap between the rich and the poor. Suffice to say, this widely used book has not only captured the essence of the above-cited conferences but gone beyond. Work of this kind from the evangelical world is significant and makes clear the scope for ecumenical engagement in our witness to the gospel.

LEARNING FROM THE *ANAWIM*

The term *anawim* and the theological implication are crucial for discussion of prophetic diakonia. The premise is that the *anawim* are the most faithful and responsive to the gospel of Jesus Christ and it is they who embody the call to discipleship. The *anawim*, the true people of God, "the remnants," are found in every society and every nation. This section will include a brief introduction to the term and a fellowship bearing the name Anawim Satsang. Introducing the Anawim Satsang is indicative of our search for other ecclesial formations and our aim to realign the mission of the church to the *missio Dei*. This process is not unique to India. In other parts of South Asia, certainly in the northern parts of Sri Lanka which this writer is associated with, missional churches are emerging and embodying the "bruised reed" of Isaiah (42:1–4). The term "*anawim*" will be familiar to students and teachers of Christian theology. *Anawim* is derived from the Hebrew *Inwetan*, being the plural for *anaw*. Literally, it means "stooped, bowed, lowered, and overwhelmed." Sr. Joan L. Roccasalvo CSJ refers to the *anawim* as the "poor of every sort."[14] They are vulnerable, without earthly power, and are socioeconomically oppressed. Roccasalvo

---

14   Joan L. Roccasalvo, "The Anawim: Who Are They?" Catholic News Agency, December 5, 2012, https://tinyurl.com/4ktwzf4a.

refers to Mary the mother of Jesus as an *anawim*, the favored of God, who remained faithful to God in times of difficulty. It is the *anawim* who are the "true people of God," who have visions of reversals and become ambassadors of this good news (Luke 1:47). The foundational principles for these arguments come from Fr. Albert Gelin in his work *The Poor of Yahweh*.[15] It is noteworthy to highlight that Fr. Gelin's work was very influential in the ministry and writing of Gustavo Gutiérrez. Drawing from the apostle Paul, Gelin posits Jesus as the *anawim* of God. In the text from Philippians 2:6–7, the writer points to Jesus who emptied himself, taking the form of a servant, a powerless *anawim*. In pursuit of this motif, Gelin, drawing from 2 Corinthians 8:1–9, points to the reason, "he did this so that we might become rich." The Hebrew Bible, or the Old Testament, is replete with the term and understanding, more specifically in the psalms and the prophetic literature (Psalm 149:4, Isaiah 60:21, 63:8, Hos. 2:23, to cite a few examples).

The *anawim* are present in every nation and continent. In the recent past, it took the death of George Floyd, among many other Black Americans, to expose the brutality of the police in the United States and the systemic evil in our societies. The Black Lives Matter (BLM) movement has been reignited and strengthened. BLM and the Poor People's Campaign, championed by Rev. William Barber II among others, have already had an impact in other parts of the world. Musicians, artists, civil society institutions, and politicians have expressed angst and hope. Racism is back on the agenda of global politics and governance. While the "gasping for breath" caught the imagination of many all over the world, similar cases raised their ugly head in India. Over centuries, in every generation, there is a defining moment and a dominant spirit that inspires and guides. The defining moment or moments of the last two decades (culminating in the last two years) is one

---

15   Albert Gelin, *The Poor of Yahweh* (Collegeville, MN: Liturgical Press, 1964).

of crumbling structures and systems, be that economics, politics, culture, and more specifically, religion. Metaphorically and physically the death knell of this colossal crumbling was made visible in the cruelty of the pandemic and the ongoing damage caused by the inaction related to climate injustice. Less than prudent political acumen and an astute political will have brought us to the brink of global disaster. False prophets abound, and now is the time for women and men from a prophetic tradition, anchored in mysticism and truth-telling (rooted in *agape* love), to be witnesses. For it is truth alone that will set all people free. It must be noted, however, that "the crumbling" has had positive results. Significant rethinking and reconfiguration have happened in many spheres of life. An example, yet to be evaluated and documented, is a sharp decline in materialistic ways of living and a search for deeper meaning. Certainly, a steep decline in religious faith and practice and a simultaneous upsurge in a search for spirituality and spiritual practices have occurred. Both trends are to be critically examined and we need to draw from the best of all that is life-affirming and life-sustaining. It is in this context that we define a dominant guiding and inspiring spirit. Working from biblical tradition (1 Cor 13), this writer draws on virtues of hope, faith, and love. While affirming the primacy of love, hope must be lifted up as the *zeitgeist* for the global community. This is not wishful thinking, but rather an exercise of faith made manifest in our walk as disciples of Jesus Christ.

The *anawim* that the author is associated with include women and girl children from the *devadasi* tradition in South India[16] and grassroots communities of peasants and agricultural

---

16   In southern India a *devadasi* was a female artiste dedicated to the temple for life. Documentary evidence suggests that in Karnataka the system was practiced for over ten centuries. In the period from the sixth to the thirteenth century, *devadasis* had high social status and were even affluent. However, in modern times the

workers in the Chittoor district of Andhra Pradesh in South India. For the purposes of this chapter, the emphasis will be on the latter. The *anawim* in the contemporary context of Chittoor are:

- First-generation Christian believers and "pastors."

- Grassroot churches and house fellowships.

- Outside the purview of national federating structures (National Council of Churches in India and Evangelical Fellowship of India.)

More than 90 percent of them belong to the Dalit or tribal communities, living in chronic conditions of dynamic poverty and victimization, experiencing less-than-hospitable relations with mainline denominational churches. When inspired and supported, individuals are more than able and willing to assume leadership and spearhead faith-inspired community action. This was made manifest in the most recent Christian Response to Covid in Chittoor (CRCC), a subject that we will return to as a case study.

Our conviction is that the above sections of people have the *potential, resilience,* and *zeal* to build up their own communities. This will blossom with ongoing nurture, drawing from the liberative principles and perspectives in the Bible (a rereading of the text), the study of the Constitution of India, social analysis, and communication skills. As opposed to standing by itself, the pedagogical task is one of exploring intersectionality and weaving a mosaic that leads to holistic formation.

The Anawim Satsang (fellowship) is an ecumenical fellowship of community churches, house fellowships, and mainline churches, committed to prayer, unity of churches, and public

system has fallen into disrepute and is associated with "temple prostitution." Visthar, the civil society institution, founded by this writer is actively involved in the rescue and rehabilitation of young girls trapped in this tradition.

witness. Anawim Satsang (AS) is a deliberate choice and reflects a cultural and spiritual identity. The choice of name is a conscious affirmation of our identity as an ecumenical fellowship, based in India, committed to the spirituality of participation and solidarity with the poor and a social engagement coming out of faith inspiration. Inspired by the trinitarian God, we draw from Christian Scripture and Indian counter-culture traditions. In name and structure, the Anawim Satsang (fellowship) has been more than three years in the making and is committed to a search for alternatives. In the context of mainline denominational churches going through a decline in their vocation and membership, the Anawim Satsang is a tentative, faith alternative and is a search for realignment in an uncertain and fragile world. It is rooted in:

1. A *conviction* that it is inspired by the Holy Spirit of God.

2. A *commitment* to affirming the *anawim* as authentic messengers of the gospel.

3. A *confession* that we are a *Satsang*, a fellowship, *a sacred space*; physical and spiritual.

4. A *congregation* of the faithful, to be in partnership with other congregations, in the mission of God.

As one of the founders of the Anawim Satsang, I am convinced that our work is in keeping with the global movement of promoting missional churches. The missional church is an emerging faith movement, a departure from the denominational/historic churches. Ironically, early in the last century (1934), Karl Hartenstein, a German theologian, laid the foundation for the current discourse. Coining the phrase *missio Dei* (the sending of God) Hartenstein drew attention to and contrasted the *missio Dei* with *missio ecclesia* (the mission or sending of the church). The theological shift is from seeing mission *as an **activity** of the church* to *an **attribute** of God*. In India, and especially coming out of the tradition of the united/uniting church (CSI), the inspiration for this movement comes from Bishop Lesslie Newbigin. Michael Goheeen, who gained his PhD from the University of Utrecht, has made a significant contribution on Lesslie Newbigin's missionary ecclesiology. Significant literature on the subject exists. *Transforming Mission, Paradigm Shifts in Theology of Mission* by David J. Bosch (Dutch Reformed Church in South Africa) is a case in point. Drawing from the Bible, the author points to the church as sent by Jesus Christ (John 17:18; 20:21), sent with the cross (1 Cor 1:18; Acts 28:31), sent in community (Acts 2:42–47; John 13:34–35), sent to every culture (John 1:14; Matt 20:28), and sent for the reign of God (Luke 4:43; Acts 28:31). To quote the author, we have begun to see that the church of Jesus Christ is not the purpose or goal of the gospel but its instrument and witness. God's mission is calling and sending us to be a missionary church in our own societies.[17]

MODELS OF PROPHETIC DIAKONIA

In response to the request for case studies emerging from India, I offer experiences from my own engagement. It is noteworthy to state that my engagement, spanning close to four decades, includes years in ministry both as a layperson and as an ordained minister of the Church of South India. More importantly, my engagement and learning have been through the church and "secular" civil society organizations. I had the good fortune of serving my church, the CSI, as the founding director of the diaconal ministry and the Protestant church of Switzerland as the first Indian national to head their services of relief and

17   David Bosch, *Transforming Mission: Paradigm Shifts in Theology of Mission* (Maryknoll, NY: Orbis, 1991).

development in India.[18] This section will reflect the experiences of pathos and hope of large numbers of people, pushed to the margins by discriminatory and prejudicial policies of political and social institutions. The irony of course is that India, a neighbor to Myanmar, is a functioning democracy with a growing number of wealthy persons. It is a democracy with a constitution and constitutional culture that merits a quality of inclusion, caring for the most vulnerable, diversity of religions, languages, ethnicities, an independent judiciary, and free and fair elections. Yet, we see chronic poverty and unbridgeable gaps in wealth, and growing levels of intolerance based on fabricated and biased information, resulting in violence and untold misery for those already in the margins.

This sharing comes from a sense of shared responsibility. While the case studies are "local" in nature and reflect an engagement with grassroots communities, simultaneous attempts were made to respond to structures and systems that dehumanize at a wider level. Certainly, one situation that calls for collaboration and partnership between churches and Christian organizations in India and Myanmar is that of the Rohingya people. This is a shared responsibility: to challenge the sociopolitical positions of both governments (Myanmar and India) in contributing to an international scandal caused by callous neglect and actions of exclusion, resulting in the displacement of Rohingyas from Rakhine state and the grossly inhospitable manner in which the Indian state responded to the news. Let me corroborate by drawing from a "key influencer" and the national organization he represents. Mohan Bhagat is the president of the Rashtriya Swayamsevak Sangh (RSS), which, translated into English, means "national social service organization." RSS and Bhagat are powerful influencers of the ruling party in the government, the Bharatiya Janata Party. Speaking at Nagpur, the headquarters of the RSS, Bhagat

18   Hilfswerk Evangelischen Kirchen de Schweiz (HEKS).

declared, referring to the Rohingyas, "any decision on them should be taken by keeping in mind that they will definitely be a threat to national security and integrity."[19] I dare say that Bhagat's words echoed the sentiments of thousands of "educated" Indians across the country. In an almost disrespectful manner, the statement raised the bogeyman of national security and integrity of the (Indian) nation. To state the obvious, the "they" were Muslims across the border. In discussions during workshops leading to this publication, participants reflected on this shared shame and picked this up as a concern for a prophetic diakonia. Key questions that occupied our minds included the notion of the enemy: By whom and how is this created? Equally significant is the dismantling of the concept of neighbor.

Returning to a more recent local engagement is the work of the Anawim Satsang in response to the pandemic. This ecumenical initiative was facilitated under the banner of Christian Response to Covid in Chittoor (CRCC). The CRCC is a modest initiative of the Anawim Satsang which received an overwhelming response from churches and civil society institutions and partly focused on supporting the government of Andhra Pradesh in their efforts toward relief and care. The CRCC reached vulnerable persons in need of care, irrespective of caste, color, or creed. The core convictions of the CRCC included:

1. Primacy to the unity of churches in prayer and service.

2. Christian faith and spirituality of engagement are key to the process.

3. Emphasis on grassroots community engagement in which leaders of the community will be strengthened to conduct the tasks they set for themselves. The anawim will be the prime movers.

---

19   The Wire, September 30, 2019.

4. The Anawim Satsang will coordinate the process and draw from a variety of resource persons and institutions.

5. Youth from the community will continue to serve as the backbone to the engagement.

Toward this end the very first task of the Satsang was investing in youth. It is in and through CRCC that we saw the impact of our training of youth. Labeled as Leadership for Social Transformation (LST), the formation of youth was aimed at equipping the church for the *missio Dei*. The participants of LST were mobilized for an intensive engagement in Covid relief, awareness, and educational campaigns. An outcome of this program, besides participation in the campaign, is the curriculum that can be adapted and applied. Noteworthy of mention is that LST is an ongoing initiative and made possible with the support from the Global Ministries, USA.

It is true that the virus did not carry the tag of rich and poor. However, for the poor, it was not only an issue of poor physical health, but a *survival* issue, a *dignity* issue, and a chronic *mental health* issue. Lack of Covid-appropriate behavior, vaccination hesitancy, communication gaps between the communities and government departments, fear of the third wave, and lack of proper medical infrastructure at the village level form the basis of the case studies.

1. Individuals and families who lost their jobs in the informal economy were vulnerable to being at greater risk of falling prey to lenders providing credit on terms constituting debt bondage.

2. Covid-affected persons from the "dominant" communities, while in quarantine refused to eat meals cooked by Dalits. Even in schools, students brought

homemade meals, for fear of contracting the virus through food cooked by Dalits.

3. No dignified burials for Dalits and Christians. Burial sites included riverbeds and unknown forest areas. This has been the case for Dalit Christians even prior to Covid.

4. School children from Adivasi communities enrolled in government schools were denied midday meals due to the closure of schools thereby increasing levels of malnutrition.

5. Survival became an insurmountable issue when the adults/parents were unable to get a daily wage/work.

6. The shutting down of schools followed by an almost immediate shift to online teaching worsened the inequality in learning among children. It also pushed vulnerable children out of schools; hence issues such as child labor, girl child marriages, child/human trafficking, bonded labor issues, mental health issues due to uncertainties, addiction, drug use, violence, and engagement in criminal activities have become rampant.

7. Many adult persons with disabilities yearning for dignity of life and labor are being denied jobs due to their physical condition, despite the fact that they have undertaken formal education, including a few who are college graduates. Many companies consider it inauspicious to have people with disabilities in their reception areas.

8. It is estimated that two hundred children lost their parents due to Covid in Chittoor alone. While the

government of Andhra Pradesh is paying compensation, the children's mental health and safety issues need to be addressed. An allied important need is the sensitivity of their guardians. A safe space for these children is crucial, especially for female children.

9. Unemployment is a severe problem. In the Yadamari mandal of Puthalapattu constituency, two private school teachers committed suicide due to the closure of private schools. Many qualified (graduate) teachers have shifted to daily-wage labor in agriculture to sustain their families. There is also huge mental stress on the middle-class families to shift their children from private schools to government schools as they are not in a position to pay fees.

As a result of the very intensive engagement under the banner of CRCC, the Anawim Satsang is equipping member churches and civil society institutions to sustain their zealous efforts in specific areas. This includes engagement in a campaign leading to securing a burial ground for Christians from the Dalit background, a survey of children who have lost parents due to Covid, and an assessment of mental health issues among persons with disability and the unemployed. This focus will lead to outcomes that will include:

1. Securing a site from the state government for the purpose of a burial ground as a right of the community.

2. Requiring the government to be accountable for children orphaned due to Covid.

3. Initiating a program and proposal for working on a holistic mental health initiative for vulnerable groups

in the community, standing with those severely impacted by Covid.

4. Beginning an ecumenical initiative of working with children with disabilities.

Many other cases were used for reflection during the workshops leading up to this publication. These included initiatives undertaken exclusively by Christian faith communities and interfaith collectives responding to issues of corporate greed and environmental disasters and the persecution of religious minorities subjected to policies of cultural nationalism. If I were to single out one key learning from four decades of engagement, it is this: peace with justice is a gift of God, and simultaneously it is our mission goal. Social change anchored in peace with justice comes from those excluded, marginalized, and ostracized. As a servant of the gospel committed to prophetic diakonia, I can only be in solidarity and play a supporting role. Merely being on the margins faced with chronic levels of poverty does not automatically qualify one to be an agent of change. It is those made conscious and yearning for change who become the leaders. My engagement provided me with many opportunities to collaborate with multiple actors involved in various forms of social action drawing inspiration from a range of ideologies and religious faith persuasions. Their resolve toward social change has been inspirational and triggered in me a significant learning curve. The scope for a multifaith and interfaith engagement in a prophetic diakonia is a subject for another paper, but is a crucial topic. Partnerships in the mission are not to do with churches and Christian institutions alone.

FOREBEARS IN PUBLIC WITNESS

Recently I was invited to lead a reflection on public witness in my diocese. Listening to participants, I was reminded again of the barriers to an engagement in public witness. I imagine it is the dichotomy in our understanding of Christian faith and public engagement and of the theological and political interpretation of respecting authority. I realize it is easier said than done; however, an emphasis must be made that personal faith and public engagement are not two ends of the spectrum. Rather, the former is the inspiration for the latter. It is the consciousness that the God we encounter in the Bible and through Jesus Christ is the one who calls us to witness peace with justice, rooted in love, in the public space.

Our faith forebears have walked this path. Dietrich Bonhoeffer is a case in point. For the purposes of our ongoing study, we would do well to consider the Barmen Declaration and the more recent Kairos Palestine Document. The full title of the latter is "A Moment of Truth: A Word of Faith, Hope and Love from the Heart of Palestinian Suffering." The Barmen Declaration is a document of the German Bekennende Kirche, a movement for revival within Protestant churches in Germany in the 1930s. It was a bold faith movement, resisting Hitler's attempts to make churches an instrument of National Socialist propaganda and politics. The Barmen Declaration was an attempt to evolve a three-church (Lutheran, Reformed, and United) consensus to oppose pro-Nazi German Christianity. This is a significant and defining document, drafted by Karl Barth and Hans Asmussen from Reformed and Lutheran traditions, respectively. It was a call to resistance and an immediate response to the Nazi seizure of power in 1935. More specifically, the resistance was directed against the dominating "Führer Principle" as the organizing "German prophet," and preaching racial consciousness as the source of revelation alongside the Bible was at the core of the act of resistance. The declaration itself is in the format of affirmation and denouncement, drawing on the Bible. The document concludes with *Verbum Dei manet in aeternum*, "the word of God will last forever."

CONCLUSION

As indicated in the introduction, I have approached this task of writing and co-editing as a fellow pilgrim and co-worker. It is my hope that this will open up conversations on the subject of prophetic diakonia. Being part of this project has vindicated my position on the need for persons from diverse backgrounds to engage in study and reflection leading to fresh insights: be it theological, social, or pedagogical. Finally, as Dr. Ram Lian Thang argues in his chapter *"Interfaith Dialogue as the Relevant Characteristic for Making Peace among Christians and Buddhists in Myanmar,"* the way forward is for persons of varied religious faiths to come together in creative and constructive acts of peace with justice. The public witness must go beyond any one religious faith. It is a witness to the truth that unmasks untruth and love that drives out hate.

PART III

CONTEMPORARY ISSUES AND THE "HOW" OF PUBLIC WITNESS

9

THE SILENCE OF THE CHURCH IN MYANMAR
A Self-Reflective Approach

Lal Tin Hre[1]

*Silence in the face of evil is itself evil: God will not hold us guiltless.
Not to speak is to speak. Not to act is to act.*

—Dietrich Bonhoeffer

INTRODUCTION

An issue that many Christians grapple with is "the relationship
between church and state," or the interrelatedness of church and
politics. While some churches have been deeply involved in the
social, economic, and political issues, others have been silent and
kept themselves away from the affairs of society and state. This
chapter will examine Myanmar society in brief and outline some
possible reasons and factors why churches in Myanmar have been

---

[1]   Lal Tin Hre has served at the Association of Theological Education
in Myanmar (ATEM) office as an executive secretary since 2009.

silent amidst social-political-economic crises for almost six decades. My reflections and suggestions will be underlined in the last section.

MYANMAR: A BRIEF INTRODUCTION

Myanmar (formerly known as Burma) was the second most beautiful country in Asia in the 1960s, only after Japan. Given her high yield of rice, Myanmar was known as "the rice pot." In the sphere of education, Yangon University, in Yangon, was one of the best universities in Southeast Asia to which hundreds of international students came to study. The land itself was known as "Golden Land" (*Shwe Pyidaw*) because of the natural resources—such as quality jade, gold, iron, hardwood, and the like. The second-most-prized gem in the world was found in Kachin State: Karin Dean notes that Myanmar is the biggest jade producer in the world.[2]

In 1962, General Ne Win seized state power and introduced "socialism," which he called "Burmese way to socialism" as he thought it was best suited for the people in Burma. His governance made Myanmar one of the poorest countries in the world. In 1978, the twenty-fifth year of Ne Win's coup, the United Nations Organization (UNO) identified Myanmar as "the poorest country in the world," and it was, thus, listed by the UNO as the Least Developed Country (LDC). The country had a national debt of 3.5 billion US dollars (USD) and currency reserves of between 20 million and 35 million USD, with debt service ratios standing at half the national budget.[3] The International Monetary Fund granted a huge amount of money to the Burmese government.

2   Quoted in Pum Za Mang, "Burman, Burmanization and Betrayal" in *Studies in World Christianity* 18, no. 2 (2012): 169–88, quote on 177.

3   Saphir Athyal, *Church in Asia Today: Opportunities & Challenges* (Singapore: ALCWE, 1996), 349.

Unfortunately, the money failed to reach the people.[4] The land is endowed with rich resources but most people in Myanmar are extremely poor. A Buddhist monk stated that everything in the country has collapsed since Ne Win's regime in 1962.[5] Myanmar was one of the very first countries that enthusiastically endorsed the United Nations Universal Declaration of Human Rights in 1948 but has infringed upon the human rights of people in general and ethnic minorities in particular.

Since General Ne Win's coup, the military regime has been accused of being responsible for systematic crimes against humanity—political oppression, religious persecution, massive human rights violations, sexual violence, rape, mass murder, religious persecution, and ethnic cleansing of marginalized ethnic groups, especially of the Chin, Kachin, Karen, and Shan. General Than Shwe led the country even further into isolation and destruction by uprooting democratic and civil society institutions, as a result of which Myanmar became vulnerable to human rights violations and economic exploitations by both internal and external powers.[6] Thus, Myanmar is regarded as one of the most oppressive countries in the world today. Hilary Clinton, the then US secretary of state, told the junta to "end the violent repression of minority ethnic groups in some of the world's longest civil conflicts."[7] "Peace" in Burma is generally seen by the military government as the total elimination of ethnic rebellions and the imposition of law and order.[8] The current suffering of the people

---

4   "2008 Constitutional Talks" by U Ko Ni, Tamwe-Yangon on September 18, 2013.

5   *D. Wave* 3, no. 13, Monday, March 31, 2014.

6   Oliver Byar Bowh Si, *God in Burma: Civil Society and Public Theology in Myanmar* (Las Vegas: self-published, 2014), 2.

7   *New York Times*, December 1, 2011.

8   Byar Bowh Si, *God in Burma*, 11.

in Myanmar can be attributed to ethnic conflicts, poverty, and decades of military rule.

Myanmar is accused of being complicit in mass atrocities committed against Rohingya Muslims during army counterinsurgency in northern Rakhine state in 2017. The case was brought by the Republic of Gambia (Africa) to the International Criminal Court (ICC) in The Hague in December 2019.[9] The State Counsellor Daw Aung San Suu Kyi appeared before the International Court of Justice (ICJ) to defend her government against charges of genocide.[10] Despite some concrete reforms under the leadership of the National League for Democracy (NLD) violence, dehumanization, incidents of indiscriminate killings, civil wars, assassination, and rape of women take place every day, and villagers have been forced to leave their homes and become refugees. Abductions have also become common in the country.[11]

---

9   The Rohingya people are a Muslim-Indo-Aryan ethic minority in Buddhist-majority Burma and have lived in Rakhine state in particular for generations. However, the state government deems them illegal immigrants and rejected the use of the term "Rohingya." It was estimated that the total number of Rohingya Muslims exiled to the border of Myanmar and Bangladesh was about 700,000.

10   *The Mirror*, December 11, 2019. Several Muslim, Hindu, and Catholic religious organizations, the Ramakrishna Mission Society, the Myanmar Evangelical Christian Alliance (MECA), and others, have lent their full support to the state counsellor through the state daily newspaper. See *The Mirror*, December 11, 12, and 13, 2019.

11   Since ethnic groups are no longer safe in their homeland, hundreds of thousands of the Chin, Kachin, and Karen have left their homes behind for their safety. The number of Chin refugees living in Mizoram state in India is currently estimated at 100,000, and there are an estimated 50,000 Chin refugees in Malaysia. Karen refugees living along the Thai border number over 130,000, and Kachin refugees scattering in the border areas in northern Burma are also estimated at 100,000. Quoted in Pum Za Mang, "Burman, Burmanization and Betrayal."

The following poem was written by the director of an NGO and has been widely circulated in civil society *fora* in Yangon:

I . . . Myanmar Civil Society

I have . . . mythical land and cornucopia trees
Grow with suppleness and passive resistance;
I . . . live and life through grassroots and
Bridge heaven and earth;
I . . . reconciling the fractured land
Deposit myself for a verdant generation;
I . . . guardian of chances for youthful future
Dancing with uncertain fire inside of the havoc's games;
I . . . vibrate solo of peace and delightful lyric
Singing among the world of children;
I . . . raft when flood of misery
Propel to space of opportunity;
I . . . dissolving the weakness and
Sustain to nurture to stand on their own;
I . . . hug people to be aware of
How Mother Nature loves you and to respect her;
I struggle every single instant and
Keep on flowing for Endless journey.
I . . . Myanmar Civil Society.

POSSIBLE REASONS FOR THE SILENCE OF THE CHURCH

This chapter takes a different position; not the historical documentation or record of military actions, but rather it attempts to pinpoint the possible reasons and causes why churches in Myanmar have been silent despite experiencing inhumane sociopolitical oppression, the denial of social justice, political liberty, religious freedom, human rights, and even ethnic cleansing. How does the church in Myanmar interpret and present Christians as the "light of the world and the salt of the earth?"

Many issues deserve our attention, but we cannot attend to them all here. I came up with the following reasons why churches in Burma are so silent on the issues. Salai Pum Za Mang, who teaches at Myanmar Institute of Theology and who is a prolific writer, asserted that the church in Burma (Myanmar) has been silent in the face of such inhumane socio-political evils, especially by the horrendous military regime, because of two basic factors: the separation of church and state, and the subjugation of church to authority.[12] After addressing these two factors, we can examine other factors which I think are important.

First, on the concept of separation of church and state, there are numerous opinions and concepts related to this, from the early church days through the centuries. One of the seven Baptist distinctives is "the separation of church and state"[13] and the subjugation of the church to political authority. This concept led to the belief that the state is secular, and the church is religious. According to the 2014 census, Myanmar is religiously very diverse. Buddhism is practiced by 87.9 percent of the people, whereas Christianity is practiced only by 6.2 percent, Islam by 4.2 percent, and Hinduism by 0.5 percent of the population.[14]

---

12   Pum Za Mang, "Separation of Church and State: A Case Study of Myanmar (Burma)," *Asia Journal of Theology* 25, no. 1 (2011): 43.

13   Quoted in Edward. T. Hiscox, *The New Dictionary of Baptist Churches*, 1859. See Fundamental Baptist Institute, fbinstitute.com.

14   Department of Population Ministry of Labour, Immigration and Population MYANMAR (July 2016). *The 2014 Myanmar Population and Housing Census Report Volume 2-C*. Department of Population Ministry of Labour, Immigration and Population MYANMAR, 12–15.

Even though the constitution guarantees religious freedom, Buddhism is the favored religion. On the one hand, the Myanmar constitution clearly mentions that "religious orders (including pastors) are not eligible to cast their votes in the general election as it is related to politics."[15] On the other hand, the churches in general, including Christian ministers, simply think that there will be no impact on the state even if the churches get involved in social issues and that they keep themselves away from the state. Lap Yan Kung, professor at Chung Chi Divinity School, Hong Kong, rightly says, "One of the characteristics of the Baptist tradition is the separation between politics and religion, and it may become an excuse for the church in Burma to refrain from politics."[16] The former general secretary of the Myanmar Council of Churches (MCC), Rev. Smith Ngulh Za Thawng, asserted that the majority of Christians in Myanmar are Baptists. Baptists traditionally uphold one of their distinctives, namely, the separation of church and state. I suppose this may well be one significant factor of churches' noninterference in sociopolitical matters in Myanmar.[17] One of the prominent leaders in the Zomi Baptist Convention (ZBC) also said in an interview, "being a Baptist organization, the ZBC firmly believes in the principle of 'separation of church and state.'" From the era of the socialist regime, the SLORC and SPDC, the ZBC has always governed itself by this principle. When the government became involved in ZBC matters, it developed into a conflict between ZBC and the government.[18] Hence, churches

---

15 Constitutions of the Republic of the Union of Myanmar 2008, Chapter IX, Article 392 (a).

16 Lap Yan Kung, "Love Your Enemies: A Theology for Aliens in Their Native Land: The Chin in Myanmar," *Studies in World Christianity* 27, no. 2 (2009): 93.

17 Personal email message to Lal Tin Hre, dated October 20, 2020.

18 Salai Za Uk Ling and Salai Bawi Lian Mang, "Religious Persecution: A Campaign of Ethnocide against *Chin* Christians in Burma," unpublished research paper.

do not want to be involved in the affairs of state, and the state also does not interfere with the church's activities, ironically not recognizing theological degrees offered by Bible schools and seminaries. He continues by saying that "One of the major hindrances to the work of ZBC has always been the government's policy to promote Buddhism at the expenses of other religions." This is known as *Amyo, Batha, Thathana,* or "one race, one language, one religion." This refers to the creation of a country based on three Bs: "Burman, Burmese, Buddhism."[19]

Second, the misinterpretation of Scripture and Romans 13:1 in particular: "Let every soul be in subjection to the higher powers: for there is no power but of God; and the powers that be are ordained of God" (RSV). The Baptist Church, the largest and most influential church in Myanmar, adheres strongly to the Baptist tradition and its distinctives. Therefore, the Myanmar Council of Churches (MCC) maintains silence on issues related to the government.[20] The Christian churches in Myanmar never come out

---

19   Za Uk Ling and Bawi Lian Mang, "Religious Persecution."

20   Smith Ngulh Za Thawng outlines the involvement of MCC in the Myanmar government in this way. The first phase was military rule (1962–2010; revolutionary council, 1962–73, one-party socialist government, 1974–88, socialist constitution, SLORC/SPDC military rule, 1988–2010). During this period, there was no state constitution and most of the time the country was ruled by order (military and party), meaning there was no rule of law, freedom, human rights, etc. In my opinion, our church leaders felt it was no use to speak to deaf ears or to hit a brick wall with one's head. And I assume they opted to apply the Scripture text "to be wise as serpent and harmless as dove." During my tenure in the MCC office (2000–5) while Gen. Khin Nyunt was powerful as Secretary-1 (S-1), annual Christmas dinners were used as open fora of dialogue at which MCC used to choose preachers who could speak prophetic messages publicly in the ears of S-1 and other ministers (generals) who accompanied him. On the other hand, S-1 regularly gave Christmas greetings which were public statements of the military regime

onto the streets for demonstrations, whereas the Buddhist monks have gathered several times for public demonstrations.

I fully agree with Pum Za Mang, who suggests that the church in Myanmar, with an overemphasis on the theory of subjugation to the authority and separation between church and state, is too submissive to the authority and is mostly silent in the face of political oppression, religious persecution, ethnic genocide, and human rights violations brought about and perpetuated by the repressive military regime. Consequently, the presence of Christianity, Christian seminaries, Christian churches, Christian pastors, and Christians in Myanmar can offer "little to nothing for the liberation of Myanmar from their social, political, and economic sufferings."[21] Samuel Ngun Ling in *Communicating Christ in Myanmar* asserted that "civil governments, rulers and magistrates are to be respected, and in all temporal matters, not contrary to conscience and the Word of God, to be obeyed; but they have no jurisdiction in spiritual concerns and have no right of dictation

---

and were usually kind words to Christians and ethnic groups that appeared in full in the following day's newspapers. They were very helpful in many instances. I think we had written two or three letters to both Gen. Saw Maung and Gen. Than Shwe which were not made public. Since 2001, MCC and CBCM (Catholic) jointly organized a week of prayer for reconciliation and peace in Myanmar during September and October every year which was intended to be a public witness of Christian participation in national peace. During the same period, by special permission of S-1, Bishop Sotero (Loikaw) used to write Christmas messages on every Christmas Day about peace and unity which appeared in daily newspapers. The second phase is multiparty democracy (2011 to date), a much more open phase than before. Here, I note the occasional statements and messages made by Cardinal Charles Bo which I found are quite open and frank. See his personal letter to Lal Tin Hre, dated October 20, 2020.

21   Pum Za Mang, "Separation of Church and State: A Case Study of Myanmar (Burma)," *Asia Journal of Theology* 25, no. 1 (2011): 44.

to, of control over, or interference with, matters of religion; but to protect all good citizens in the peaceable enjoyment of their religious right and privileges."[22]

Third is the fear of the brutality of the authoritarian regime. According to Freedom House, Burma has become one of the three most brutal and cruel nations in the world, third only to Cuba and North Korea. Evidence-based data show this statement to be true and correct, especially when political-economic demonstrations have been held in the country. A nationwide protest for democracy and socioeconomic reform was held in 1987 as a result of the withdrawal of the Burmese currency and on several occasions in August and September in 1988. By the end of the year, it was estimated that 10,000 people, including protesters and soldiers, had been killed, and many others were missing. Aung San Suu Kyi remarked on the event, on September 22, 1988, "I would like every country in the world to recognize the fact that the people of Burma are being shot down for no reason at all."[23]

The infamous Insein Central Prison, located in Yangon Division, is notorious worldwide for its inhumane conditions, corruption, abuse of inmates, and use of mental and physical torture. From 1988 to 2011 it was run by the military junta of Myanmar, named the State Law and Order Restoration Council (SLORC), and was used largely to repress political dissidents.[24] In May 2008, over one hundred prisoners were shot by guards at the prison resulting in the deaths of thirty-six inmates. One of its most famous prisoners is the Nobel Peace Prize–winning human rights activist Aung San Suu Kyi, who has been confined to Insein on three separate occasions in 2003, 2007, and 2009. Than Win Hlaing quoted from Assistance Association for Political Prisoners (AAPP) in his *Khin Nyunt's Biography* that 124 prisoners have died in Insein Prison

---

22   Ngun Ling, *Communicating Christ in Myanmar.*

23   Insein Prison–*Wikipedia.*

24   8888 Uprising–*Wikipedia.*

and other places. Some have died in the same year as or a few years after their imprisonment. Most of them were supporters of the NLD Party and university students.[25]A further four inmates were later tortured and killed by the prison guards who believed they had been the ringleaders of the initial protest that culminated in the mass shooting in 1988. It was estimated that the number of casualties surrounding the nationwide prodemocracy protests called the 8888 Uprising[26] range from hundreds to 10,000. Military authorities put the figures at about ninety-five people killed and 240 wounded.[27]

It would not be an exaggeration to say that space does not allow us to mention all the unjust deeds and brutal actions in this short chapter. However, I would dare to say that all the people in Burma have been overwhelmed by "fear"—fear of soldiers, fear of the police, fear of jail, fear of authorities members, fear of poverty, fear of teachers, fear of robbers, and so on. In this context, Aung San Suu Kyi, in her book *Freedom from Fear,* reflects on her greatest hopes and fears for her fellow Burmese citizens.[28] U Ne Win's order clearly indicated the merciless actions of the Burmese authoritarian regime toward the people. He said: "If the army shoots, it hits there is no firing into the air to scare."[29]

It is sad that the churches in Myanmar have no voice at all in any demonstration for different reasons, while hundreds of

25   Than Win Hlaing, *U Khin Nyunt (or) The Crowner of Every Cases* (Yangon: U Lwin Oo, 2014), 217–27. It is so painful that five died while they were in the hands of the police force; see 217.

26   This nationwide demonstration was usually called the "8888 Uprising," and it was Burma's transition to democracy that resulted in the first free election being held. The ruling NLD was born in the aftermath of the 8888 Uprising.

27   Than Win Hlaing, *U Khin Nyunt.*

28   Aung San Suu Kyi, *Freedom from Fear* (London: Penguin, 2010).

29   Bertil Lintner, *Outrage: Burmese Struggle for Democracy* (Hong Kong: Review Publishing Company, First Publishes, 1989), 19.

Buddhist monks come out onto the streets and join the demonstrations. Buddhist monks have held rallies several times, while no Christian organization has ever supported the reform movements. A Myanmar Catholic recounts how, behind the calm and the apparent freedom of movement, is hidden the most savage oppression, which prevents anyone to step "outside of the lines." "We are like half statues, half human beings: we can feel and see the suffering of our people, but we cannot speak." The same idea is stated by Smith Ngulh Za Thawng, former general secretary of MCC who says that the political leaders give their deaf ears to church leaders in Burma. He compares talking with the government leaders like hitting a brick wall with one's head." And I assume they also opted to apply the Scripture text "to be wise as a serpent and harmless as a dove."[30]

Fourth, the emphasis on the eschatological future. Out of various eschatological perspectives, many Christians in Burma put a stronger emphasis on *futuristic eschatology* than *realized eschatology* and are very fond of singing hymns like Jim Reeves's country gospel song, "This World Is Not My Home," though we are living in this world. Albert E. Brumley's "I'll Fly Away"[31] was a very influential hymn among many Christians in Burma. As has happened elsewhere among Christians, there is a tendency among Burmese Christians also to separate the earthly kingdom, which is evil, from the heavenly kingdom, which is holy and pure.

30   Personal email message to Lal Tin Hre, dated October 20, 2020.
31   "I'll Fly Away" is a hymn written in 1929 by Albert E. Brumley and published in 1932 by the Hartford Music company in a collection titled *Wonderful Message*. It has been called the most recorded gospel song and is frequently used in worship services by Baptists, Pentecostals, Nazarenes, the Churches of Christ, and many Methodists. See https://en.wikipedia.org/wiki/I%27ll_Fly_Away. Still, some evangelical pastors fully adhere to the notion of dispensationalism and place their emphasis on the Second Coming of Jesus, followed by His one thousand-year reign.

More evidence of this concept is found in a hymn book called *Khristian Lenkhawm Hlabu*[32] originally produced in the Mizo language but translated into many Chin dialects. More than half the book comprises hymns of yearning for the new world, New Jerusalem, and the land beyond the Jordan River. A good number of Christians, especially the Chin people, said that they have a very strong desire to leave this world, renounce worldly things, and go to heaven, the New Jerusalem. Ironically, the Chin people mourn their dead seriously and the mourning period is usually very long.

In this context of neglecting the present issues, the church in Burma comforts itself that this world is full of misery caused by its nature. Therefore, the church does not pay much attention to social issues. A very common notion prevailing among Christians in Burma is that the churches that express concern for social issues are regarded as liberal and advocate a social gospel. The evangelical churches have prioritized the gospel of salvation, with an emphasis on spiritual salvation. At the same time, they have issued a memorandum on social issues similar to the ecumenical faction. A case in point is the support extended to Aung San Suu Kyi by the MCC, along with Myanmar Evangelical Christian Alliance (MECA) in defending the Rohingya cause in the ICC at The Hague in The Netherlands.

Fifth, Christians are a minority in Myanmar. As stated above, Christians make up 6.8 percent of the total population, primarily among the Kachin, Chin, and Karen ethnic groups. This is because of missionary work in these respective areas. About four-fifths of the country's Christians are Protestants, in particular, Baptists of the Myanmar Baptist Convention; Roman Catholics make up the remainder. Christians were the fastest-growing religious group in

---

32   *Khristian Lenkhawm Hlabu* is a compilation of hymns composed by the Mizo local people with their tunes, normally used during funerals, which they are able to sing the whole day and night.

Burma in the last three decades; today, even though that growth gap has narrowed close to the general population, they still are the fastest-growing religious group.

Burma had been and still is described as the "land of the pagodas," where the wheels of Buddhism (the light of Southeast Asia) and the cross of Christ (the light of the world) have been experienced in the abode of southeastern Asia's peninsular region. The State Law and Order Restoration Council (SLORC) of the military government has made repeated claims that there is religious freedom of worship, and no discrimination exists on religious grounds. The written law and cultural practices overlapped in many instances as to make it clear that Buddhism is simply favored by the state. This is now not only reaffirmed by the SLORC government, but Buddhism also enjoys a special distinctiveness or status over other religions and has the state's backing in all its activities.[33]

After Aung San was assassinated, U Nu adopted the Buddhism as the state religion as a means of "national integration." Buddhism, indeed, had been inseparably intertwined with Myanmar national identity, as an old saying so clearly put it: *Buddha bata, Myanmar Lumyo* (to be a Myanmar is to be a Buddhist).[34] "National unity" means the assimilation of all ethnic minorities in Burma into being Burmese—"Burmanization." This idea resulted in the curtailment of freedom of unfavored religions. Various types of political restrictions and religious discrimination have been imposed on Christians in the years beginning from 1962 when General Ne Win took power. To Burmese Buddhists, the Christian religion is nothing but a window "screening for political and cultural expansion of the westerners." The prohibition of the construction of church buildings and Christian infrastructure can

---

33   *The New Light of Myanmar*, January 5, 2003, 9.

34   Za Uk Ling and Bawi Lian Mang, "Religious Persecution: A Campaign of Ethnocide against Chin Christians in Burma."

be seen in many places across the country.[35] Since the early 1980s, Chin communities in various villages and towns have erected wooden crosses on mounds and hill tops beside their villages and towns to symbolize their faith in Christianity and to remind themselves of the fact that Christianity has played an important role in shaping their modern society and culture. The destruction of crosses started around the early 1990s with the rapid increase in army battalions established across Chin state. Since then, almost every cross in all major towns in Chin state has been destroyed by the regime. Destruction of crosses is usually ordered by the town authorities or by army battalion commanders. There is abundant evidence that since the early 1990s, the regime had destroyed several churches and removed crosses placed on top of mountains in at least five townships in Chin state. In many cases, crosses were replaced with Buddhist pagodas and Christians were forced to contribute labor and money for their construction. The regime is also prohibiting the construction of new churches and has ordered construction of several churches under construction in towns and villages in Chin state to stop.

THEOLOGICAL REFLECTION

We have explored the possible roots of the silence of the church in Myanmar, and now we conclude the discussion with my personal reflections in the light of public theology or public witness. Subordination or subjugation to the political authority in contemporary Myanmar is simply a betrayal of Christ, who was persecuted, arrested, tortured, and condemned to death for the causes of social justice, political freedom, racial equality, and just peace.[36] In response to the question of the separation of church and state,

---

35   Za Uk Ling and Bawi Lian Mang.

36   Pum Za Mang, "Separation of Church and State: A Case Study of Myanmar (Burma)," 53.

Max L. Stackhouse argues that "the separation of church and state does not mean the segregation of theology from public life and from the attempt to guide political and economic life through persuasion, preaching, and teaching."[37] It is clear that the church in Myanmar fails to play any significant role in resisting the junta's campaign of genocide, criticizing the regime's brutalization of ethnic civilians, or condemning the government's violations of human rights, and it has remained silent.

Indeed, Myanmar Christians, especially church leaders and theologians, must responsibly oppose the state in nonviolent ways if the state is a violator of people's rights and identity. There is no justification for the silence of the church in the face of violence and oppression. Edmund Za Bik, former professor of MIT, made a remarkable observation:

> If our theology does not come to grips with our situational realities, theology becomes barren, non-existential, fossilized and disorienting. Theology should be academic, but not divorced from the hard realities of life. Burmese theology should be dialectic between academic and involvement, between commitment to Christ and solidarity with the victims of injustice and suffering, between the ritual celebration of the cross and the struggle for human wholeness, freedom and dignity.[38]

I would say public theology implies that the church is not just a private matter, a relationship with God; rather, it should be regarded as a public matter that should empower the church to address public issues for social justice, freedom, and human rights,

---

37   Max L. Stackhouse, *Public Theology and Political Economy: Christian Stewardship in Modern Society* (Grand Rapids, MI: Wm. B. Eerdmann, 1987), 30.

38   Edman Za Bik, "Liberation Now," *RAYS MIT Journal of Theology*, 2.

and to do so in the public sphere. The church must denounce social evils in society and oppose state power not in a violent way but in nonviolent ways. In the light of this thought, the church is called upon to address public issues in society, because the role of the church is not narrowly confined within the decorated compound of the church edifice, but goes far beyond the comfort zone of the church boundary to enter the public sphere in order to address public issues there for the betterment of public life.

The church is an agent of Christ's holistic liberation and full humanization of those economically exploited, politically oppressed, socially marginalized, materially poor, and ethnically alienated in societies. Ideally, the Bible is truly a book of liberation. Myanmar, as elsewhere, is indeed entrusted with the divine mandate and authority to stand for truth, to defend the weak, to side with the oppressed, to champion human rights, and to combat any sort of oppressive force, including state power, if and when it inflicts miseries and suffering on its own citizens, because when the church stops being the voice of the voiceless and the oppressed in the country, it stops being the true Christian church. The church is to be called as the *salt of the earth* and *the light of the world*. In the context of Myanmar, the church ought to apply the text from Scripture: "to be wise as serpent and harmless as dove" (Matt 10:16) in its engagement with the state.

10

ECOLOGICAL PROBLEMS AND THE ROLE OF PEOPLE IN THE PRESERVATION OF NATURAL RESOURCES

Naw Amady Htoo

This chapter attempts to explore the question of environment and ecology in Myanmar in the context of prolonged militarization and the onslaught of modernity and development. It will also attempt to present alternative perspectives and mandates to the ecological problem in Myanmar.

The word "ecology" comes from the word "oekology" which is derived from the Greek word *oikos* meaning "house," "habitat," and "logos." It refers to the biological study of the interdependence of different organisms that live on earth (plants, animals, birds, fish, and humans), and their natural environments.[1] The term "ecology" or *oekologie* was coined in 1866 by the German biologist Ernst Haeckel to describe the study of the relationship between living organisms and their environment.[2] Along with the word "ecology,"

---

1   Jey J. Kanagaraj, "Ecological Concern in Paul's Mission and Theology," in *Ecological Challenge and Christian Mission*, ed. Krickwin C. Marak and Atul Y. Aghamkar (Delhi: CMS, 1998), 58.

2   R. L. Sarkar, *The Bible, Ecology, and Environment* (Delhi: ISPCK, 2000), 59.

Ken Gnanakan suggests that it is the study of animals and plants and their interrelationship and environments. Moreover, this word refers to the balance, harmony, and interrelatedness within a given environment.[3] According to James D. Talapati, ecology has been defined as the study of the relationship between organisms and their environment.[4] The word "environment" refers to the complete range of physical and biological conditions that surround human beings. Human beings are part of a particular environment. Human beings and other organisms, such as trees, plants, animals, and so on, cannot exist outside of a given environment. "Environment is the term used to refer to nature and all that surrounds it. Sometimes it was used to refer to creation."[5]

ECOLOGICAL PROBLEMS IN MYANMAR

Over the decades, Myanmar has experienced cyclones, storm surges, floods, landslides, earthquakes, drought, and forest fires. In May 2008, the most overwhelming danger came in the form of Cyclone Nargis. This hit the country and caused considerable damage to the lives and properties in the Ayeyarwady Delta region. Thousands of people died, and thousands of families were made homeless. Subsequently, in mid-February 2016, Myanmar experienced a severe El Niño-related event, including extreme temperatures, unusual rainfall patterns, dry soil, elevated risk of fires, and an acute water shortage. In addition, Myanmar has experienced floods over the past decade. The cause of all this ecological crisis is pollution.

---

3   Ken Gnanakan, *God's Word: A Theology of the Environment* (Cambridge: Cambridge University Press, 1999), 2–3.

4   James D. Talapati, "A Christian Understanding and Response on Ecology," in *Green Gospel*, ed. Thomas Samuel and Matthew Koshy Punnackadu (Tiruvalla: Christava Sahitya Samithi, 2010), 70.

5   Gnanakan, *God's Word*, 2.

The word "pollution" comes from the Latin word *pollution*, which means "defilement" or "uncleanness."[6] There are three types of pollution—air pollution, water pollution, and soil pollution. Air pollution is the contamination of the air, either indoor or outdoor. A physical, biological, or chemical alteration to the air in the atmosphere can be termed pollution. It occurs when any harmful gas, dust, or smoke enters the atmosphere and makes it difficult for plants, animals, and humans to survive as the air becomes dirty. According to Robert Parham, the industrialized nations are facing an increasing amount of air pollution. One in every five people on the earth is exposed to harmful air.[7]

Myanmar is facing the double burden of indoor and outdoor air pollution. The households in many places in Myanmar are used to cooking with kerosene, wood, or crop waste, and this contributes to indoor air pollution. Indoor air pollution also includes household cleaning products and painting supplies that emit toxic chemicals. The cause of outdoor air pollution includes indiscriminate mining, the burning of fossil fuels, mechanized agriculture-related activities (the most hazardous gases in the atmosphere are the by-products of ammonia), and manufacturing industries that release large amounts of carbon monoxide, hydrocarbons, organic compounds, and chemicals into the air thereby depleting the quality of air. Water pollution is mainly caused by toxic waste and raw sewage. Soil pollution may be the result of indiscriminate discharge of industrial waste, deforestation, excessive use of fertilizers and pesticides, unscientific garbage disposal, and climate change. Consequently, soil pollution harbors a broad spectrum of negative impacts that affect plants, animals, humans, and the ecosystem

---

6   Robert Parham, *Loving Neighbors across Time: A Christian Guide to Protecting the Earth* (Birmingham: New Hope, 1991), 41.

7   Parham, *Loving Neighbors*, 43.

as a whole.[8] Add to this the fact that cyclones, earthquakes, and global warming can be caused by overharvesting the renewable resources provided to us by creation. The depletion and destruction of precious resources such as energy (e.g., electricity), forests, the rich bio-diversity, and mineral resources is of serious concern for us in Myanmar.

Human beings have an obligation to prevent and protect, love and care for the environment, and reduce their impact on our natural resources by recycling and reusing whenever possible, and reducing the depletion of those materials whose extraction is devastating the planet. Planting trees and grass and reducing the use of chemicals, charcoal, water, paper, chop-sticks, and all materials made with wood and bamboo must be pursued with a passion for Mother Earth. In this way, we can prevent the depletion of natural resources and the destruction of nature and build beautiful environments. To prevent further damage, I propose that the church and seminaries consider the following alternate perspective and mandates.

STEWARDSHIP DOMINION MANDATE

Genesis 1:1–31 tells us the creation story: "God saw everything that he had made, and indeed, it was very good" (1:31 NSRV). However, egocentric human beings and their anthropocentric worldview influence the world and are destroying creation in various ways. Myanmar was once known as a country abundant in natural resources. However, the people did not care to protect the natural resources, which eventually were destroyed by human greed. This needs to be exposed by studying the intrinsic factors leading to

---

8   Conservation Institute.org, https://www.conservationinstitute. org/wp-content/uploads/2018/06/soilwashing.jpg, accessed February 20, 2023.

the present state of affairs and exercising theological imagination to reverse the trend. This is the task of the public witness.

Genesis 1:28 says, "God blessed them, and God said to them, 'Be fruitful and multiply, and fill the earth and subdue it; and have dominion over the fish of the sea and over the birds of the air and over every living thing that moves upon the earth'" (NRSV). The text describes that God gave the responsibility to human beings to have dominion (rule) over all the creatures on earth. However, people misinterpreted the text, which led to much of the destruction of creation. According to Robert Parham, God's command to humans is to "have dominion" over the earth. Too often people interpreted "dominion" to mean "domination." The words "dominion" and "domination" are radically different. The idea of domination has contributed to the exploitation of nature for humankind's own immediate use. But "dominion" carries the connotation of the Hebrew *Rabadah* and does not allow for the ruthless assault on nature. "Dominion" means human rule over nature as a servant king who rules with justice and peace.[9]

In addition, Ken Gnanakan argues that the word "dominion" had a political implication. The word also implied power and authority gained through conquest. He accepted that ultimate dominion belongs to Yahweh alone. The "dominion" in Genesis 1:28 means God shares dominion with humans over nature.[10] It is God who gave the responsibility to humans to name the entire creation and take care of living things as stewards. Ken Gnanakan quotes Douglas John Hall, from his book *The Steward: A Biblical Symbol Come of Age*, to drive home his point thus:

> The steward is a particularly apt metaphor for humanity because it encapsulates the two sides of human relatedness, the relation to God on the one hand and to

---

9   Parham, *Loving Neighbors*, 23–25.

10   Gnanakan, *God's Word*, 52.

non-human creatures on the other. The human being is
as God's steward, accountable to God and responsible for
its fellow creature.[11]

It means that the steward has responsibility to God as the creator
as well as to creations. Furthermore, "dominion" is the stewardship under God, responsible to God for taking care of nature, "for
the earth is the Lord's and the fullness thereof" (Ps 24:1). Psalm
8:6–8 also expresses human dominion over nature. This can and
should be embodied by the Christian faith community and all
peoples committed to seeing the earth as neighbor.

However, the environmental and ecological crisis is worsen-
ing in Myanmar. Prevention and protection strategies are urgently
needed. According to James A. Nash, the ecological crisis is not due
to a single problem, but rather a massive mosaic of intertwined
problems that adversely affect humans and every living thing.[12]

The problem of global warming comes from deforestation, overusing energy, and the consumption of fossil fuels. So,
the strategies against global warming are threefold. First, energy
conservation and efficiency must be the focus. At a practical level,
electrical appliances must be turned off when not needed. Second,
fossil fuel consumption must be reduced because 80 percent of
world energy comes from fossil fuels (oil, coal, and natural gas).
Third, the destruction of forests must be drastically reduced,
and simultaneously, there is a need to plant more trees. Revers-
ing existing environmental problems and meeting increasing
demand for firewood requires the planting of many more trees.[13]

---

11   Gnanakan, 131, quoting from Douglas John Hall, *The Steward—A Biblical Symbol Come of Age* (Eugene, OR: Wipf & Stock, 1990).

12   James A. Nash, *Loving Nature: Ecological Integrity and Christian Responsibility* (Nashville: Abingdon Press, 1991), 23.

13   Parham, *Loving Neighbors*, 36–38.

In addition to this, slowing the rate of human population growth, the preservation of forest areas, and debt for nature swap are factors that can lead to reforestation.[14]

The depletion of the ozone layer is a major factor and is well documented. This depletion has been caused by a synthetic chemical made from chlorine called chlorofluorocarbons (CFC). To reduce chlorofluorocarbons, General Motors demanded that their dealers recycle CFCs in car air conditioners.[15] To reduce air pollution, mass awareness is needed to reduce industrial waste, the use of carbon dioxide, and tobacco smoke and to promote the planting of more trees.

To reduce soil pollution, people need to reduce their use of chemicals, nitrate fertilizers, and toxic insecticides and practice the principle of reduce, reuse, recycle, especially plastic, vigorously. To reduce water pollution rivers, lakes, and coastal waterways need regeneration.

Insect species are also at risk of extinction. They have been endangered by soaring population growth, which has resulted in grinding poverty and unbridled greed for exotic plants and animals. To protect at-risk species, natural habitats in the form of parks, ecotourism reserves, zoos, botanical gardens, and aquariums are needed to preserve biodiversity.[16]

LOVING AND CARING MANDATE

God created the earth and God wants all human beings to love and care for his creations. Per Larsson, in his book *Your Will Be Done on Earth*, suggests that God loves the world and tries to care for it.

---

14   Parham, 57.
15   Parham, 38–40.
16   Parham, 53.

God cares for his creations by natural law.[17] The natural laws are to be seen in the Old Testament and the New Testament. Some examples are the prohibition of planting fields with "two kinds of seed" (Lev 19:19); ensuring that domestic animals are permitted to rest on the Sabbath (Exod 20:8–11); the animals that "belong to an enemy are to be treated with respect" (Exod 23:4–5); "destroying the bird's nest by the road was forbidden" (Deut 22:6–7); and "not to destroy the trees of the enemy" as commanded by God (Deut 20:19–20). Moreover, the New Testament commandment of "loving your neighbor as yourself" implies caring for the earth. This means protecting the environment and the diversity of nonhuman life in the world. Jesus's teaching in Luke 12:6–7 shows us that "God cares not only for the human being but also the sparrow." Therefore, loving and caring for the environment is important in Myanmar to save the country's natural resources.

CONCLUSION

Myanmar is not alone when it comes to the earth being ravaged by human greed. The policies of the state, the world over, are one of complicity with the exploitative actions of corporations. Crony capitalism in Myanmar is a case in point. Development, following a "Western model," is marketed and peddled by the media. Development is projected as the answer to the suffering of the poor. Discussions and public debates on issues of environmental impact assessment, sustainability, and the symbiotic relationship between humans and other life forms are nonexistent.

Public witness on ecological and environmental concerns calls for a critique of the present—a critique based on disaster to

---

17   Per Larsson, *Your Will Be Done on Earth: Ecological Theology for Asia, An Ecumenical Textbook for Theological Schools* (Hong Kong: Clear-Cut Publishing, 2004), 49.

a common heritage, the earth, and a critique of extreme anthropocentric world-views, industry-centered development projects,
and poor governance. Alongside this critique is the need for constructive action. Preserving and sustaining church and common
properties, reducing our carbon footprint, and enhancing efforts
to recycle are but a few examples.

The task ahead is large. No struggle for justice can ignore
the cry of the earth (earth "groans," Rom 8:22); recognition of the
earth as our neighbor sheds a different light on how we see ourselves, God's earth, development, and indeed the greater common
good.

11

SOCIAL TRANSFORMATION AND SOCIAL MOVEMENTS

Van Lal Thuam Lian

This chapter argues that Myanmar needs a public theology that engages in the social issues of wider society within and outside Christianity. The current contextual theologies in Myanmar are more concerned with indigenization or enculturation, that is, changing the outer layer of society, engaging only in intellectual and theoretical discourses. But to make the presence and witness of Christianity dynamic and effective in the public sphere of Myanmar, social transformation through social movements/actions is an essential task of public theology in Myanmar today. Therefore, the aim of this chapter is to challenge the present contextual theologies in Myanmar to make deeper and wider engagement in social issues so that the Christian gospel creates social transformation through faith-based social movements and actions. The first part of the chapter deals with definitions of society and social transformation, and the second part with the role of religion or theology in society and social movements as plausible ways of social transformation.

SOCIETY

The word "society" is derived from the Latin word *socius*, which means companionship or friendship. Companionship means sociability, which is the main element that defines the true essence of society. It indicates that human beings always live in the company of other people. The human being is a social animal and cannot live alone. Humans need a society for living, working, and enjoying life. Society has become an essential condition for human life to arise and to continue; human life and society always go together. Society consists of people, and within society there is mutual interaction and mutual awareness. Society also depends on similarity. There is cooperation and division of labor in society. Society also exercises social control on individuals. Society is not static but is dynamic.[1]

As society changes, it requires transformation so that it is always *inclusive, peaceful*, and *accessible to everyone*. In his comment on André Beteille's idea of two types of society—harmonic and disharmonic—John Desrochers rightly observes that modern societies are disharmonic and unstable because people's views of the world and ideology are increasingly shaped by the values of social justice and equality, while the organizational (economic and sociopolitical) systems lag behind and contradict this new pattern of thinking. He also states that this disharmonic state or "contradictions between the organizational and meaning systems of modern societies are pointers to a stormy, but hopefully more just, future."[2] This observation and assessment is correct in present-day Myanmar society too. Having observed that society is

---

1   Asui Tallanao, *Introduction to Sociology: Text with Notes for B.A. Sociology (First Semester) of Mizoram University* (Aizawl: Alpha-Plus Publishing House, n.d.), 174.

2   John Desrochers, *Methods of Societal Analysis* (Bangalore: Center for Social Action, 1977), 28–29.

unstable and needs transformation, let us now turn to the definition of social transformation.

WHAT IS SOCIAL TRANSFORMATION?

K. Thanzauva defines the term "social transformation" as "a process of discernible and significant change in the form, structure,
system, function and condition of society."[3] "Social reform,"
another term for "social transformation," "refers to any attempt
that seeks to correct any injustices in a society . . . with the aim
of improving the quality of life. Social reform is a kind of social
movement that aims to make gradual change, or change in certain
aspects of society, rather than rapid or fundamental changes."[4]

These social changes can affect people's lives either in a
constructive way or in a destructive way. This chapter applies the
terms "social transformation," "social reform," and "social change"
interchangeably to mean a positive and progressive change moving forward, similar to development; in other words, as a positive
and progressive development.

The underlying assumption of social transformation is that
human beings are, first of all, transcendental beings created with
the potential for self-improvement. They are, at the same time,
social beings, because true humanity is realized only in relationships with others. True humanity is co-humanity. Since a
human being is a social being, the self-improvement of individuals becomes meaningful in relation to human society. The Second Vatican Council states: "for by his [sic] inmost nature man
is a social being; and unless he relates himself to others, he can
neither live nor develop his potentials." This view is explicitly

---

3   K. Thanzauva, *Transforming Theology: A Theological Basis for Social
Transformation* (Bangalore: Asian Trading Corporation, 2002), 1.

4   https://aimplb.org/social-reform/#:~:text=A%20Social%20Reform%
20refers%20to,any%20injustices%20in%20a%20society

expressed in the Christian concept of the image of God. Macquarrie rightly states that the image of God is not a fixed "endowment" or nature, but a potentiality to move outward and upward, and to live in relationship with God and others. Therefore, we should think of "transformation" in terms of social transformation. In fact, the change of individual persons occurs in human society; therefore, change is always in some sense a social change. All those who strive for social transformation should recognize the truth that all social realities are created mostly by human beings and are therefore changeable.[5]

It is obvious that social transformation as an attempt to correct any injustices in a society with the aim of improving the quality of life is an essence of religion or public theology. Therefore, we will now turn to see what religion or theology has to do to facilitate the transformation and development of society.

SOCIAL FUNCTION OF RELIGION

To understand the social function of religion, it may be helpful to follow Niklas Luhman's idea of two dimensions of religion: religion as function and religion as performance. *Function* means what religion does to its adherents in terms of providing belief systems and meaning and celebrating rituals so that it can maintain its existence and status quo in society. On the other hand, religion becomes *performance* when it tries to respond to issues and problems (like economic poverty, political oppression, environmental degradation, etc.) that the various systems in society have caused. Through performance, religion establishes its importance for wider society.[6] It may not be wrong to assess that Myanmar

---

5   Thanzauva, *Transforming Theology*, 2.
6   Felix Wilfred, *Asian Public Theology: Critical Concerns in Challenging Times* (Delhi: ISPCK, 2010), 323–24.

Christianity still holds traditional theology that is catering to the function of Christianity. Myanmar needs a public theology that supports the performance of Christianity for social transformation in Myanmar.

Desrochers argues that all religions unavoidably exercise a social function. He summed up the two basic social functions of religion as follows:

> **Prophetic or revolutionary function**: religious protest against politico-economic injustices and plea for a new society.

> **The submissive function of religion**: (1) legitimation: religion supports the status quo; (2) rationalization: it explains the status quo; (3) compensation: it offers otherworldly rewards for the oppressed; (4) social control: it influences social behavior by the promise of after-life rewards and punishments.[7]

Here it can be observed that German sociologist Niklas Luhmann's idea of "performance" resonates with Desrochers's "prophetic social function."

Christian leaders and theologians, as a whole, have practiced the submissive function of religion in the sociopolitical sphere of Myanmar. Therefore, the ordinary public has hardly witnessed the prophetic voice and action of Christian leaders in Myanmar. While the prophetic social function of religion is power for social transformation, Christianity in Myanmar has allied with the submissive function. Therefore, Christian elites (church leaders and academicians) have a more challenging step to take further if we truly have a commitment toward social transformation in the public sphere, from writing peer-reviewed articles to doing public-reviewed actions.

---

7   Desrochers, *Methods of Societal Analysis*, 73.

What Myanmar churches are doing now is social service, whereas our prophetic call is social action or social justice. Here it is helpful to quote the Grand Rapids report "Evangelism and Social Responsibility," as quoted by John Stott, to distinguish between social service and social action:[8]

Social Service	Social Action
Relieving human need	Removing the causes of human need
Philanthropic activity	Political and economic activity
Seeking to minister to individuals and families	Seeking to transform the structures of society
Works of mercy	The quest for justice

Having learnt that social services or submissive functions of religion are a kind of means of supporting current injustices and evil systems, Christian leaders and theologians are challenged to take more prophetic engagements in the sociopolitical public sphere of Myanmar. For this purpose, social movements are plausible ways for Christians to work with people from other faiths or even secular people for the transformation and development of society.

WHAT ARE SOCIAL MOVEMENTS?[9]

Social movements are groups of people who join together to take part in social action to address social problems. They usually focus on large social issues such as environmental degradation,

---

8   John Stott, *Issues Facing Christians Today*, 4th ed. (Grand Rapids: Zondervan, 2006), 26.

9   This section is an excerpt from Rory McLaughlin, *Politics: Ideas, Institutions and Actors, A Civic Education Course for Myanmar*, student's book (Yangon: Mote Oo Education, n.d.), 136–38.

women's rights, or land rights. Social movements attract many different organizations because they focus on issues that affect large sections of society.

Social movements generally focus on advocacy rather than providing services. They often try to influence government to make laws or policies that address the issues and concerns of that movement. Like many advocacy NGOs, social movements are closely related to the idea of social activism.

Many social movements want to do more than just influence the government. They rely on grassroots support and bottom-up power to create social change. Social movements have often been associated with the idea of civil disobedience and social justice. They often use direct action strategies such as demonstrations and occupations.

There are two main types of social movements:

Issue-specific movements: Certain events or issues create so much popular support or anger that social movements grow up around them. Narmada Bachao Andolan, in India, is a good example of this kind of movement. The movement started with the specific issue of the creation of the Sardar Sarovar Dam on the Narmada River. The movement's objective was to stop the dam from being constructed to protect the people who live there. It grew into a bigger movement that opposed other big dam projects and policies of the government that supported them. This kind of movement usually has clear leadership and a higher level of organization but does not often last very long.

Generic movements: Compared to single-issue movements, generic movements generally last longer and focus on broader issues. The environmental movement and the women's movement are examples of

generic movements. Environmental movements protest against many kinds of unsustainable policies and
actions. Likewise, women's movements put pressure
on the government to create or change policies that
address different issues faced by women.

Generic movements represent many different actors who
share the same goals and values. For example, the environmental
movement is a label for a large number of individuals, CSOs, and
issue-specific movements. All of these have separate organizations
and independent leadership and often have different views on the
kind of social change they want to achieve.

SOCIAL MOVEMENTS IN MYANMAR

To understand the power of social movements for social transformation, it is helpful to look at some recent social movements in
Myanmar. The first one is the Saffron Revolution. This was a protest initially led by Buddhist monks in 2007 against the military
government's decision to raise oil and gas prices. It was named
the "Saffron Revolution" as it was mainly Buddhist monks who
were involved in the protest and saffron alludes to the traditional
color of the robes worn by the monks. This is a good example of
an issue-specific social movement in Myanmar.

When the military raised the price of energy overnight without warning, the most immediate effect was on the poor. Buses
raised fares to a level the poor could not afford. Buddhist monks
noted that people could no longer donate the usual amount of
food to monasteries because of economic deprivation, and some
people were bringing their children to temples and asking the
monks to feed them because the families could no longer do so. As
a result, monks in Pakkoku started demonstrations on September
5, 2007. The demonstration moved to Yangon, where thousands

of young monks marched quietly through the streets without political slogans.[10] In response to this challenge to their authority, the military responded brutally, attacking monastic protestors. As David Steinberg rightly observes, this demonstration resulted in the military becoming concerned about the repression of the Buddhist monks and the danger this posed to their grip on power, and this accelerated the process of the military's political transformation toward democracy after earlier interminable delays.[11]

Another example of a single-issue social movement is the campaign against the construction of Myitsone Dam on the Ayeyarwady River. The construction of the Myitsone Dam was a hydroelectric project financed and led by a state-owned Chinese company, China Power Investment Corporation (CPI), with the consent of the military junta. The dam was projected to produce 6000 megawatts of electricity by 2017. CPI would provide most of the 2.5 billion US dollars of investment for the project and would receive 90 percent of the electricity generated. Myanmar would receive the other 10 percent. After a fifty-year period, Myanmar would get the ownership of the project.[12]

Before 2011, only a few people in Myanmar were aware of protest movements against the Myitsone Dam project, which were active only on the internet, as the government imposed censorship of newspapers and strictly controlled or blocked internet (website) access. But following the 2010 election and some relaxation of censorship, people came to learn about the project, especially when the chief executive officer of the Eleven Media Group, Dr. Than Htut Aung, warned that the future of the Ayeyarwady

10   David Steinberg, *Burma/Myanmar: What Everyone Needs to Know* (Oxford: Oxford University Press, 2010), 138.

11   Steinberg, *Burma/Myanmar*, 143.

12   Ye Htut, *Myanmar's Political Transition and Lost Opportunities* (2010–16) (Singapore: ISEAS, 2019), 155.

was under threat from a powerful neighbor in January 2011. The weekly journals published by Eleven Media started a campaign against the dam project and were soon followed by other media and activist groups. The anti-Myitsone Dam movement gained momentum when Aung San Su Kyi issued a "Save the Ayeyar-wady" statement on August 11, 2011. As a result, on September 30, 2011, President Thein Sein announced that he would suspend the Myitsone Dam project for his term in office as he was concerned that further protests in different parts of the country would lead to a political crisis.[13] This is a good example of the power of a social movement that resulted in a welcome sociopolitical change or transformation in Myanmar after its independence from Britain.

Now, we examine an example of generic social movements. Myanmar Egress, a prominent civil society organization in Myan-mar, was founded in 2006 by Dr. Nay Win Maung (1962–2012) and his intellectual friends who were committed to state-building through positive change in a progressive yet constructive collab-oration and working relationship with the government and all interest groups, both local and foreign. Egress was set up with the mission of "promoting and nurturing democracy through the ren-ovation of the highly intelligent and politically motivated citizenry of the country (capacity-building and supplier of change agents); feeding-related policy inputs to the governing body (Think Tank); public opinion shaping via public media and opinion polls; and promoting issues on environment that in turn will serve the long-term benefit of the country."[14]

The main objectives of the organization are to promote civil society organizations in the country and to help young people to prepare to face the challenges of political deadlock in the coun-try and globalization around the world. Due to the long political

13   Htut, *Myanmar's Political Transition and Lost Opportunities*, 156.
14   http://myanmaregress.org/about/, last accessed March 22, 2020.

impasse in the country, Myanmar and its people have been facing a plethora of social, political, and economic problems. Regardless of the ongoing sociopolitical and economic problems in the country, Myanmar is not short of young people who are keen to work for their nation. Many young people also understand the need to work together by forming social and professional organizations. However, most young people in Myanmar lack the necessary knowledge and expertise to do what they wish to do or should do for their country. The country's education system does not prepare young people to meet the needs of the new economic system and to face other challenges. Most young people cannot afford to study at private academic and technical training schools in their own country, let alone study in foreign countries. The members of Myanmar Egress individually organized some short training courses and workshops for young people from different parts of Myanmar.[15]

Thus, the main aim of Myanmar Egress was, first and foremost, the training and education of young adults—the generation that had not had the chance to go to university, and those who could be catalysts for change.[16] Ko Kyaw Thu, a fellow at the Oxford-based Reuters Institute for Journalism who wrote his master's thesis on Egress, said the organization had played a "crucial role in giving political education to the younger generations in a country where there was previously no formal institutions that taught political sciences."[17] As Egress focused on a peaceful transition to democracy in Myanmar, the leading founder Nay Win Maung accepted the 2008 constitution and the military-led process of democratic transformation. Therefore, Myanmar Egress made a positive impression on military leaders and they

---

15   http://myanmaregress.org/about/, last accessed March 22, 2020.

16   Marie Lall, *Understanding Reform in Myanmar: People and Society in the Wake of Military Rule* (London: Hurst & Co., 2016), 22.

17   Ko Kyaw Thu, https://tinyurl.com/2adb5bms

cooperated closely in the reform process of Thein Sein's government. Ye Htut, the presidential spokesperson, even criticized that "one or two individuals from Egress took all the credit for the Myanmar Spring and boasted that all the president's speeches and policies came from Egress."[18] This showcases that Myanmar Egress has been pivotal in Myanmar's political transformation toward democracy.

When we look at the above three examples of social movements in Myanmar, we can clearly see the power of social movements for social transformation and that these movements work beyond racial and religious boundaries for the common good of the people.

CONCLUSION

Social movements are inclusive ways of engaging in a wider society where people from different faiths can work together in the task of social transformation seeking the common good of the whole society. Modern societies are disharmonic and unstable, so they always need social change or transformation. To transform society with the values of peace, equality, and justice is an indispensable task of religions, and Myanmar Christianity is not exempt from this social function. Therefore, Myanmar's contextual theologies must give great consideration not only to inculturation/indigenization or theoretical discourses but, more importantly, to social action and justice. Liberation theology "is an attempt to make religion an instrument of social transformation,"[19] and therefore, Myanmar needs a public theology that is more liberative, prophetic, and transformative in the public sphere.

---

18   Htut, *Myanmar's Political Transition and Lost Opportunities*, 79.

19   Thanzauva, *Transforming Theology*, 12.

12

DISPLACEMENT, MIGRATION, TRAFFICKING, AND SEXUAL VIOLATION

Van Lal Hming Sangi

INTRODUCTION

Trafficking, migration, and sexual violence have a long history, have been an issue since the beginning of human history, and are recognized as universal phenomena enduring for centuries. This trend has continued and seems to have increased in the twenty-first century. The current movement of people has been called the "global nomadic age."

As transnational migration increases, the world today witnesses an alarming trend of migrant smuggling and human trafficking. Human trafficking is thus intimately linked to the undercurrents of global migration. Migrant smuggling is a complex crime that takes different forms in different parts of the world.[1] While emphasizing the significance of an international framework for action to implement the Smuggling of Migrants

---

[1]   Mathews George Chunakara, "Transnational Labor Migration, Human Trafficking, and Asian Diaspora: Responses of Churches," in *Migration, Human Trafficking and the Asian Diaspora: Report of the International Consultation* (Bangkok: CCA, 2018), 13–39.

Protocol, the UN observes: "Although the vast majority of the member-states of the United Nations have ratified the Smuggling of Migrants Protocol, most do not have dedicated action plans or strategies to respond to the issue. Where migrants are simply detained and returned to countries of origin without investigating the actors involved in smuggling those migrants, the criminal processes at work continue unchallenged."

In this chapter I will discuss the following: migration, human trafficking, human trafficking in Myanmar, and conflict and displacement in Myanmar.

MIGRATION

The United Nations Human Development Report on "Human Mobility and Development" states: "Migration contributes to human development and it is a motive power, and it increases individuals' finance, health, and education." This trend of migration has impacts at various levels on most countries in the world, sending, transit, or receiving country, or any of these two or all three categories. Most of the growth in the global population of international migrants has been caused by movements toward high-income countries, which host 64 million migrants. The number of international migrants includes 26 million refugees or asylum seekers, or about 10 percent of the total. Although a majority of the world's transnational migrants live in high-income countries, low- and middle-income countries host nearly 22 million, or 84 percent of all refugees and asylum seekers. In 2017, 48.4 percent of international migrants were women. Female migrants outnumber males in all regions except Africa and Asia. Migrant workers, those who migrate for employment, and their families account for about 90 percent of transnational migrants. Transnational migrants today are a very mixed group, including seasonal workers, temporary contract workers, skilled migrant workers, unskilled workers, students, asylum seekers and refugees, workers with irregular status, and victims of trafficking and forced labor.

There are various factors that contribute to labor-related transnational migration. The increasing trend of transnational migration is also a consequence of globalization, which is characterized not only by the liberalization of trade, services, investment, and capital but also by the transnational movement of people in search of better lives and employment opportunities. The economies of the migrant-labor-receiving countries also demand labor forces to cater to the needs of their domestic labor demands in various sectors. At the same time, migration also helps a large number of migrant workers to improve their economic conditions back home.[2] Migrants workers' rights and security require specific and special protection in all circumstances. However, these groups of transnational migrant workers are often denied legal protection that is otherwise available in their home countries, and they continue to face exploitation and denial of their right to decent labor and human rights. Legal protections to ensure their labor rights are not adequately established in many countries where they work. The basic human rights of migrant workers are too easily violated or denied.

HUMAN TRAFFICKING

Human trafficking, known as "modern slavery," or the widespread buying and selling of human beings, constitutes one of the most alarming issues facing contemporary humanity. Human trafficking exists because of the demand to exploit human persons. Traffickers exploit cultural traditions, prey on the most vulnerable in society, and take advantage of those living in poverty. For human trafficking to be a lucrative business, there must be a demand for

---

2   Chunakara, "Transnational Labor Migration, Human Trafficking, and Asian Diaspora: Responses of Churches."

the use of women and children. Human trafficking cannot exist or thrive unless people demand the services or provide "the market" for them. The concept that a human person may be considered or treated as an object or commodity is at the heart of the demand side of human trafficking.

Human trafficking and the demand which drives it is an extremely complex issue. The United Nations Convention Against Transnational Organized Crime emphasizes the use of force, fraud, abuse of power, and deception in its definition. This highlights the illegal aspects of trafficking and the demand for human persons.

> Trafficking in persons shall mean the recruitment, transportation, transfer, harboring or receipt of persons, by means of the threat or use of force or other forms of coercion, of abduction, of fraud, of deception, of the abuse of power or of a position of vulnerability or of the giving or receiving of payments or benefits to achieve the consent of a person having control over another person, for the purpose of exploitation. Exploitation shall include, at a minimum, the exploitation of the prostitution of others or forms of sexual exploitation, forced labor or services, slavery or practices similar to slavery.

In this definition, the eradication of human trafficking and demand relies on the legal system to curb and stop criminal activity.

Another definition of trafficking and demand is proposed by Donna Hughes, a professor in the women's studies program at the University of Rhode Island. She highlights sexual exploitation in her definition of demand.

Hughes has divided the demand side of sex trafficking into three components: the person who purchases sex acts from women (the pimps, traffickers, brothel owners, and corrupt officials);

those who profit from prostitution and trafficking; and the culture which encourages demand by normalizing prostitution, lap dancing, or other commercial sexual activities. Each of these must be addressed to eliminate the demand for sex trafficking.

To halt trafficking and demand using this definition would center on a threefold strategy of:

1. care of women and children trafficked,

2. prosecution of the "johns" and pimps, and

3. changing the cultural norms and attitudes toward commercial sexual activities.

The third definition of trafficking and demand looks at basic marketing principles to understand the phenomenon. Kevin Bales, a consultant to the United Nations Global Program on Trafficking in Persons, defines trafficking and demand as an economic exchange in which trafficked people are the "products" that produce a profit. He notes that trafficking is only possible in an economic context in which workers can be enslaved for profit. However, a larger social context must exist that allows for such exploitation. Bales proposes two steps to eradicate human traffickers and demand. First, he relies on the implementation of human rights on behalf of the victims of trafficking. Second, he calls for a public redefinition of the activity.[3]

MIGRATION AND HUMAN TRAFFICKING IN MYANMAR

Migration within Myanmar and across its long borders, which abut Thailand, Laos, China, India, and Bangladesh, is subject to

---

3   Cited from "Mission in the Context of Empire: Response to Human Trafficking," in CWM Regional Assemblies Review 2015, 18–20.

a range of drivers which are complex and are critical in affecting how and why people decide to move. Of the 53.9 million people in Myanmar, 70 percent live in rural areas. Following the general election held on November 8, 2015, there have been dramatic economic and cultural changes that have brought an increase in foreign investment and have also been a driver of urbanization and rural-to-urban migration. Many people migrate internally as they want to improve their livelihoods, follow their family members, get married, attend schools and universities, or avoid poor socioeconomic conditions. In 2014, 9.39 million people were internal migrants (which is approximately 20 percent of the population). Regionally, Myanmar has grown to be the largest migration-source country in the greater Mekong subregion. The Myanmar government estimates that there are 4.25 million Myanmar nationals living abroad. Regionally, drivers of migration can include higher wages in neighboring countries, conflict, and environmental migration due to natural disasters, among other factors.

It is reported that up to 70 percent of migrants living abroad are based in Thailand, followed by Malaysia (15 percent), China (4.6 percent), Singapore (3.9 percent), and the United States (1.9 percent). The IOM estimates there could be as many as three million Myanmar migrants living in Thailand as of 2016. The highest numbers of migrants, according to the latest census, came from Mon state (427,000), Kayin state (323,000), and Shan state (236,000).[4]

Migrants are often vulnerable to poorer health access and treatment and IOM works with the Myanmar government and a range of international and local partners to improve migrant health outcomes. Migrants, whether traveling regularly or irregularly, can become victims of trafficking, and smuggled migrants are exposed to abuses such as extortion, debt bondage,

---

4   IOM, Countries: Myanmar, https://www.iom.int/countries/myanmar, accessed March 3, 2020.

and physical exploitation. Myanmar migrants in the region send large amounts of remittances which help boost the economy, much of it through unofficial channels. While official estimates are that Myanmar received only USD 118 million in remittances in 2015, the then Ministry of Labor, Employment and Social Security estimated that remittances could be as high as USD 8 billion.[5]

CONFLICT AND DISPLACEMENT IN MYANMAR

Patterns of forced migration in Myanmar are structured by the changing nature of conflict in the country. While acutely vulnerable, internally displaced persons do live in those few areas of the country that are still affected by significant armed conflict, where the phenomenon of forced migration is more widespread and complex.

The Guiding Principles on Internal Displacement define internally displaced persons as "persons or groups of persons who have been forced or obliged to flee or to leave their homes or places of habitual residence, in particular as a result of or in order to avoid the effects of armed conflict, situations of generalized violence, violations of human rights or natural or human-made disasters, and who have not crossed an internationally recognised state border" (UNHCR, 1998).

According to the Ashley South Analysis there are three types of displacements in Myanmar.

The first type is armed conflict-induced displacement, which occurs either as a direct consequence of fighting and counterinsurgency operations or because armed conflict has directly undermined human and food security. This type of forced migration is linked to severe human rights abuses across Karen state, in

---

5   IOM, Countries: Myanmar.

eastern Tenasserim division, southern Mon state, southern and eastern Karenni state, southern Shan state, and parts of Chin state and Sagaing division.

The second type is state–society conflict-induced displacement, which is generally post-armed conflict caused by military occupation or "development" activities. This type is forced migration and could be due to confiscation of land by the *tatmadaw* (military) or other armed groups, or due to infrastructure development, for example. It could also be a product of predatory taxation, forced labor, and other abuses. All of the border states and divisions are affected by militarization or development-induced displacement, including Arakan (Rakhine) and Kachin states, as well as many urban areas.

Both these types of migrants are internally displaced persons whose displacement is the result of conflict—either active, armed (type one), or latent conflict, or the threat of the use of force (type two).

A third type is livelihood vulnerability-induced displacement, which is the primary form of internal and external migration in and from Myanmar. The main causes include inappropriate government practices and policies, limited availability of productive land, poor access to markets resulting in food insecurity, lack of education and health services, and stresses associated with the transition to a cash economy. Type three displacement occurs across the country, especially in remote townships. Type three movements involve a particularly vulnerable subgroup of economic migrants and result from limited choices faced by marginal populations. As such, they constitute a form of forced migration. Migration due to opium-eradication policies is included under this because the causes of the movement are related to livelihood issues; with the exception of some war areas, people are not ordered to move (opium eradication-induced migration could, however, also be considered under the second type of forced migration, due to the forcible nature of the opium bans, the severe shock to livelihoods involved, and the links to development activities). There are important links between these three types of displacement, each of which undermines traditional livelihood options and depletes people's resource base.[6]

Trafficking and displacement are gendered phenomena related to the discrimination against women who are denied

- education,

- economic opportunities,

- the right to own land,

- the right to inheritance, and

- the right to take decisions.

The crime of human trafficking consists of three core elements: the act, the means, and the purpose (see table).[7]

ACT	by	MEANS	For	PURPOSE
Recruit		Threats/violence		Force labor or services
Transport		Coercion		Sexual exploitation
Transfer		Deception/fraud		Slavery/servitude
Harbor		Abduction		Forced organ removal
Receive		Abuse of power		Exploitation

How do the root causes of trafficking impact women?

---

6   Ashley South, "Conflict and Displacement in Burma/Myanmar," Burma Library, accessed February 21, 2023, https://tinyurl.com/mr3bm5ak.

7   United Nations, "Human Trafficking," accessed February 21, 2023, https://tinyurl.com/38p6m4df.

- micro factors such as violence within the home or community or;

- macro factors such as gender-based discrimination and economic policies result in a lack of livelihood options in countries of origin.

Traffickers are mainly targeting women and girls. The vast majority of the identified victims of trafficking for sexual exploitation are females, and 35 percent of the victims trafficked for forced labor are also females, both women and girls.[8] Trafficking and demand is an economic and social relationship between two people involving very unequal power, exploitation, and violence. Such a moral economy can only exist in a subculture that defines some people in a way that makes exploitation possible. A public redefinition must precede changes in behavior. The application of basic human rights takes place in a cultural context, and extending basic rights to all members of the populace only takes place gradually as understandings change. The demand side of trafficking is not, therefore, properly understood as the demand for a trafficked victim's prostitution, labor, or services. Rather, demand must be understood expansively, as an act that fosters any form of exploitation that, in turn, leads to trafficking. To foster is to "support . . . encourage or help to grow (or) to promote the growth of . . . "

THE SOLUTION IS IN UNDERSTANDING THE PROBLEM

Broadly speaking, the institutions of state and civil society engage in reactive rather than proactive agendas. Invariably, the civil society response is a social and justice response to the agenda that is directly or indirectly perpetrated by the state. A broad categorization can be made as follows:

---

8   UNODC elaboration of national data.

State	Civil Society
Migration	Patriarchy
Globalization	Discrimination
Displacement	Unemployment
Violence	Illiteracy
Poverty	Conflict and unrest
Emergency	

It is therefore important for both state and civil society to:

- recognize the human rights of the rescued adult/child (a rights-based approach);

- ensure rescue does not take away the dignity of the persons (lead to stigmatization, further vulnerability, and such);

- identify the source/causes of the vulnerability of those being trafficked (NB: there can be more than one source, for example, discrimination based on gender and ethnicity/religion/(dis)ability/poverty. The last mentioned is important for both prevention as well as rehabilitation);

- ensure opportunities for the person to voice their opinion/concern and needs;

- ensure the steps taken for rehabilitation are such that the person is safe so that he/she is not retrafficked.

The key strategy is to reshape mainstream discourse, policy, practice, advocacy, and research in order to:

- develop compassionate hearts to listen to the voices of the vulnerable, the trafficked, and migrants;

- make media more sensitive toward the projection of trafficking cases;

- develop societal perspectives on trafficking and prostitution leaving the morality discourse in various religions;

- understand trafficking beyond dominant discourse;

- depart from one-track practice of rescue, rehabilitation, and reintegration of victims;

- understand the complexity of the issue in its various dimensions;

- develop innovative models of rescue, rehabilitation, and reintegration of trafficked victims with a rights-based approach.

The goal is to ensure survivors live a dignified life free from exploitation.

WHY FAITH-BASED ORGANIZATION?[9]

In conclusion, drawing from Christian Scripture, I point to the core principles of justice and compassion. Clearly, Christian discipleship requires us to take our neighbors' pain—caused by the structures and systems of society—seriously.

1. The heart of the Christian faith focuses on God's unconditional love and relational nature. From the

---

9   "Understanding Human Trafficking," paper presented by AATW, Global Alliance Against Traffic in Women at Global Consultation on Human Trafficking: Challenges Before Church and Church Related Organizations (Bangkok, Thailand, 1–3 December 2019).

very beginning of the Bible, the writer of Genesis describes God as the creator who has made people in his own image (Gen 1:27).

2.   Throughout the Bible, there are also repeated calls to God's people to remember the "widows." In a well-known passage of the gospels, Jesus is speaking to a crowd. When some of his disciples try to prevent the children and their families from approaching him, Jesus reprimands them, saying, "Let the little children come to me, and do not stop them; for it is to such as these that the kingdom of God belongs" (Luke 18:16).

3.   Jesus also speaks out forcefully against anyone who might take advantage of children and their trusting nature: "If anyone causes one of these little ones—those who believe in me—to stumble, it would be better for them to have a large millstone hung around their neck and to be drowned in the depths of the sea. Woe to the world because of the things that cause people to stumble! Such things must come, but woe to the person through whom they come!" (Matt 18:6–7).

4.   From these examples, it is evident that, in Christianity, God values children very highly and expects his followers to ensure they are protected.

The Christian church has a rich tradition of social justice teaching. The central elements of the church's teaching are: the world is God's creation; women and men are made in God's image; human beings are called to be in right relationship with all people and the environment; and the life of each individual has inherent dignity and sacredness. Human dignity is not an earned privileged but rather the basic right from which all other human rights flow.

Solidarity is a primary social principle. Human beings are born social, through the cooperation of their parents with God's plan. Each person's growth in strength and knowledge comes through relations with others. No one is or can be "self-made." Interrelationships and interdependences are societal requirements, not individual options.

13

THE WORKING CLASS AND THEIR PROBLEMS

Min Thang

INTRODUCTION

Myanmar is known for its diversity of ethnic communities, cultures, religions, and languages. Since independence, ethnic minorities in particular have been engaged in a political struggle to defend themselves and, in the process, they are influencing centralized Bamar politics in the country. The majority of the population are Bamar and Buddhist, therefore after independence, the Burmese Buddhist area favored nationalized race (Bamar) and Buddhism as the state religion. This has influenced national politics aided by the military to the present day. In this situation, the working class faces many challenges, not only economic, social, and political, but also in terms of the imbalance of power in Myanmar society.

Theo Tschuy rightly suggests that most nation-state ideologies are formulated by the dominant power sectors in a given state. They often impose their beliefs on the rest of the population, especially on minority groups, and if necessary by force of arms. These ideologies have become violators of human rights and initiators of social, economic, political, religious, and ethnic conflicts, a situation that persists to the present.[1] Eric O. Hanson commented that the political-religious issues in global politics emerged from four major factors and institutions: the economy, the military, communication systems, and political systems. The international economic system with its enormous income stratification cries out for social justice. The global military system poses issues of war and peace between nations, within nations and between nations and nonstate groups. The international communication system threatens traditional personal and communal identities and values. Religious actors naturally focus on human rights in the global political system.[2]

This chapter examines the working class and their problems in Myanmar. What does "the working class" mean? Who are the working people? What has the International Labor Organization implemented in terms of child labor, child soldiers, human trafficking, and forced labor in Myanmar? Under the political transition of Myanmar, child labor, forced labor, and gender discrimination in the workplace are the main problems and challenges today. Amidst this dilemma, what do the Christians do in relation to such social issues? Christians are called upon to raise a prophetic voice in public life under democracy government of Myanmar today.

BACKGROUNDS AND CONTEXT OF MYANMAR

The people of Myanmar have faced one socio-politico-economic crisis after another. They have suffered throughout different historical periods after Burma gained independence from Britain. In

---

1   Theo Tschuy, *Ethnic Conflict and Religion: Challenges to the Churches* (Geneva: WCC Publications, 1997), xii.

2   Eric O. Hanson, *Religion and Politics in the International System Today* (Cambridge: Cambridge University Press, 2006), 60.

Myanmar the issues of national identity are complex because the country is a multiethnic and multireligion state. In such cases, many ethnic Bamar do not see a difference between the word "Myanmar" and the word "Bamar" (Burmese). Today many ethnic minorities view their identity as Burmese/Myanmar. The issues of nationalism and national identity remain complex and challenging.[3] As the result of more than forty years under military rule many ethnic minorities have lost their basic human rights, equality, government employment, and power-sharing as citizens of Myanmar. Since 2014 Myanmar has been reforming from an authoritarian form of government and transitioning to democracy.

Since 2014 there have been various changes in Myanmar sociopolitically, but sadly the threat to freedom of religion remains significant. However, one cannot ignore the severity of the political and economic challenges. While there is no doubt about the significance of church and state engagement in the political transition of Myanmar in social, political, and working-class issues in various ways, during the transition to democracy, there seems to be a severe threat in Myanmar from the conflict arising from different religious, social, economic, and political ideologies. There are issues of church and state (religion and politics) which are involved in all these threats today. The experience of authoritarianism has shocked a new generation into economic-political thought at a deeper level than the arguments taking place between political parties and also between church and state today. Decades under military regime totalitarianism created problems in Myanmar in the sphere of church and state relations. Historically, Christianity has been closely linked with most of the types of political structures which have existed in Myanmar. Though "the church and state are legally separated . . . the state is friendly to religion and cooperates ungrudgingly with churches and other

---

3   Marie Lall, *Understanding Reform in Myanmar: People and Society in the Wake of Military Rule* (London: Hurst & Co., 2016), 185.

religious bodies." As a rule, Christians cooperate with citizens of the country in which they live, they share life with their fellow citizens, and they are partially embodied in laws and institutions.[4]

Ethnic and Religious Diversity

There are different ethnic groups living in Myanmar, and there is a strong correlation between religious loyalty and ethnic divisions. The Burmese are predominately Buddhist. Whereas the other ethnoreligious groups are predominately Christian, the Arakanese are split between Buddhists and Muslims. Buddhism entered Myanmar from India in the early seventh century and along with it came Hindu-Buddhist cosmological ideas. The Burmese/Bamar embraced Buddhism. Christianity was introduced during British colonial rule by British missionaries who evangelized among the ethnic people of the hill country, converting the Chins, Shan, Karen, Kachin, and other ethnic groups to the Christian faith. The coincidence of ethnicity and religion has deepened the divisions between ethnic groups in Myanmar.[5] The cultural background of Myanmar is Theravada Buddhist. Buddhism was introduced to most Burmese peoples during the lifetime of Gautama Buddha (563–483 BCE) and Buddhist culture has influenced Myanmar's politics, economics, education, and so on. Thus, Buddhism in Myanmar has a long history and is rooted in the life of the people. Generally, Buddhist culture, especially its language, has influenced the Burmese people. It is true to say that one cannot ignore Buddhist culture in developing theology in Myanmar context.[6]

---

4   John C. Bennett, *Christians and the State* (New York: Charles Scribner's Sons, 1958), 3.

5   Peter Church, ed., *A Short History of Southeast Asia* (Singapore: Wiley, 2009), 109.

6   K. M. Y. Khawsiama, *Towards a Ludu Theology* (New York: Peter Lang, 2013), 104.

Political Background

For many decades Myanmar was under British occupation. Since 1962 Myanmar has a secular state that consistently fostered a policy of religious plurality. Both the revolutionary council of the socialist state and the SLORC of the transitional state support the secular philosophy of the political leaders. In 1962, the leadership in Burma has sought to develop state–society relations around a nondivisive set of goals that includes religious tolerance. In the socialist era, state policy sought to bring the Buddhist *Sangha* under state control. The activities of foreign, mostly Christian, missionaries were restricted and mission schools were taken over by the state.[7]

Since independence, the relationship between the Burmese state and religions, particularly Buddhism, has been strongly consolidated. In 1960, Buddhism was declared the state religion and it has become part of a nationalistic resurgence. Representatives of all the religions, including Christianity and Islam, protested strongly against the state favoring Buddhism. General Ne Win, who succeeded U Nu, oversaw a militaristic response with great efficiency. In 1964–65 the government abolished all previous parliamentary acts concerning Buddhism. In 1973 the constitution did not mention Buddhism as a state religion, and Myanmar has become a secular state with a socialist government.[8] After the political independence of Myanmar, the predominant ethnic group was the Bamar. They applied the policy of single language (Burmese) and single religion (Buddhism). Christianity was brought to Myanmar first by

---

7   Helen James, *Governance and Civil Society in Myanmar: Education, Health, and Environment* (London and New York: RoutledgeCurzon, 2005), 51–52.

8   S. Batumalai, *An Introduction to Asian Theology* (Delhi: ISPCK, 1991), 326.

French Franciscans in 1554[9] and later by the Protestant missionary Adoniram Judson in 1813.

THE PROBLEMS AND CHALLENGES
OF THE WORKING CLASS IN MYANMAR

Myanmar's ethnic states, which are blessed with a wealth of natural resources and biodiversity, have been cursed by the unsustainable extraction and sale of those resources, which has fueled
armed conflict and exacerbated the problems of the working class.
Instituting a system of developed federal management of natural
resources could play a key role in resolving conflict and building
lasting peace in Myanmar. Military offensives into resource-rich
ethnic areas have expanded the Myanmar Army's presence in
places previously controlled by de facto ethnic governments.
Resource projects have collected huge revenues for the army and
the central government but have not benefitted local populations,
thus causing an economic problem for the working class in Myanmar. Constitutional powers place natural resource ownership,
control, and management fully in the hands of the central government. Ethnic women in rural areas are marginalized from natural
resource governance. Resource projects are causing environmental destruction, human rights abuses, and the loss of livelihoods,
with unique impacts on women.[10]

Religion is included on national identity cards,[11] and this
results in various forms of discrimination against non-Bamar ethnic groups and non-Buddhists in the workplace, in government

---

9   *The Official Catholic Directory of Myanmar* (Yangon: The Catholic
     Bishops' Conference of Myanmar, 2007), 7.

10   "Resource Federalism: A Roadmap for Decentralized Governance
     of Burma's Natural Heritage" (2017), 2.

11   Jonathan Fox, *A World Survey of Religion and the State* (Cambridge:
     Cambridge University Press, 2008), 104.

jobs, and in the military, resulting in a reduction in their life opportunities. Because Buddhism is the national religion, Christianity and other religions are referred to as "foreign" religions and "ethnic minority community" religions[12] by non-Buddhists in Myanmar. As a result, all governments in recent decades have put pressure on ethnic minorities and Christians in Myanmar. For example, for decades under the military government, Christian citizens were forced into cooperating on public works projects such as the construction of roads, bridges, and other public structures. Sunday was a favorite day for "recruiting" labor, because soldiers could surround a church where a service was being held and easily corral enough people.[13]

The total population of Myanmar is about 52 million, among which 65 percent are of working age and about 28.6 percent are under fifteen years of age. This is an impressive working-age population compared to other countries. Despite having a large available workforce, firms in Myanmar are currently facing shortages of skilled workers. Many young people in Myanmar lack formal education and English-language proficiency, and this renders them unqualified for many jobs. In addition, experienced and skilled workers usually find jobs with attractive salaries abroad. Qualified workers who remain in the country demand high salaries. The government of Myanmar tried to tackle this problem by stipulating in a new law that all unskilled positions should be filled only by citizens of Myanmar. There are also specific rules and regulations regarding skilled workers contained in the foreign investment law.[14]

---

12   Samuel Hugh Moffett, *A History of Christianity in Asia*, vol. 1 (Bangalore: Theological Publication in India, 2006), 508.

13   Eugene Morse, *Exodus to a Hidden Valley* (New York: Reader's Digest Press, 1974), 4.

14   Rajan Acharya, "Myanmar Labor Market Beyond 2015," Medium.com, June 11, 2016, https://tinyurl.com/bdzarcw6.

Under the reform government, in 2015 Myanmar tried to abolish all child labor and child soldiers. The International Labor Organization (ILO) had registered more than 2000 complaints, from issues of underage employment in the army to traditional forced labor, bonded labor, human trafficking, land issues that led to forced labor, forced cropping, pottering in conflict zones, and forced recruitment into the military and into infrastructure projects.[15] Capitalism involves structured relationships between labor and capital that result in the alienation of workers from the most important aspects of their labor. Workers are also alienated from the product they produce. Their energy is invested in those products, but workers do not own what they produce. Workers are alienated from their fellow workers as a result of capitalists promoting competition among them for the available jobs at subsistence wages.[16]

WORKING CHILDREN IN MYANMAR

In Myanmar, child labor is another significant social problem. According to the census taken in 2014, 1.65 million children between the ages of ten and seventeen years were engaged in employment in Myanmar. This includes child work and child labor defined by the International Labor Organization (ILO) as including both paid employment below the minimum working age, which in Myanmar is sixteen years, and children engaged in unpaid, often hazardous, household services. Industrial sectors, agriculture, forestry, and fishing employed the largest number of children in Myanmar. More than 210,000 (2 percent) between the ages of ten and seventeen years were actively looking for

15   Lall, *Understanding Reform in Myanmar*, 80.

16   James Farganis, ed., *Readings in Social Theory: The Classic Tradition to Post-Modernism* (New York: McGraw-Hill, 2014), 30.

employment.[17] Early school dropout rates are very high, with large numbers of children failing to complete primary school, middle school, and in particular high school. The incidence of Burmese children working has been shown to depend on household income, social class, and structural factors. Parents, in particular the father's education level and skill level of employment, have an impact on whether children work. Whether children live in urban or rural and middle- or working-class areas plays a role in whether children work and the types of work they engage in. Many of those who live in rural working-class areas are, like their parents, employed in the agricultural sector. Those who live in industrial areas are likely to be engaged in factory work and are more likely to have been recruited by brokers or employers. More boys than girls are working and boys tend to begin at an earlier age than girls. However, girls who are working tend to have a double load of paid work and domestic work. The type of work they engage in is influenced by both gender and age. The idea of children laboring in farms, factories, and construction sites goes against conceptions of childhood and children in the international community. However, these need to be located in cultural and historical contexts and contrasted with differing notions of childhood in Myanmar.[18] In Myanmar, Chin state has one of the lowest child labor rates and Shan state the highest. Children in Chin state had the highest current school attendance rate and was among the lowest never-attended-school rates.[19]

---

17   Su-Ann Oh, "Drudges or Providers? Working Children in Myanmar," *Perspective: Researchers Atiseas–Yusof Ishak Institute Share Their Understanding of Current Events*, 2.

18   Oh, "Drudges or Providers? Working Children in Myanmar," 1.

19   "Census Atlas, Myanmar: The 2014 Myanmar Population and Housing Census," accessed February 21, 2023, https://tinyurl.com/3bvs8r2p.

FORCED LABOR PARTICIPATION: MALE AND FEMALE

The working class comprises those who engage in waged/salaried labor, especially in physical labor occupations and industrial work. Working-class occupations include blue-collar jobs, some white-collar jobs, and some pink-color jobs. Members of the working class rely for their income exclusively upon their earnings from wage labor; thus, according to the more inclusive definitions, the category can include almost all of the working population of industrialized economies, as well as those employed in urban areas of nonindustrialized economies or in the rural workforce.[20] "Working class" is a socioeconomic term used to describe persons in a social class marked by jobs that provide low pay, require limited skill and/or physical labor, and have reduced education requirements.[21]

In Myanmar the proportion of males participating in forced labor is higher than the proportion of females. In 2014 approximately 85 percent of males aged fifteen to sixty-four were actively employed or looking for work. For females in the same age group, the proportion was just fractionally over a half. There are also gender differences in the age-specific forced-labor participation rates. In 2014 the rates for men were consistently high, at between 85 and 95 percent for all age groups between twenty and fifty-nine years. The maximum rate at which women participated in the forced labor (about 60%) was between the ages of twenty and twenty-four. Whereas almost 70 percent of men aged sixty to sixty-four were reported in the census as still working, fewer than 30 percent of women were still actively employed.[22]

---

20   Wikipedia, "Working Class," https://en.wikipedia.org/wiki/Workingclass, last accessed July 11, 2019.

21   https://www.investopedia.com, last accessed July 11, 2019.

22   "Census Atlas Myanmar," 54.

Forced Labor

The Burmese military has used forced labor to build roads and dams, harvest sugarcane and other agricultural products, sweep for mines, build military bases, lay railroad tracks, and restore tourist sites and clear land. In ethnic regions, the military required farmers to carry supplies, clean barracks, and build roads without pay. Forced laborers can be seen at road construction sites breaking rocks with pickaxes, sledgehammers, and small hammers under the hot midday sun.[23]

In 2015, females constituted 54 percent of the working-age population while males constituted 46 percent. Of the working-age population, 71 percent lived in rural areas and 29 percent lived in urban areas. About 65 per cent of the population in the country constituted the labor force and the remaining 35 per cent were outside the labor force. The labor force consisted of 79.9 percent males and 51.4 percent females, and for both males and females, the labor force participation rate was higher for males than females.[24] The proportion of males in the employment ranged between 72.8 percent and 83.8 percent, while for females it was between 34.8 percent and 62.3 percent, and for all persons it was between 55.5 percent and 70.4 percent. Among males, out of the 15 states, regions, and union territories only in Chin state was the proportion of people employed below 70 percent; six of the remaining states had a proportion above 80 percent. Among females, the proportion who were in employment was below 50 percent of the working-age population in eight states and

23 "Labor in Myanmar," Facts and Details.com, accessed February 21, 2023, https://tinyurl.com/3emxfktu.

24 "The Government of the Republic of the Union of Myanmar Ministry of Labor, Immigration and Population Department of Labor: Report on Myanmar Labor Force Survey-2015" (Nay Pyi Taw, International Labor Organization, 2016), 33–34.

regions, while only two states have a proportion that is above 60 percent.[25]

Gender

The type of work and the age at which children begin working were influenced also by gender. In most employment more boys than girls are engaged in work. Boys were two times more likely than girls to be employees. However, girls are more likely to have a double load of work, undertaking outside employment as well as domestic work in the home. The type of work boys and girls engaged in was determined by age and gender. Boys under thirteen years of age and between thirteen and fifteen years old were found to work predominantly as servers in teashops, while boys aged sixteen and above worked mostly on construction sites where they carried rubble or were involved in building work. Girls aged thirteen to fifteen and sixteen and above said they worked mostly in garment and food factories, followed by restaurants.[26] Less-educated women from rural areas were more likely than the overall average to claim that action has been taken relating to their demands. Where action has not been taken, they are more likely to identify social norms as the reasons. Almost 90 percent of less-educated women are from rural areas.[27]

---

25   "The Government of the Republic of the Union of Myanmar Ministry of Labor, Immigration and Population Department of Labor: Report on Myanmar Labor Force Survey-2015," 36.

26   Oh, "Drudges or Providers?" 8–9.

27   MyJustice 2018, "Searching for Justice in the Law: Understanding Access to Justice in Myanmar Findings from the Myanmar Justice Survey 2017" (London: British Council, 2018), 80, https://tinyurl.com/7uy7wmvy.

Discrimination in the Workplace

The constitution protects the right of all citizens to choose their occupations (Article 349) and provides that women should receive equal pay for work of similar value (Article 350).[28] However, many fields are dominated by male workers. Thus, antidiscrimination laws protecting working conditions should include penalties for sexual harassment in the workplace. In Myanmar discrimination against certain groups is an across-the-board issue affecting all industry sectors. In workplaces, women; people from ethnic and religious minorities; lesbian, gay, bisexual, and transgender (LGBT) people; individuals living with HIV; and people living with disabilities face discrimination. Discrimination against certain groups is prevalent in law, policy, and practice in Myanmar and often leads to human rights abuses against them. It is not only the authorities who are discriminatory. Discrimination occurs in families, in the workplace, and in the form of the wage/salary imbalance in society. Moreover, some individuals face discrimination on multiple grounds, for example, women who are members of ethnic minorities or women with disabilities.[29] "The National Convention in Burma (Myanmar): An Impediment to the Restoration of Democracy" suggests the existence of violations of the most basic human right, freedom from discrimination, as recognized in the UN Charter, the Universal Declaration, and the Convention on the Rights of the Child, a treaty to which Myanmar is a party.[30]

---

28   "Constitution of the Republic of the Union of Myanmar (2008)" (Yangon: Ministry of Information: 2015), 249.

29   "Briefing Paper: Combatting Discrimination by Business and in the Workplace in Myanmar," June 2017, https://tinyurl.com/ynz6fwt6.

30   Janelle M. Diller, *The National Convention in Burma (Myanmar): An Impediment to the Restoration of Democracy* (New York: International League for Human Rights, 1996).

In the decades under the military government, injustices and abuses of power fueled an opposition that emphasized the rule of law as an aspiration and core tenet of any dialogue on reform. The process of building a society based on the rule of law is a complex and challenging one. It requires the reform of justice sector institutions as well as deeper changes to established practices and attitudes. The rule of law underpins the functioning not only of the judiciary but of the executive and legislative branches of government as well.[31] People in Myanmar commonly understand the concept of justice to be about equality and fairness. However, few connect the role of the law to promoting a fair and just society or protecting people's rights. Instead, the law is viewed as a tool to maintain order and control. This affects how people engage with the law and justice-sector institutions.[32] The majority of women are illiterate and confined to doing household chores in some communities in Myanmar.

POVERTY AND STRUCTURAL FACTORS

Government intervention is required to improve adult wages and address child labor problems, but the likelihood of such action is questionable because some industries dominate the government. In addition, some industries are major foreign exchange earners and this creates conflicts of interests between government and industry representatives and pervasive corruption. Despite the minimum working age and constitutional protection given to protect children from economic exploitation, child labor can interfere with their education and development. Governments lack implementation measures and do not enforce the law. Despite being signatories to many conventions, there is no meaningful enforcement of any of these provisions and child labor is increasing in

31   MyJustice 2018, "Searching for Justice in the Law," 10.
32   MyJustice 2018, 83.

developing Asia countries. National and international organizations consider community participation as a critical component in collaborative efforts to resolve the child labor problem.[33]

The reasons for children working are complex. It was established that "poverty was not necessarily the sole cause of child labor, but rather the two (poverty and labor) were jointly symptomatic of poor access to education and healthcare, landlessness, migration, and the effects of decades of armed conflict and human rights abuses," particularly in ethnic minority areas. A significant finding was that being a migrant is an important determining factor in child employment. Children work because of a variety of internal and external factors that affect the household economy and it is likely that the income from children's employment is an economic necessity for many families and serves also as a buffer against misfortune.[34]

In the 2014 census the total population of Myanmar was about 52 million. This implies that many people in Myanmar, especially in the rural areas, exist just above the poverty line. There is a lack of proper social protection, social safety net, and social insurance. Low public spending on healthcare also means that when a family member falls sick, the family has to either sell off assets or borrow money at an exorbitant interest rate, thus entering a vicious debt cycle which is very difficult to break.[35]

In 2014, urban areas seemed to offer employment opportunities in a wider variety of sectors, but they also tended to have significantly higher unemployment rates than rural areas. In Myanmar it appears that the "big city" fails to live up to

---

33   Gamini Herath and Kishor Sharma, "Labor and Economic Development: Emerging Issues in Developing Asia," in their *Child Labor in South Asia* (Abingdon: Routledge, 2007), 6.

34   Oh, "Drudges or Providers?" 4.

35   Moe Thuzar, "Human Security and Development in Myanmar: Issues and Implications," *JICA Research Institute* (March 2015): 15.

expectations of easy-to-find well-paid jobs and that people who move there in search of work are often disappointed. Though the labor force generally has a significantly larger proportion of male than female participants, women do a lot of work on the farm in many rural societies, as well as undertaking domestic duties. In Myanmar as a whole, there is a slightly larger proportion of males than females in the workforce. The labor force information that emerged in 2014 reflects that children in the workforce, including girls, are working rather than attending school. A very large proportion of working children are employed in the primary sectors of the labor force. Whereas about one third of the employed population in cities like Yangon and Nay Pyi Taw have at least completed high school, in most districts and townships with predominantly rural populations, less than one fifth of the workforce have completed this level of education.[36]

Migration

Migration within and beyond Myanmar's borders is and has long been mixed. People move as migrant workers, traders, refugees, asylum seekers, and stateless people for marriage and as victims of trafficking. The reasons people migrate are complex, cutting across economic, social, and political factors. Limited rural livelihoods, economic opportunities elsewhere, persistent civil conflicts, and social aspirations and desires are all drivers of migration.[37] Myanmar has become the country with the highest number of migrants. This is mainly a result of people fleeing conflict taking place in the border areas between the armed forces and insurgent groups, as well as semi- and unskilled workers seeking what they perceive as an attractive income in the

---

36   "Census Atlas Myanmar," 51.
37   *Building Labor Migration Policy Coherence in Myanmar* (Yangon: International Labor Organization, 2017), 6.

labor-scarce higher-income ASEAN economies. Intercommunal tensions between Rakhines and Rohingyas in 2012 led to some 144,00 people being displaced in Rakhine state—most of them without citizenship and living in fragile environments, and other working-class people, particularly unskilled women and children. In Kachin state some 100,000 people were displaced. International and local humanitarian organizations have direct access to internally displaced persons (IDPs) in government-controlled areas. The governments of Myanmar and Thailand are discussing the situation of displaced persons along the Thai–Myanmar border, most of whom are in refugee camps or are undocumented workers in Thailand. There are various displaced persons who work in Thailand and the government responses to migration thus far lack policy coherence. The migrant worker issue is dealt with mainly by the Ministry of Labor, which has no jurisdiction over IDPs and which provides peripheral inputs to the negotiations on the liberalization of skilled professionals. INGOs, the UN, and the government of Myanmar all have the potential for building local civil society capacity to take on the bridge-building role in postconflict peacebuilding and reconciliation efforts and to strengthen nascent capacities among civil society groups that are participating in national, bilateral, and regional discussions on cross-border migrant labor issues.[38]

Child Education

In Myanmar child law states that children have the right to engage voluntarily in work permitted by the law, as well as detailing rights relating to hours of employment, rest, and leisure. The minimum working age is fourteen. Employment contracts must be approved by and registered with the relevant township office of the labor

---

38   Moe Thuzar, "Human Security and Development in Myanmar: Issues and Implications," *JICA Research Institute* (March 2015): 12–13.

department. An employer convicted of failing to sign an employment agreement can be punished with imprisonment for up to six months or with a fine, or both. The employees' wage/salary was 3,600 kyat per day for eight hours of work in 2015.[39]

Today Myanmar is engaged in one of the longest civil wars in the world, resulting in large numbers of workers fleeing to neighboring countries for work; the majority of these workers are from rural areas of Burma. The workers in the survey were employed across a number of industries, including fishing, construction, retail trade, hotels and restaurants, household service, food processing, agriculture, forestry, and quarrying. Incomes earned varied widely across these industries; the highest-paid were those engaged in quarrying and the lowest were in agriculture and forestry. A majority (62%) of those surveyed were men.[40] Education is expensive at all levels, whatever the formal commitments of the state. Remittances can assist in the payment of school fees and can provide the wherewithal for children to attend school rather than working for family survival.[41]

THE INTERNATIONAL LABOR ORGANIZATION: IMPLEMENTATION IN MYANMAR

Today in a global context the most shocking event and sensitive moral issue brought to public attention is the problem of child

---

39   Nang Kay Si Kham, Fabian Lorenz and Luther Law Firm, "Myanmar Employment Law," August 6, 2018 (Luther Law Firm Limited, 2018), https://tinyurl.com/557frh63.

40   Sean Turnell, Alison Vicary, and Wylie Bradford, "Migrant-Worker Remittances and Burma: An Economic Analysis of Survey," in *Dictatorship, Disorder and Decline in Myanmar*, ed. Monique Skidmore and Trevor Wilson (Australia: ANU Press, 2008), 73.

41   Turnell, Vicary, and Bradford, "Migrant-Worker Remittances and Burma," 66.

labor and this continues to be recognized as one of the major challenges for the international and national community. In earlier decades the problem of labor was not acknowledged at the national level in Myanmar. Under the military government, there was an increasing commitment to the adoption of measures to prevent and abolish the "worst forms" of child labor in Myanmar. After the transition of Myanmar (from 2014) coherent actions were developed to reduce poverty and increase education and human rights protections, all of which are essential to eradicating child labor. Child labor is an important issue in Asia, particularly in Myanmar. The ILO estimates that in 2000 about 211 million children aged between five and fourteen were engaged in some form of child labor.[42]

Myanmar ratified the Forced Labor Convention in 1955 during a short period of parliamentary democracy. The convention prohibits the imposition of forced labor, which it defines as "all work or service, which is exacted from any person under the menace of any penalty and for which the said person has not offered himself/herself voluntarily." There are a number of exclusions in the convention: compulsory military service, normal civic obligations, prison labor, cases of emergency, and minor communal service.[43] The ILO's efforts to tackle forced labor in Myanmar represent a rare example of success in influencing the behavior of the past military regime. Under the military regime, there was forced labor, mostly in villages, to complete assigned work without pay. The United Nations and other international actors have engaged successfully with the abuse of human rights and imposition of forced labor in Myanmar by regimes. In 2000, Myanmar's persistent violations of the Forced Labor Convention led the

---

42   Gamini Herath, "Child Labor in Developing Countries: Review of Theoretical and Empirical Issues," in *Child Labor in South Asia*, ed. Gamini Herath and Kishor Sharma (Aldershot: Ashgate, 2007), 11.

43   Richard Horsey, *Ending Forced Labor in Myanmar: Engaging a Pariah Regime* (London and New York: Routledge, 2011), 7.

organization for the first time ever of the invoking of a provision in its constitution allowing it to take action, including trade measures, against a defaulting state. The objective of the ILO was to bring an end to the practice of forced labor in Myanmar.[44]

The ILO was created in 1919, at the end of World War I, by the Paris Peace Conference within the framework of the League of Nations. In 2007, the ILO had 181 members states. The establishment of the ILO was the result of a strong movement of opinion aiming to improve the conditions of workers. This movement was fueled by interventions of scholars, political scientists, and artists throughout the nineteenth and twentieth centuries, which had accompanied the consolidation of the Industrial Revolution and its sometimes-catastrophic impact on social structures and the ordinary lives of human beings, including children. The idea was to establish at the international level some authoritative source of minimum standards aimed at regulating the world of work, including social protection for workers, in order to effectively reply to the usual objection against initiatives taken at national level in order to improve the condition of workers.[45]

The Core Conventions and the ILO Declaration on Fundamental Principles and Rights at Work

In ILO Convention there are eight conventions relating to four areas (namely freedom of association and effective recognition of the right to collective bargaining, the abolition of forced labor and child labor, and the elimination of discrimination in employment

---

44   Horsey, *Ending Forced Labor in Myanmar*, 2.

45   Anne Trebilock and Guido Raimondi, "The ILO's Legal Activities Towards the Eradication of Child Labor: An Overview," in *Child Labor in Globalized World: A Legal Analysis of ILO Action*, ed. Ciuseppe Nesi, Luca Nogler, and Marco Pertile (Aldershot: Ashgate, 2008), 18–19.

and occupation) which have been identified by the ILO as being fundamental to the rights of people at work, irrespective of the level of development of individual member states. Eight fundamental conventions are:

- Freedom of Association and Protection of the Right to Organize Convention, 1948 (No. 87)

- Right to Organize and Collective Bargaining Convention, 1949 (No. 98)

- Forced Labor Convention, 1957 (No. 29)

- Abolition of Forced Labor Convention, 1951 (No. 105)

- Equal Remuneration Convention, 1951 (No. 100)

- Discrimination (Employment and Occupation) Convention, 1958 (No. 111)

- Minimum Age Convention, 1973 (No. 138)

- Worst Forms of Child Labor Convention, 1999 (No. 182)[46]

After 1988, there were massive demonstrations across the country against the crumbling of human rights under the military government in Myanmar. It is said that there were serious human rights abuses, including extra-judicial execution, torture, and forced labor being committed by regime against civilians, particularly in ethnic minority areas. The military government had ordered many unjust things to be done, one of the worst being forced labor. The government has tried to present these practices in religious terms, as a form of donated religious labor, but the fact is that Buddhism does not accept forced labor. Buddha was

---

46   Trebilock and Raimondi, "The ILO's Legal Activities Towards the Eradication of Child Labor," 23.

against any kind of oppression and the very concept of forced labor is offensive to Buddhism. The poorest villagers were forced into work in many places, particularly in ethnic minority regions. This is the result of the lack of systematic and effective governance in the country. The problem is that government leaders are uneducated and ineffective. Their authorities are trying to avoid allegations of forced labor by pressuring monks to request that people give their labor.[47]

THEOLOGICAL REFLECTION/REPONSES

Awareness and compliance with labor rights is far from complete in Myanmar. The fragmented legal framework, its often poor and arbitrary implementation, and the country's authoritarian political history have impacted labor relations, specifically the models and forms of interaction between employers and employees that are practiced in enterprises. Labor unions were long forbidden under law and have only recently been allowed. Labor associations are important for social dialogue.[48] Today child labor, forced labor, child soldiers, and human trafficking are a global experience from which no country is protected. The ILO estimates that 20.9 million people are forced into labor every year all over the world. According to a global report released on July 19, 2018, Myanmar ranks eighteenth out of 167 countries in the Global Slavery Index. Modern slavery identified by the report included people smuggling, forced labor, the purchase of slaves with money, forced marriage, and forcing under-age children to work and selling them,

---

47   Horsey, *Ending Forced Labor in Myanmar*, 122.

48   Thomas Bernhardt, S. Kanay De, and Mi Win Thida, "Myanmar Labor Issues from the Perspective of Enterprises: Findings from a Survey of Food Processing and Garment Manufacturing Enterprise" (International Labor Organization, Myanmar Center for Economic and Social Development, 2017), viii.

in addition to normal slavery. In the case of human trafficking 11.99 percent involved men and 88.01 percent involved women. It has been found that a majority of women who illegally migrate to neighboring countries for jobs fall victim to forced marriages. In domestic trafficking cases, prostitution and labor exploitation is common knowledge. Doing public theology is necessary and concerns the people of Myanmar, particularly women and children, human trafficking, child labor, and working-class rural areas.

Public theology offers an open forum for all those who are inspired by their religious beliefs and convictions, who wish to engage themselves in the liberation of the poor and the marginalized.[49] Myanmar depends heavily on agriculture, which is practiced extensively in rural areas and which is therefore the predominant occupation of many poor families. A significant amount of child labor takes place on farms, not least because poor families cannot afford to engage labor due to poverty. Over the course of decades, we have witnessed not only various social, political, and military conflicts and religions instability, but also a challenging relationship between economic factors, child soldiers, forced labor, and child labor. The church and state must respond positively to such situations. The churches in Myanmar need to express the task of prophetic imagination and ministry to bring to the attention of the public those whose rights have been denied for so long and suppressed so deeply that we no longer know they are there.

What needs to be taught in the churches and societies in Myanmar are the biblical and theological foundations for justice and love. Since the welfare of working children is a real issue, it is important to examine the nature of child labor, human trafficking, forced labor, women, migration, and discrimination in the workplace and in society. However, today child labor is still a controversial issue and many jobs fall outside the law. Low wages, irregular hours of employment, exploitative slavery, terrible

---

49   Felix Wilfred, ed., *Theology to Go Public* (Delhi: ISPCK, 2010), xi.

working conditions, and a lack of contracting power all characterize child labor in many countries. Child labor is the basis of
economic activities in many Asian developing countries and many
consumer goods, including export commodities such as carpets,
clothing, and agricultural goods. Child labor also involves a range
of potentially hazardous tasks, such as gem mining, construction, commercial farming, and transporting goods and services.
Poverty, the absence of accessible schools in the villages, and the
shortage of teachers prevent children from attending school and
keep them in employment with meager returns. It is estimated
that about 60 percent of world's children live in developing Asia
and about 19 percent of these children are victims of child labor
practices.[50]

DO THE CHURCHES IN MYANMAR RAISE THEIR PROPHETIC VOICE IN PUBLIC LIFE?

The churches in Myanmar need to be aware of the social issues
on all the above. The churches' duty to engage in social involvement is necessary and needs to increase in the current climate.
The economic situation in most Asian countries is miserable and
in others it is uncertain. A new culture of consumerism and competition has invaded the Asian regions and these elements have
no regard for ethics and no interest in the future. Lack of political
justice has exhausted natural resources and increased the miseries
of Asians.[51] Sociopolitical and economic liberation is a key priority
in the church's activities in Asia, given the presence of massive and
dehumanizing poverty among the Asian peoples. Today, in most
of the Asian countries, women, children, and ethnic minorities

50   Herath and Sharma, "Labor and Economic Development: Emerg-
      ing Issues in Developing Asia," in *Child Labor in South Asia*, 3.
51   Evelyn Monteiro, "Asian Churches and Public Theology," in *Theol-
      ogy to go Public*, ed. Felix Wilfred (Delhi: ISPCK, 2010), 176.

are some of the most marginalized groups in society. They are not merely excluded from mainstream life in society but remain the most powerless, controlled, discriminated against, and underrepresented groups.[52]

Colonial theology and its missions were part of a colonial agenda to plunder the rich minerals, land resources, and human labor of the country and to destroy its arts and crafts. There emerged a loss of identity for national Christianity because the people in the colonies were taught to disregard their way of living. During the early missionary period, the missionaries presumed the people outside Europe were "pagan" and that they were without any concept of God.[53] In Myanmar, the participation of women, ethnic minorities, children, and the working class (rural/villages, farmers) and the consideration of basic human rights in decision making and empowerment are still not being addressed today. As a result, women and children are continuing to struggle against sexual exploitation, forced labor, female infanticide, sexual abuse, and violence. This demonstrates that the churches in Myanmar have failed to participate in social involvement in order to respond to the challenges and burning issues of today. The churches in Myanmar have been silent and have isolated themselves from social, political, and economic issues in public. This isolation also led to the isolation of Christian thinking, which is conservative. Apart from small-scale participation, the church still has not daringly and deeply reflected upon the situation of socioeconomic and political issues, child labor, forced labor, migration, human trafficking, and discrimination in the workplace based on gender and ethnicity in Myanmar.

After 1962, when Western missionaries left the country, Burmese Christians were ill prepared. Christians have not been

---

52   Monteiro, "Asian Churches and Public Theology," 178.
53   Cited by M. P. Joseph, ed., *Confronting Life: Theology out of the Context* (Delhi: ISPCK, 1995), 6–7.

educated in the ways of power politics and the role of democracy in changing the structure of society. They had to learn rapidly how to relate Christian social witness and responsible living in society.[54] Under the military and Bamar governments, people of non-Bamar ethnic and non-Buddhist backgrounds found themselves discriminated against by their Bamar Buddhist counterparts in education, employment, and at various levels in the civil service. Even those in the army and police serving successive governments were systematically denied promotions in rank on the sole basis of their ethnicity and religion.[55] Through the decades Christians have been forced to contribute both money and labor to building Buddhist pagodas, roads, and other activities on the Christian Sabbath day. Many Christian pastors have been tortured and killed in Myanmar. However, even today many Christian churches and organizations do not give voice to the oppressed, the working class, women, child laborers, child soldiers, marginalized groups, and so on in public discourse on sociopolitical and religious issues in Myanmar.

CONCLUSION

In conclusion, it is time for the Christian community and churches in Myanmar to become involved in sociopolitical, religious, and public issues such as child labor, forced labor, human trafficking, and so on in order to facilitate justice under transition to a democratic government. Christian churches cannot isolated themselves from state and society. The Christian churches should be the light of the world and salt of the earth in the present day. They need to teach a biblical and theological foundation for justice in

---

54   Batumalai, *An Introduction to Asian Theology*, 329.

55   Za Uk Ling and Bawi Lian Mang, *Religious Persecutions: A Campaign of Ethnocide against Chin Christians in Burma* (Canada: Chin Human Rights Organization, 2004), n.p.

Myanmar. Under the weight of oppression, suffering, isolation, and other pains, the churches are called to be a living reality and our theology should be a living theology in socioeconomic and political issues in public life.

The aim of this chapter is not only to preach to the Christian churches in Myanmar but to bring into the light the various social issues such as child labor, human trafficking, women's rights, and discrimination in the workplace which people have been facing in their daily lives in the course of their employment. Moreover, today the leaders of most of the Christian churches and other minority religions are well aware of the issues on the ground. This need not be the case with mainstream Buddhism. The churches and their leaders cannot escape from the reality of the social struggles in Myanmar and oppression by the powerful and the elite in church and society. However, Christian citizens and churches must be a voice for the voiceless and stand for the oppressed and the marginalized on social issues in present-day Myanmar, in the pursuit of justice for all.

14

MY STORY, OUR STORY

Lalrindiki Ralte

THE BEGINNING

This particular story began when I was studying for my Master's in Theology in the Department of Social Analysis in Tamil Nādu Theological Seminary (TTS), Madurai,[1] between 1996 and 1998. In those days we discussed a lot about food security during lectures and seminars. The necessity of ensuring food security and food availability at the local community level and in the country and the different forces which thwart this were the main topics of our deliberations.

When the time came for me to submit my proposal for the thesis work as part of our course requirement, I opted to address the issues and problems we faced in my home state, Mizoram. Being miles away from Mizoram, which is in the northeastern corner of India, I had to spend considerable time and energy to reflect upon the different issues and concerns in my state so that I could choose the most appropriate topic for my thesis.

I was born and brought up in Aizawl, the capital of Mizoram, and our house is by the side of a local market. When I pictured the market in my mind, I saw a group of people who had come from the surrounding villages to sell their vegetables in this market. For

---

1   Madurai is a city in the state of Tamil Nadu, South India.

many necessities, Mizoram has to depend on products from other parts of the country. One of the few items which Mizoram has is the vegetables produced by villagers to ensure food availability and security. So, I decided to focus my research on this group of villagers who produced their own vegetables and brought them to the local markets to be sold. As I was preparing my proposal, I also came to realize that the vegetable vendors from the villages are overwhelmingly women. Hence, I decided to gain an understanding of this group of people and their role in our economy.

UNDERSTANDING THE ISSUES

My research helped me to understand many of the issues and concerns of the present-day Mizo tribal community which one is unable to discern without a critical analysis. Some of these are:

1. The Mizo women vegetable vendors belong to the laboring class in the increasingly class-divided Mizo tribal community, which is split into an educated elite and the toiling masses. At the same time, they are the ones who uphold and sustain the rich traditional knowledge of the community which is a result of their intimate relationship with their natural surroundings.

2. The vegetables they cultivate in their *jhum* (garden) and the ones collected from the surrounding forests provide food availability in terms of vegetables to the whole Mizo community. However, deforestation, climate change, the use of chemical fertilizers, and the privatization of land are seriously threatening their livelihoods.

3. Their trade is a combination of the traditional tribal subsistence economy and modern-day subsistence local market. But the increasing penetration of the

profit-oriented market economy is taking away the crucial space for these women to sell their vegetables in the different local markets in Aizawl. Due to lack of space in the market area they are forced to sell their vegetables in congested places by the roadside and are often compelled to sell them at a low price, which makes their efforts not worthy of their hard labor.

4. Many of the women vegetable vendors from the villages are the main earners in their families and hence they enjoy mobility and have a say over their income and in taking decisions concerning family matters. The male members of the family also support them by taking care of household chores in their absence. However, their space is severely limited and controlled by the Mizo patriarchal values governing family and society. The moment the women return, most of the household work will be handed over to them by their husbands or other male members and their role in decision making does not go beyond their respective family circle.

    Hence, the Mizo women vegetable vendors have to bear the double burden of household chores *and* work outside the home, in the *jhum* (forest) and in local markets. This is often unacknowledged and taken for granted by others. The land is also registered in the name of the male family members (husband/father), who are considered to be the head of the family. Even though the women play such a crucial role in upholding the economy of the household and the community, these vegetable vendors are deprived of their access and control over resources such as land and homestead in the case of being widowed or separated from their husbands since they are not officially the owners of the family's private assets.

5. The Mizo women vegetable vendors take their faith and religion seriously. Many of them left mainline churches and joined smaller indigenous Christian groups where they feel more comfortable and get more recognition, which they expressed as having the freedom to dance as much as they wanted to and the opportunity to preach once in a while. Their experiences and observations reflect the impact of the elite-oriented and patriarchal church institutions of the mainline churches in Mizoram on women, particularly women from the toiling class. The hard human labor needed in their occupation, their struggle against environmental degradation, the lack of acknowledgment of their crucial contribution in the economy of the tribe, having no proper place in the local markets, and the overall marginalization of the toiling class in the socioeconomic and political life of the community are theologically explained by them as the curse of God as found in Genesis 3:17–19.

INTERCONNECTIVITY OF ALIENATION, MARGINALIZATION, AND SOLIDARITY

In my attempt to fulfil the academic requirements I got an opportunity to enter the lifeworld of the Mizo women vegetable vendors. Even though all of us are from the same Mizo tribe there is no doubt that our class differences, education, and toiling classes provided unequal opportunities and prospects in life. But, as women, we share many similar experiences in the Mizo patriarchal church and community, such as marginalization, discrimination, alienation, and vulnerability to threats and abuse. The refusal of women's ordination by my church and the patriarchal customary law marginalized and alienated me and other Mizo women in religious life and obstructed our access to and control over land and other resources. As a woman I am also vulnerable to patriarchal violence and abuse. This is the story shared by women in patriarchal communities and society everywhere, irrespective of religion, class, caste, tribe, ethnicity, and nationalities.

I have also come to realize that there are many other women vegetable vendors from different tribes and communities all across northeastern and other parts of India who are playing the same crucial role in upholding their respective communities and families. These women vegetable vendors represent other subsistence workers—women and men—in various parts of the country, such as small peasants/farmers, Adivasi communities, Dalits, traditional fish workers, local artisans, construction workers, and so on. In the same way, in neighboring countries such as Myanmar and Bangladesh and in other parts of the world subsistence workers continue to toil in order to sustain the lives of their respective communities in many ways. Most of them are marginalized and invisible in the wider society and they have to struggle against the onslaught of the capitalist market economy, the ecological crisis, marginalization, and the trivialization of their crucial contributions.

Identification of common experiences among marginalized and invisible groups in various parts of the world brings about not only better understanding but compassion and solidarity among them and those who choose to journey with them. Thus, the threading of one story into another story with compassion and solidarity creates our common story. It is this common story which inspires and motivates diverse people to come together, to reach out to one another, and to struggle together against life-negating forces in various situations and under different circumstances.

15

FEMINIST PERSPECTIVES ON WORSHIP AND PUBLIC WITNESS

Van Lal Hming Sangi

I would like to draw our attention to the formulation of a women's theological perspective for their liberation. This theological formulation is very useful and challenges women to find and to rediscover the image/symbol of Jesus. That formulation can be called "Jesus as a dancer for women." In various cultures, joy and celebrations of any occasion may be expressed through dance. Even in Scripture, dance is mentioned on many occasions. Likewise, dance is as important now as it was in the past. If we study the Chin people, dancing has played a vital role. The sound of the drum, song, and dance cannot be separated throughout our history.

The most important aspect of dance in Chin society is the equal participation of men and women, which has a powerful liberating dimension. Men and women dance together as the expression of their gratitude to God. This is not only a sign of their gratitude, but also a symbol of their commitment to God. Dancing is regarded as a sign of the spiritual liveliness of the church. However, dance and women are linked together in church life today. It is felt that women are more inclined to dance, as they are more emotional than men and are assumed to be less able to control themselves. Hence, more women have participated in dancing during worship services. However, there is a need to investigate why women participate in dancing.

In order to understand the reality of Chin women, we need to analyze the socioeconomic, political, and religious life of the people first. As there is continuity from the past to the present, we may need to look at the pre-Christian society that has impacted women's condition in society today. One consideration is that "traditions die hard" in our attitude toward women. Let us look at briefly the situation of women in the Chin community.

EXCLUSION OF WOMEN IN DECISION-MAKING IN FAMILY AND SOCIETY

The practice of patriarchy is the root cause of discrimination against women and their exploitation and marginalization in our society. In this male-dominated structure, women are regarded as the "weaker" sex, "inferior," and "subordinate" and debarred from active participation. Traditionally, they were excluded from the decision-making processes in the family and in the village environment. Even after Christianity entered the Chin hill regions, this exclusion continued in the administrative setup of the church, and women were not included in decision-making bodies. As far as woman were concerned Christianity did not bring remarkable changes; rather it re-enforced patriarchal attitudes toward women.

VIOLENCE AGAINST WOMEN

Domestic violence: The objectification of women through the practice of bride price is one of the causes of physical violence, and this might also cause sexual violence among married couples. Physical violence is the most usual form of violence women face in Chin communities. Women have been beaten for giving birth to girls, for not working hard enough, for complaining, and many other things. When women can no longer tolerate their violent husbands, the solution is often to go back to their parents' home. Separation from their children and financial dependence are the most common reasons women give for being unable to leave their alcoholic, abusive husbands. Mostly, women think that it is shameful to be beaten and they try to hide this. Many neighbors and close relatives think that it is better not to intervene as women tend to change their minds after the immediate crisis has passed. Nobody makes reports to the police or court about being beaten, except when they want to file for divorce. When a woman leaves her violent husband and seeks refuge with her parents, and when her husband apologizes and comes to take her back, she is usually pressured to forgive him and go back to him. Currently neither the civil authorities nor the churches provide domestic violence shelters.

Violence against women outside the family: In the past, traditional Chin law treated sexual violence as a serious crime and the penalty was often the same as for murder. Forgiveness, which has been embedded in Chin customs, is further strengthened by Christianity and is now frequently applied in solving rape cases and other acts of physical violence. The current practice places more emphasis on forgiveness and reconciliation between the two families, and peace and harmony in the community, while neglecting justice for the survivor. The exclusion of women from decision-making processes is another barrier for women attempting to access justice. In many cases, women have no power to decide whether to report the assault and seek formal justice or to reconcile in the traditional way. Instead, their male guardians take decisions on their behalf. Moreover, men still dominate the system, so when rape cases are resolved using traditional laws, both the lawmakers and judges are men. Moreover, victim blaming, gossip, and fear of losing face and earning a bad reputation discourage women from reporting rapes and seeking justice.

EXCLUSION OF WOMEN IN THE CHURCH

In traditional religious practice in Chin society, women play a crucial role in cultural ceremonies and festivals and preside over the worship of household gods. Over the course of time, religious functions were gradually restricted to male priests only. Even after the Chin people embraced Christianity, women were not permitted to hold any significant positions in the church. In the early years of Christianity in Mizoram, there were "Bible women,"[1] evangelists, and preachers in the Presbyterian Church. In the Baptist Church women were ordained as elders from early times. As a whole, women are excluded from decision-making bodies or leadership roles in most of the churches even today, except in women's fellowship. However, the participation of women at the grassroots level is well recognized. Although it has been debated at various levels in PCM, the issue of women's ordination has made only slow progress. It is argued that there are no constitutional, biblical, and theological barriers to women's ordination but there is a problem with sociocultural attitudes. The mindset of the members is that ordination should be confined to men folk only. To date we have had only one probationary female pastor in the whole of PCM. The structure and constitution in the church is still patriarchal, with all the associated hierarchical systems. The church has also failed to analyze gender-related issues, which never find a place

---

1   Title given to women laity who taught the bible.

on the church's agenda. As a result, there are imbalances in the church's theological reflection.

This long absence of the female voice has impoverished the churches, intellectually and spiritually. Inherited theologies and traditions have given the church a legitimacy to subjugate women. Undoubtedly, our cultures have also helped to form the myths against women which abide in the church.

Ultimately, these two major factors reinforce the fundamental theology which defines women as inferior to men by divine decree, beginning with the discussion of a theological theme with Scripture, continuing to doctrine, and ending with practical application. Hence, our theological perspective has been one-sided biocentrism, which has resulted in the suppression of women's theological voice. The absence of a specific contribution from women's perspective in theological thinking exposes the prevailing theology as "a dying theology," for it is not nurtured by the life experience of whole of humanity.

CONCLUSION

As noted in the introduction, women express and turn their feelings into dancing in church and in communal singing. "Dance" has become an important theological way to identify oneself with Jesus Christ. This means people dance to express the inner feeling they have for Jesus because women understand from the Bible that Jesus never rejects dancing (Luke 6:23; 15:25). It is estimated that 85 percent of the dancers in the churches today are women. Critical reflections show that it is imperative for women to get involved in dancing because this is the only platform for them to express their inner joy, happiness, and contentment. Beyond this, the church does not give women the chance or the space to share their spiritual insights.

Dance can be regarded as a divine intervention in human affairs, especially to women whose humanity is being denied. God can work through dance to empower women to resist evil forces, to give them hope for liberation, and to encourage them to work to transform the oppressive patriarchal structure of the church and society. "Dance" is a way of transcending the many suppressive social and ecclesial conditions and can empower a person in the struggle for structural transformation.

The experiences of women include their total exclusion from full-time ministry, an exclusion that denies "women's totality of being." This oppression is expressed powerfully through dance that calls for the full liberation of women. As the psalmist rightly sings, "You turned my wailing into dancing" (Ps 30:11). The image of Jesus as a dancer symbolizes the identification of Jesus with the suffering, the oppressed, and marginalized women. This image also symbolizes Jesus as the physical and spiritual healer of human beings from their oppressive situations, especially women. In order to fight against the power in the hands of men, Chin women feel relieved if they dare to dance in front of others.

Romans 12:2 came to my mind: "Do not conform to the pattern of this world, but be transformed by the renewing of your mind. Then you will be able to test and approve what God's will is . . . his good, pleasing and perfect will." This message reminds me to think "out of the box" and with eyes open to see the reality of the situation around us. In patriarchies, men made laws and customs and gave orders, and these laws, customs, and orders dehumanize and violate women's dignity and humanity. The same thing can happen anywhere in different forms. We should not turn a blind eye. We all can be part of the voice for the voiceless, speak for the marginalized and those who are vulnerable to any form of exploitation. We should not conform to the pattern of this world. I believe each one of us can be transformed by renewing our minds.

GUIDELINES FOR DISCUSSION

1. Can the church still claim to stand for a "theology" representing the whole people of God if it excludes women's theological contributions?

2. Empire can be in our family, community, and church. Have we ever asked ourselves, churches, or communities: What empire made them vulnerable?

3. What can we do to prevent vulnerable people being exploited?

4. Will we let exploitation and discrimination happen and ignore it because it's not our problem?

Note: I am indebted to Prof. Dr. Lalnghakthuami, my former professor at Aizawl Theological College, for her book, *Understanding Jesus: Indigenous Women's Perspective,* in preparing this short chapter; to Ninu (Women in Action Group) for their research work, "Women as the Others"; and the Association of Theologically Trained Women of India—Mizoram Branch for the book *Study on Women's Status.*

16

LIVING LIFE AS WITNESS
The "How" of Public Theology

Dhyanchand Carr

There came a point in my life as a teacher of the Bible and biblical theology when I had to do my own thinking on the vision of God as an existential necessity. The opportunities to get involved, from time to time, in the struggles of the Dalit people provided the basic inspiration for a rethinking process.

A PERSONAL STRUGGLE WITH THEODICY

The term "Dalit" is a name chosen by themselves to describe the crushed and trampled-upon nature of their lives as outcastes by religion and culture with indescribable levels of indignity imposed, compounded by physical oppression very similar to the sufferings of the Blacks in the United States subjugated as chattel slaves. The Dalits are learning to break free from the caste system and to struggle for their freedom and dignity. This, for a theologian, threw up the question of theodicy sharply.

- Why did the poor Dalit people suffer indignity, abuse, and physical hardship of indescribable levels if God was the God of the poor?

- How can God allow blatant injustice and cruelty to be justified in the name of God?

- If God was powerful and compassionate with a special leaning toward the oppressed, why did God not intervene to liberate them and give them freedom and restore their dignity?

The oppression of the Dalits is at least three thousand years old. Though this exercise has public theology and theological education in Myanmar as its focus, I am not hesitant to start with a reference to the problem of Dalit liberation since we have already taken note of a number of stories of people's struggles. We have seen the story of Dr. Ambedkar and his significant contribution to the fight against the religiously sanctioned caste system of the Hindu religion. However, I am referring here to the profound influence the Dalit struggles have on anyone given to the traditional theological perspective of God as sovereign Lord in control of history.

The Indian caste system makes nearly a quarter of the population "outcastes." They are deemed untouchable and made to live in the outer reaches of villages, a real apartheid which has existed for three thousand years. Thus ostracized from socializing with the rest of the human community, they are however loaded with a lot of dirty and difficult jobs for a pittance of a wage. Thus, they are kept in a state of abject poverty and always with a complete sense of loss of dignity and self-worth. They are denied entry into the temples as their presence is deemed defiling even of the deity. All this happens in the name of God as God is responsible for everything that happens. There are, of course, other legitimizing reasons offered in the name of God, reasons such as white supremacist claims to enslave African people and oppress them at will, patriarchal oppression against women, and wealth accumulation through the economic system called capitalism. All such legitimizing tendencies using God's name sharpen the question of theodicy—if God is good and powerful and is committed to justice, how could such things happen in human history?

TRUE VISION OF GOD AND LIBERATION FOR ALL

In addition to the question of theodicy, the questions of the legitimacy of the doctrine of election and predestination consciousness which most Christians cherish with relish also need to be questioned. This led to the most commonly accepted theory of atonement, which is that Jesus was put to death by the empire of Rome and the religious leaders with God directing the whole drama so that the death of Jesus could be reckoned as just punishment for the sins of the whole world. For God was bound by the moral necessity of punishing the sinners, that is, the whole of humankind, and God did this by making the sinless Jesus to suffer as a substitute. God satisfied God's self that justice had been done and God became free to forgive those who believed in God's offer of salvation and by this God is just and infinitely compassionate.

The problem is, however, if sinners got away then "the sinned against" found no reprieve. This problem was solved by declaring that sinners (the oppressive slave owners, tyrants, misogynists, racist/casteist supremacists, imperialist marauders, and capitalist exploiters, those involved in the rape of the earth), as well as the sinned against (the victims), were all sinners and equally deserved God's punishment. In other words, the sufferings of the sinned against were in fact also God-ordered, for nothing happens beyond God's sovereignty. If we honestly wrestle with the problem on behalf of the oppressed this will lead us to very different conclusions. First, the almighty God should be seen as having chosen to be self-abdicating and, therefore, becoming vulnerable and suffering together with those who suffered unjustly.

This self-chosen vulnerability was in fact due to God respecting the freedom that God had granted to humans.

The real sinners, however, are those who presume legitimacy through religion and culture and get away with their arrogant atrocities because God has chosen to be nonintrusive out of deference to freedoms granted. Strictly speaking, they could be forgiven and reconciled with God only if they sought forgiveness from those they had been hurting with impunity and got reconciled with them first. But they, like Cain of old and his descendants like Lamech, control religious thinking to make people who are on his side believe that they need no forgiveness because God was on their side. Their mega sins are committed with assumed divine approval and they enjoy divine blessing to prosper in their entire endeavor. But, in fact, they are the ones who need repentance and reconciliation with those whom they hurt with impunity and so with God too. Only then will justice and peace prevail. This can be substantiated by hermeneutically expounding Scripture with care.

There had indeed been other theologians who had, more or less, come to the same conclusion. But why then have their thoughts not caught up with the church? The church's liturgy and theology seem to have undergone little change. Sins are understood only in moralistic terms and corporate sins which are committed with presumed religious and cultural sanctions are rarely recognized as sins. It is this question we should make the church at large face.

As we learned, Bonhoeffer had undergone a profound conversion in a Black church, during his postdoctoral studies at Union Theological Seminary, New York. Rev. Powell had emphatically preached that in the context of racist oppression suffered by the Black community God was a co-sufferer. As a result, Bonhoeffer had come to believe in the theological significance of the "Blackness" of Jesus. The Jesus of the Western theological tradition as a whole was declared as the depiction of a fascist Jesus. It was this conversion that made Bonhoeffer take up the cause of the Jews, seeing them as people of the Black Jesus. The late James Cone wrote on Black theology a few years later and had asserted the theological significance of the Blackness of Jesus and also Jesus as the "first *lynchee.*" This meant that what is envisaged in our statement of a theological position to undergird public witness to God's Just Reign is not new. However, insofar as it is new to most Christians in Asia, "a new vision of God"—the self-abdicating and co-suffering God—is quite an appropriate theme.

We shall therefore venture upon a biblical exegetical journey so that this chapter becomes part of a textbook for public theology. In this theological journey, the emphasis would be on the self-understanding of Jesus Son of Man—the human one and his understanding of his impending death as a death in solidarity with the collective of the oppressed of human history. This indeed would be new to most traditional Christians because Christian theology is traditionally done ignoring Jesus's self-understanding and his understanding of his impending death. Alluding to such neglect, Philip Yancey writes in his *Jesus I Never Knew* that, even as a regular churchgoer, he had not heard much of what Jesus thought and taught. Most Christians, while adoring Jesus as savior, rarely ever give his self-understanding as the Son of Man and his understanding of his impending death any theological relevance. For them, his death was God-ordered as a substitute's death to bear their sins. They never care to check whether that was in fact how Jesus thought of and spoke about the meaning of his death. Of course, he spoke of the bloodshed as the blood of the new covenant for the remission of sins. Any covenant is between two parties. Who were the two parties between whom the new covenant was sealed by the blood of Jesus? Such questions are never asked. One party is the Son of Man, Jesus, and the other party is the victim collective of the oppressed unjustly made to suffer. Even if not all of them are violently killed, almost all of them die a slow death due to the lifelong oppression they had suffered.

Under the traditional understanding, we assume we belong to the elect and are predestined for salvation and therefore have little difficulty in accepting the theological thinking of a sovereign almighty God whose decisions must be accepted even if they seem blatantly arbitrary, unjust, and partial. Without any question, we have also accepted the legal fiction of atonement based on the understanding that God's nature demands retributive justice and unless God's wrath finds satisfaction all are doomed for eternity to suffer in hell. It is strange to note that worship of mammon goes hand in hand with the worship of God in the traditional way. It is so because traditional Christianity, with its emphasis on personal salvation after death, has no qualms in accepting the exploitative and earth-plundering globalized trade as a God-ordered way of economy. They do not find the abuse of Scripture by racial supremacists and male gender supremacists in any way abhorrent.

COUNTERING THE DISTORTED VISION OF GOD IN THE CHURCH

If only Christian believers would learn to look away from the distorted vision of God that makes them ineffective and useless to God and begin to see and know God as God really is they would become real children of God; that is, their sole preoccupation would become peace with justice for the whole of humankind and the restoration and renewal of all creation (Matt 5:9–10). This is what Jesus announced when he began his ministry when he said that the reign of God had drawn near. He also said that the powers of the demonic, whom he called the ruler of the world, were really in control of the world. He even alleged that his own fellow believers, with whom he worshipped every Sabbath, had been deluded into blindness by Satan, which made it impossible for them to recognize that he was the Son of God. Though they worshipped God, the parent God of Jesus, their worship was without true knowledge of God. This was because they had come to believe in the clever lies of the devil (John 8:44–56). Unfortunately, this assessment of Jesus's contemporary religion is not considered by present-day believers as in any way mirroring our own beliefs and practices.

All are agreed, however, that the whole of humankind suffers alienation from God and is also splintered and divided within itself. It is the contention of this chapter that this human predicament should be traced to a false understanding of God. Let us recall that the story of the "fall" in Genesis started with Satan sowing the seeds of doubt as to the good intentions of the prohibition to eat the forbidden fruit.

The roots of the problem of having internalized a false perception of God can be traced metaphorically to the kind of presumptive arrogance of Lamech, Cain's fifth-generation descendant, who mocks the nonretributive nature of God as God winking over the sins of the powerful wicked. Worse still is that within Christianity also this age-old tradition leads to a deliberate ignorance of how Jesus had tried to portray God. We need to learn to envision God as Jesus had portrayed God through his life, teaching, death, and resurrection. Let us recall what Jesus said to Philip. Philip asked Jesus, "Show us the Father"; Jesus replied that those who had seen him have already seen the Father and so was surprised that Philip, who had been with him so long, was to ask him to show the Father. In spite of this assurance by Jesus, Christian theology has chosen to ignore Jesus and put its trust in Paul's explication of the wrath of God and the atoning significance of the death of Jesus as the death of a substitute. If we took seriously the proclamation of God as nonretributive by Jesus, a very different vision of God would emerge. In order to test the truth of this assertion, we should be prepared for a review of the recorded history of the people of God in the first testament and also the history of Christian theology, beginning with the writings of St. Paul the Apostle. In spite of the way we have misunderstood and so continue to misrepresent God, however, God has not abandoned us or given up on us. God is limitlessly gracious and so God keeps alive dimly burning wicks hoping that one day we shall be motivated to funnel them into a conflagration. All our pride needs to be burnt away. Rather than take pride in being saved we need to become people of love and service. Of this, we could be assured without a doubt that God had inspired some dissenters to disagree with prevailing beliefs. Jesus was the most consistent among all the dissenters. We need to get to a point of doing theology paying attention to the teachings of Jesus.

SOME FALSE AFFIRMATIONS ABOUT GOD

We shall take note below of some of the fallacious and partially true affirmations about God:

- "God is all-mighty; sovereign in all that God does and so has unquestionable authority. Without God, nothing happens whether they are devastating earthquakes killing thousands in one stroke or the daily occurrence of road accidents resulting in fatalities and, famines, Droughts or floods." Such an understanding is only partially true. While correctly affirming God's sovereign right, it fails to consider that God delegated responsibility to humankind, whom God created in God's own image, to care for creation. God, out of deference to this covenant with humankind, has chosen not to interfere and meddle with the affairs of humankind. Rather, God has chosen to suffer together with the victims of abuse of the freedom God granted to humankind. It is through such identification and solidarity in suffering that God planned to save the whole world. This is the mystery of the cross.

Let us also take note of the following traditional beliefs:

- "All wars are instigated by God and God takes sides with God's chosen people." This is a near-blasphemous understanding. God's love is inclusive. God's choice of people is not to make them fight wars and indulge in the annihilation of other people, but to be a distinct people functioning as God's priests mediating God's love and justice, working for the liberation of all.

- "God makes rich and God makes poor." This is a gross misreading of 1 Samuel 2:7 attributed to Hannah, the mother of Samuel. This song provided the basis for the Magnificat sung by Mary, the mother of our Lord. The song of Mary looks forward to the day when the lopsided way in which wealth and power are distributed in human structures of economy would be reversed (Luke 1:46–55). Those who arrogate power to themselves and abuse it would be thrown off their seats of power when the Just Reign of God dawns.

- "Illnesses and deformities are caused by God as punishment." Rather, they are the work of the realm of the demonic and that is why Jesus went about driving away demons and demonstrating that he had come to bind up Satan "the strong man" and restore to God the rightful ownership of the world. We now have to understand that this work began in Jesus and has to be continued through faithful discipleship by all who are believers.

- "God is love and also very wrathful; so, he is deemed to favor the pious and punish the impious." If God is nonretributive then there is no room for wrath in God. No doubt God is anguished and deeply hurt by all the wickedness which causes misery to the poor and the vulnerable but God does not go about punishing the wicked. The responsibility to maintain justice is left to humankind. God is prepared to wait until such time as humankind learns to implement justice and, until then, suffers together with the victims of injustice. If this counter statement is true then we need to try to reinterpret the reigning theory of atonement as resulting from the death of Jesus as substitute in the place of sinners who deserve death and condemnation in eternal hell. Most certainly, Jesus's death won a victory over powers of evil and paved the way for reconciliation between God and the alienated humankind. But the death of Jesus was not masterminded by God in order that God's craving for legal justice would be satisfied.

- When significant natural disasters occur, stories of how God specially protected God's favorite believers get popularized.

These are some of the beliefs internalized by us. To our disappointment, the Bible also seems to endorse such views. But the counter statements provided also have equal biblical backing. For example, the Deuteronomist's history of Israel depicts victorious kings, including wicked ones like Solomon, as enjoying God's favor because of their piety, whereas kings who had strayed into the worship of Baal, even if their rule was efficient and people-caring, are dismissed with a bare mention of their long just reign as those who do not deserve notice. So too the teaching of the books of

Wisdom epitomized by the statements of Eliphaz, Bildad, and Zophar, the three comforters of Job, emphasizes that God will always protect and favor the righteous and will never allow the wicked to escape punishment. We should remember that, according to the writer of the book of Job, God reprimanded the three friends as those who had not spoken rightly about God.

Through an unmistakable forethought, God has enabled voices of dissent to arise from within this widely prevalent misunderstanding about the divine must of retribution. They carefully articulate dissent and get implanted into Scripture. They challenge misrepresentations of God. As mentioned above, the book of Job within the collection of Wisdom literature challenges the core views of many of the Wisdom sayings about God never allowing the righteous to suffer and never allowing the wicked to escape punishment. The author of the book of Jonah and the author of the book of Ruth challenge the view that God despised all nations other than Israel. Enticed by the history of God's special favor to Israel in the past, many psalmists raise the question of why God had abandoned them during times of trouble. But as the psalm proceeds with the lament, the psalmist comes to reaffirm faith and trust in God even while God had not yet really intervened to deliver him/them. These psalms are called Psalms of Lament. Even the prophet Jeremiah and prophet Habakkuk indulged in laments which begin with a sense of despair and then come to affirm faith in God. Habakkuk. 3:17 speaks of the prophet making a significant affirmation of faith in Scripture which asserts that even in a situation of total devastation he would continue to put his trust in God. Above all, in a most straightforward and simple way, Jesus understood God as a nonviolent and nonretributive God perfect in love; in other words, inclusive in all respects. Jesus openly declared that the laws and traditions which endorse retribution should be repealed. Such a declaration has far-reaching implications as to how to read the past recorded history of Israel which depicts God as supporting the violent wars and ethnic cleansing activities of Israel and also how we review the Christian history of indulging in anti-Jewish pogroms and in the Crusades against people of Islam as if their vindictive activities were fulfilling God's will.

God loves the unlovable as much as the lovable; the unbeliever as the believer; the poor as also the responsive and caring rich. But we have hemmed God in to be and to relate to only the so-called believers and the so-called made righteous by God. God is understood as one who can resort to violent punishments, one who supports the wars of the deemed righteous, showering the deemed righteous with health, wealth, and success. God is so portrayed by most believers in spite of the incontrovertibly different ways in which Jesus, whom we call Lord, portrayed God. The fact that Jesus emphasized the cost of discipleship and asked would-be disciples to follow him after giving up everything and bearing the cross is a forgotten challenge.

Apart from the contingent facts of human history now and then, the false understanding of God is the root cause of cultures of domination such as racism, the caste system (in India), majoritarian marginalization of the tribal communities of Myanmar, patriarchal subjugation and ill-treatment of women all over the world, and other such social evils. They are described as sanctioned by God and so get overlooked. Black theologians have described such depictions of God as god the racist, god the capitalist, and god the male chauvinist. This god does not exist but it is this god who is ardently worshipped by racists, casteists (in India), capitalists, and male chauvinists who, at the same time, claim to be pious Christians.

No doubt, the distorted portrayal of God by religion also speaks of God as love and passionately just in a most deceptive way. The problem, however, is that those who do not experience God's love because their lives are full of misery (poverty, marginalization, illness, stigma due to their supposed low birth, color, gender, sexual orientation, broken relationships, and denial of opportunities) are dismissed as unworthy of consideration because one way or the other they must have deserved it in God's judgment. So they suffer the just punishment of the Almighty God who knows best. And, if someone were to ask, "Are the deemed righteous really righteous?" Christians would say they belong to the elect and so have been conferred with the status of being righteous, the prosperous Hindus who enjoy the good things of life would say they are enjoying the outcome of merit they earned in their previous life, although in this life they don't seem to be all that good, the Islamists would say the Almighty God knows best and we do not question his righteous judgments even if it means some good persons experience misery for no known reason. By and large, everyone believes in the law of retribution. Either it gets fulfilled by fate and the law of karma (the principle of reward and punishment working out through the cycle of birth and rebirth) as in Hinduism or through election and predestination or through the inscrutable will of the Almighty God. If the wicked seem to prosper, they surely will reap the results in the next life. If the righteous seem to suffer, they are paying back what they deserved in their previous life. For Christians, the righteous who suffer must have done something wrong secretly as contended by the friends of Job. As for the wicked, if they are not punished in their lifetime their children will pay for their sins, as God had said that God would visit the sins of the father until the third and fourth generations. The law of retribution is deeply embedded in the minds of all who have some religious belief.

An imaginatively constructed Jewish prayer in preparation for the Day of Atonement questions how God could allow some just and good people to suffer. And, when such a reality persists, how can God claim to offer forgiveness to erring people? The questioner confronts God with a blunt question, "Do you not, oh God, need to be forgiven for your dereliction of duty of not caring for the good and the righteous before you offer forgiveness to us?" Of course this question shows clearly how wrong it is for us to attribute all contingencies of life to God.

How do we get out of this maze? We shall take up the different aspects of the portrayal of God by Jesus, not just in word but also in the ways in which Jesus indulged in actions of liberation, and was crucified by a conspiracy of the powers of religion and state. Following this, we shall engage ourselves in some theological reflection and see God as God really is. We shall also seek to draw out the implications of such a vision of God. There are not many statements directly speaking about God attributed to Jesus in the Synoptic Gospels. In the fourth gospel, there are clear statements about God by Jesus in which he asserts that all that he does is from what he observes the Father as being involved in. Therefore, we could construct the God-image that provided the basis for the actions of Jesus and his teaching. His teachings sometimes seem to be addressed to individuals ignoring the cultural and corporate dimensions of life as just good ethical advice. But behind such advice also is the perception of a divine portrayal and a vision of a counterculture reflecting the Just Reign of God. Jesus was not just an ethicist; he was by far a theologian most perfect. It is a pity his theology has been ignored by and large.

THE CALL TO ABRAHAM

We begin with the story of God's call to Abraham and the people of Israel, followed by God's call of the church as a body of the Risen Lord Jesus Christ on earth. This we do because not only is Jesus called son of Abraham as much as son of David, but Jesus had a particular perception about Abraham and those who are fit to be called children of Abraham. Christians believe we are children of Abraham. These tie-ups need to be understood in order to understand the God of Abraham as the God of all.

It is a mystery how God who called Abraham to leave behind an oppressive city culture and take to a nomadic life in the land of Canaan, and Isaac and Jacob following his example, eventually came to be known as a God who favors just the people of Israel, endorsing their land grabbing. Israel indulged in destructive wars and genocidal and ethnic cleansing activities in the name of God. They did all this claiming God was their God and not God of all. And, God had promised the whole land of Canaan to them as far back as Abraham.

But as Abraham continued to be a nomad and friendly to the native inhabitants, the promise was to take effect only after they returned from slavery in Egypt. These texts should clearly be read as a projection back after accomplishing the land grabbing. This development stands at variance also with God's call of Abraham saying that in him all the families of the earth would be blessed. It is at variance with God's call from Sinai that the people of Israel, who had been delivered from slavery, would be a nation of the royal priesthood. Their life would be distinctly different in that they would care for the aliens as if they were fellow citizens and their treatment of slaves would be compassionate. Priests were not supposed to own land, particularly as a people who had suffered, being treated badly as aliens in Egypt and who had been made slaves to work without reprieve because they were of foreign origin. Remembering this past they were to be different and distinct, treating slaves compassionately and accepting aliens in their midst as if they were fellow citizens. They failed badly in ignoring this charge of God. And that meant that the God they proclaimed was endorsing violence and favoring just the people of Israel. God, they claimed, forbade marriage with Ammonites and Moabites and had vowed that the Amalekites should be wiped out.

God was patient through the widely varied history of the people of God, perhaps because the tradition they kept still contained seeds of justice and interethnic amity. It is out of this tradition that the messianic hope was born. God kept inspiring prophets who denounced the entire system of sacrifices; who demanded mercy and justice and pleaded for the proper treatment of slaves, allowing them to have the Sabbath rest, the sabbatical freedom for them, the annulment of all loans in the sabbatical year, sabbatical rest for the land, and also the observance of the fiftieth year as the year of Jubilee, when everyone returned to their own property. But the people did not care to observe any of these ethical demands, but were very fastidious about maintaining the elaborate system of sacrifices and tithes. In spite of such intransigence on the part of the chosen people, the long-suffering God kept alive the hope for the Messiah for well over a thousand years, although it was incipiently a skewed hope for a political kingdom for the Jewish people which would acquire imperialist dimensions over all other nations.

This had not been left unchallenged by prophetic voices from time to time. In the meantime, however, God had prepared a remnant to accept and preserve the words of Isaiah and Jeremiah. The minor prophets spoke of the Messiah, yet to come, as one who would establish a new covenant of inward righteousness without the threatening stick of an external law of retribution. True knowledge of God would prevail when the Messiah establishes justice by dispelling all legitimizing logic of culture and politics which made some people rich and powerful but many others poor (Isa 11:1–9). This the Messiah would do by promulgating a new and powerful Word countering all legitimizing logic, which kept the poor poor. Nations would be delivered from the "love for capitalism" as it were.

MESSIANIC HOPE GETS TRANSFORMED

When the time was fulfilled, Jesus was born to the unwed mother Mary and was adopted as the son of David through Joseph. This is how the messianic hope gets transformed. The supremacist claim of the male gender is dismissed in the incarnation by the creating power of the Holy Spirit. David's line was of mixed ethnic origin; thus, the ethnic particularity of Israel got challenged. The greatly admired imperialist Solomon's legacy was ignored and Joseph, the Son of David through Solomon, was a carpenter who trained the Messiah also to be a carpenter. Prior to this long line of descendants that yielded Joseph, a perfect gentleman void of male chauvinism, there had been many tragedies. For during Solomon's reign many suffered unjustly and some were killed because of his paranoid behavior. This suffering seems paralleled by the slaughter of Bethlehem innocents. It means that just as the Son of Man was one in covenant solidarity with the Abel-Hagar community, so also the blood of many from among the Abel-Hagar community got united with the blood of the Son of Man. Thus, atonement was a corporate event. And thus, the supremacist claims of gender, race, and the worship of mammon were put down in the incarnation. This was indeed God's doing. This Jesus was made Lord and Christ on the day of Pentecost.

The messianic community came into being on the day of Pentecost. This community was grafted into the tree of the people of Israel and was given the same vocation of being royal priests for God. In this narrative the real God of inclusive love and justice was fully present. God's ultimate purpose for a new human community of peace with justice was there for everyone with eyes to see. God wanted the people of Israel and later the Christians integrated into their history to be a peculiar people but not a people with any consciousness of particularity of privilege and election. Rather, God expected that they would be a people who would suffer together with those who suffer and bear witness to the fact that God was a co-sufferer with all those who suffer unjustly (Rom 8:16–17). But God's expectation did not materialize for the people of Israel and later the Christian church developed a consciousness of election and particularity and so became exclusivist in all the ways that the word connotes. Christians wanted to be children of Abraham by imagining that they had replaced the Jewish people. The Christians also became individualistic, forgetting they were members of the body of Christ and stones in a building. As a result, they portrayed God as their God who affirmed their antagonism and hatred toward all other people.

Many thinking people with concern for those who are deprived and marginalized see no meaning in the heavenward look of many Christians who are conscious that they are saved for eternal life and are keen only to add at least a few more to their number. Usually such Christians who control the church come from the affluent middle and upper-middle classes. They simply ignore all the teachings of the Bible about God's bias toward the poor. Jesus's command to make disciples who would follow his teachings has fallen by the wayside. Such is their response to God's saving grace. So, both people with real humanistic sympathies as well as the suffering people wonder whether there was a God who was really benevolent and just to all. This narrative is briefly told in the hope that it will be understood that a true vision of God is intertwined with a distorted vision of God. And thus far only the false vision prevails without, however, stifling altogether the genuine still small voice of the spirit of God.

THE INTERTWINING OF A TRUE VISION OF GOD

The intertwining of a true vision of God with a false understanding of God persists mainly because of human unwillingness to undertake costly discipleship commitments. We assume that God is more interested in pietistic exercises and in getting us to heaven. This makes it difficult to discern the true nature of Christian hope. Jesus came announcing the nearness of the Just Reign of God for the whole of humankind and, therefore, also of all creation as

Isaiah clearly saw the two as inseparably bound with one another (Isa 11:1–9). Jesus was hopeful that he could elicit cooperation among those who were eagerly looking forward to the messianic reign in the task of throwing off the demonic powers and establish God's rule. He knew it was like sending sheep into the midst of a pack of wolves. The world would not welcome the disciples advocating a counterculture and speaking of God taking the side of the poor. There would be vehement opposition. Jesus also knew that humankind is estranged from God and therefore in bondage to the powers of evil. Therefore, reconciliation with God is fundamental to becoming true disciples of Christ. But God being grace was always willing to accept a repentant sinner. There was no need for sacrifice but just the willingness to accept the free offer of God's grace and emulate God's mercy toward all who were in the mode of lament thinking God had abandoned them.

But it is at this point, because of the internalization of a deep sense of guilt arising from an image of God full of wrath seeking appeasement, believers get co-opted by various attempts to appease God and seek to escape death and damnation. So, rather than become mindful of working for God, they are deluded into a belief of being special to God and want to remain in that relationship through piety. It is necessary to get them disentangled from a past heritage of theology, strongly supported by many well-known theologians and reinforced week after week by the church's liturgy and preaching. For this effective countering of well-entrenched spiritual self-seeking, we need to spend time listening to Jesus and understand his command to work for God's Just Reign.

For this task, we would:

- Pay attention to a few straightforward affirmations about God.

- Then move to elicit the God portrayal which undergirds some of Jesus's apparently ethical teachings, and examine sayings which depict how God's reign is to be identified. We would also note the God portrayal in some of the parables.

- Illustrate how the miracles of Jesus also enshrined kingdom values by giving a few examples.

- Then pay attention to the debates Jesus had with contemporary religious leaders.

- Then see the implications of his self-understanding as the human one (the Son of Man) to understand how Jesus interpreted his impending suffering and see if that corresponds to the traditional teaching of the church.

- As we took note of the above, we would, at each stage, draw out the image of God that underlies each aspect of the teaching of Jesus and deduce the implications for our theological task. We would see whether the vision of God that emerges corresponds with the way the church has been portraying God and teaching about God's ultimate purpose.

After this exercise we would attempt to draw out the implications for us and take note of some straightforward affirmations about God in the teachings of Jesus: God is perfect in love. This meant that God's love was inclusive and totally nonretributive. Jesus pronounced the statement about God being perfect in love after declaring that the law of retribution was incompatible with God's nature. God does not resort to any violent punishment even when God gets deeply hurt when the vulnerable and the weak are tyrannized, ravaged by wars, exploited as workers, denigrated as people of low birth, ridiculed for their sexual orientation, marginalized with regard to opportunities, and in many cases totally deprived of basic needs, and all this created by socioeconomic and political forces supported by human culture and religion.

God who is grieved chooses to be co-sufferer and keeps hoping that people who are slaves of demonic forces would repent and turn away from the devil through a realization that God was not with them but on the side of the victims. Jesus said that when the Son of Man was lifted up there would be judgment for the world; that is, the world of religion, culture, and politics ruled by the demonic ruler of the world would be exposed and the demonic ruler would therefore be cast off as all people realizing their folly of following the devil would be drawn to the "Lifted Up Son of Man" (John 12:31–36). This is an ongoing process as the cross of Christ is a "Through Time Event." This is what is meant by understanding God as perfect in love and justice. Such an understanding does not tally with the traditional understanding of Jesus's death on the cross as atonement to appease an angry God.

Jesus said, "Blessed are the pure in heart for they shall see God." These are well-known words of our Lord. But are we sure what he really meant? If we understand seeing and knowing as synonyms in spiritual language, then we should recall that our Lord was anguished over his own religious compatriots for worshiping the parent-God of our Lord without knowing who God really is (John 8:53–56). Instead, they had fallen prey to falsehood cleverly introduced into their religious beliefs and practices which had effectively clouded their vision. They had lost their ability to perceive what God was really like and what were God's purposes in calling them to be a peculiar people carrying out God's tasks in the world. The important lie among many other lies that clouded their vision of God was the lie of God being retributive and so sacrifices and tithes had become more important than justice and mercy.

Let us take note of the blinding factors which had blurred the religious compatriots' vision. These include:

1.   Forgetting that God's love was inclusive they had developed exclusivist attitudes at many levels.

2. Social exclusion of the deemed sinners like tax collectors, commercial sex workers, but with both groups Jesus maintained close friendships. The tax collectors were despised for serving the colonial government of Rome. This was hypocrisy of the worst kind. They knew many sex workers; perhaps, they had enjoyed their company and so a sex worker could walk into the banquet hall of a rich Pharisee without anyone stopping her. She went straight to Jesus, the chief guest, and paid homage to him in the way she knew best. So again their pretense of ostracizing the commercial sex workers was highly hypocritical.

3. Ethnic exclusion of the Samaritan people: If a Jew from Judaea wanted to go to Galilee, they would avoid going through Samaria by crossing Jordan twice unnecessarily rather than risk being "polluted(?)" by passing through Samaria. But Jesus habitually passed through Samaria. Once stopping by Jacob's well, he asked a Samaritan woman, who was despised by her own people for having been divorced several times, for some water to drink. Jesus entered into a theological discussion with her about true worship! And eventually revealed himself to her as the Messiah. Jesus also praised a Samaritan traveler who became "the next of kin" and helped a Jewish man who had been badly hurt by highway robbers and left for dead. But a Jewish priest and a Levite who passed by the stricken man avoided touching him, fearing the touch might pollute them lest he was dead.

4. Gender disparity was rigidly maintained by the Pharisees, whose males were known to have thanked God in public for having not been born as a woman. But Jesus

had a few female disciples who followed him from Galilee and became witnesses to the crucifixion and burial, and to them the risen Lord appeared first and sent word to his disciples to go up to Galilee to meet him (Matt 28:10). The male disciples had to learn of the empty tomb, the vision of angels, and the Lord's command to go to Galilee and meet him from the female disciples. Jesus also allowed women of "ill repute" to show their affection for him in public unabashedly and declared that sinners and commercial sex workers entered the Kingdom before everyone else, simply because in their heart there was a deep sense of repentance and they were accepted by God, whereas the religious were completely confident of their piety and goodness and thus distanced themselves from God.

5. Religiously, the Pharisees were keen to evangelize people of other faiths and get them to become Jews through circumcision. Otherwise, they maintained a distance from even the "God-fearing non-Jews" who came to worship in the synagogues. They were made to be seated separately and avoided all social interactions with them.

6. The physically challenged were deemed as suffering a curse from God due to their sins or the sins of their parents, so they were denied temple entry. But Jesus refuted that argument and went about healing them and asserting they were as much children of Abraham as the Pharisees themselves were. On Palm Sunday, Jesus encouraged the visually impaired and the lame sitting outside to enter the temple along with his entourage and he healed them inside the temple (Matt 21:14–16). Children who were following Jesus shouted

"Hosanna to the Son of David," whereas the religious leaders were enraged. They could not see what the children were able to see.

7. The attitude of the religious elite toward the poor was despicable. While they were keen to give alms in public and gain recognition for themselves, they denied those laws which affirmed the rights of the poor and the needy. For example, they had annulled the law enforcing the cancellation of all loans in the sabbatical year even when a warning existed that anyone of affluence would incur God's disapproval if the loan was denied to the poor. The fifth commandment directs children to take care of their elderly parents, but if someone gave an arbitrarily commuted sum to the temple he would be exempted from this. Jesus made a provision for his mother from the cross and asked the beloved disciple to take care of his mother. He appreciated the two-mite offering of a poor widow as something that exceeded in value, in God's sight, the value of the big offertories of the rich. For the widow's offering was all she had, whereas the rich had a lot more for themselves and gave what they could conveniently spare. It is interesting to observe that just prior to the story of Jesus commenting on the offering of the widow comes a devastating statement about the Pharisees. Some of them indulged in robbing the widows' homes (Mark 12:42f.).

8. The Sabbath healings of Jesus were the most provocative. Breaking Sabbath was considered a terrible sin. Knowing this, Jesus went about healing on the Sabbath when he saw someone with an illness or deformity among those who had come for worship. He claimed

that inasmuch as he saw his Father working to save irrespective of the Sabbath he was just following his example (John 5:17) after he had gone to Bethesda to heal a man who had suffered from semi-paralysis for thirty-eight years. This angered the Pharisees. Then on another Sabbath he healed a man born with sight impairment. He refuted the question of why he had suffered, and whose sin this was due to.

Very interestingly, it was these Sabbath healings he described as works done in sync with God's own work. Then he also said that his disciples too would do greater works; that is, they would be involved in works of redemption. Equating his work with the work of God, and claiming that similar and greater works of liberation rendering a different meaning to Sabbath would be done by his disciples, enraged the religious leaders even more. So, they started plotting to kill him (Mark 3:1–6). Once again, their reaction was supposedly on behalf of God, of whom their understanding differed totally from that of Jesus.

In short, the religion of the Pharisees mirrors contemporary conservative Christians. Even as it was rigorous, it was woefully on a wrong track, for they lacked the understanding that God's love was inclusive and God did not care for ritual and sacrifice but for justice and mercy. God accepted all, even those deemed as polluted and sinful. Jesus exposed the Pharisees' lack of understanding and challenged them which only earned their wrath even more.

THE PARABLES PORTRAYING GOD

There are parables which specifically speak about God, for example, the parable of the owner of the vineyard. He gives equal wages to all workers, even to those employed at the last hour of the day of work. God's principle is "to each according to need and to no one according to merit." The parable of the last judgment speaks of God's self-identification with those who suffer. The parable of the talents speaks about God in an ironic manner. The man who was given one talent protests and refuses to participate in the capitalist way of making money through usury as the one who is fit for God's Kingdom. Courageously he challenged the master, saying that he was a hard-hearted man. God is not like this wealthy master. It is not a parable to teach that we should diligently use our God-given abilities. The very word "talent" has gained currency because of the wrong understanding of the parable. So also, contrary to common belief prompted by Luke's preface to the parable of the unjust judge and the unrelenting widow, the meaning is not that we should pester God to receive what we need desperately. God is the opposite of the unjust judge who would answer speedily. This is what Jesus taught about prayer based on his understanding of God. For God is neither like the reluctant friend nor like the unjust judge. God is the opposite of both. The tax collector knew God better than the pious Pharisee.

THE SUBVERSIVE ELEMENTS IN THE MIRACLES OF JESUS

We have already referred to the Sabbath healings in the section on Pharisees. Now let us see those miracles which were signs of the counterculture to emerge in the Just Reign of God. For example, the very first miracle that was performed was changing water into wine when the hosts of the wedding in Cana ran short of wine. In all probability, the friends of Jesus who also attended the wedding were far too many, for which the hosts were unprepared. That is probably why the mother of the Lord takes the initiative to ask her son to do something. This is not stated openly. But Jesus understood that and made up for the shortage far more abundantly, in both quantity and quality. How does this become a sign of the counterculture that would emerge when the Just Reign of God dawns? The good quality wine was kept to the last, after all the VIPs had already feasted and drunk and the least were yet to be fed. It demonstrates that God reserves the best for the least, those who had thus far been made to wait and were expected to be satisfied with the second-best wine reserved for them. Thus, the miracle at Cana becomes the sign that God's reign was breaking in.

Similarly, the feeding of the five thousand is a sign of the Kingdom when no one would suffer want because of the selfish habit of hoarding. It was not a miracle of multiplying the five loaves and two fishes. Challenged by the example of the little lad who was ready to share what he had, all those who had kept their food packets safe, waiting for the meeting to be over at which time they could consume them privately, also came forward to give up their food parcels to be shared and so there was a great deal left over. If it was an action of simply multiplying there would have been enough for all. Where did the leftovers come from? There is no question of whether Jesus could or could not have multiplied the five loaves and two fishes. If he could convert the six jars of water into wine, multiplying the loaves would not have been impossible for him.

But a miracle of breaking down selfishness and the instinct of hoarding out of a sense of insecurity most certainly is a greater miracle and a real sign of the counterculture of God's Just Reign during which there would be just distribution and no one would suffer want. There would also be greater willingness to share with one another and this would pave the way for plenty and not just the bare minimum. There would be just governance and there would be a greater sense of community. The miracles of the healing of the leprosy-stricken and the woman experiencing severe bleeding make void the laws of purity and pollution. The leprosy-stricken man of Mark 1:40–44 was embraced by Jesus before he healed him and Jesus was also angry at the crowd who, in all probability, chided him for daring to come into the midst of "clean people." The woman who suffered from continuous menstrual bleeding was addressed by Jesus as "daughter" and was also praised for her faith, faith which gave her not only confidence in the power of Jesus to heal but also the courage to dare to "pollute" all those who she would brush past in her attempt to gain access to Jesus secretly. The miracles were indeed deeds of power, exhibiting that the reign of evil was getting defeated, and they also pointed forward to a new way of life ahead in the new creation when God will reign.

THE SON OF MAN–SELF-UNDERSTANDING OF JESUS AND ITS IMPLICATIONS FOR UNDERSTANDING GOD

It is well-known that Jesus made a reference to himself as the Son of Man over forty times in the gospels. Only Jesus used this self-designation. Nobody else addressed him that way, except the one occurrence in John 12:34 when from the audience came the question as to whom did Jesus refer as the Son of Man. These sayings are divided into earthly Son-of-Man sayings (just two), the Suffering Son of Man and Glorified Son of Man, depending on the nature of the saying.

THE EARTHLY SON OF MAN

In contrast to John the Baptist, the ascetic, the Son of Man came eating and drinking. He said that the Son of Man has nowhere to lay his head when foxes had their holes and birds had their nests. This, in all probability, was a reference to his choosing to be a homeless person, living by accepting hospitality from anyone, and particularly choosing Peter's home in Capernaum as his base, as well as for his enjoyment of hospitality offered to him by the so-called sinners. When he sent his disciples on mission, he expected them to emulate this example. In all probability this self-chosen lifestyle was to indicate the relationships that should prevail in the forthcoming reign of God. Those who had left their homes for the sake of God's reign could count upon hundreds of homes receiving them gladly. It also spoke of Jesus's total dependence on God. Not by bread alone but by every word that proceeded from God.

Jesus had said that in the matter of giving and taking we had to give freely and also receive freely. This means that the giving and taking had to be without reciprocal obligations. The giving had to be to the needy and offers of hospitality should not be merely made among equals who would return the invitation. Such a lifestyle of receiving and giving reflects God's unidirectional giving, with no expectations from the recipient. If everyone who received also gave freely to those in need the cycle of reciprocity among equals and the cycle of mandatory mutual obligation would be broken. For such reciprocity drew a narrow circle around people of same status. People of equal status relating to one another and giving to anyone holding that person in a sense of obligation defy the nature of God, who always gives freely.

In the book of Job, during the whirlwind speech by God he tells Job to observe how in the animal world all species carried out their duty of bringing forth offspring and taking care of them until the young ones grew up. Once the need for motherly care ceases the grown-up offspring becomes independent. Parents do not expect their offspring to return their obligation. But when their turn comes they bring forth offspring and take care of their young. It is in this way that human life also needs to be ordered. The homelessness of Jesus and his constant seeking to serve the afflicted challenge all of us to emulate a style of giving in a unidirectional manner. Job was disappointed because, in spite of his life of helping people in need and in spite of his offering of sacrifices to God, God did not come to his aid when he needed that desperately. It is to this kind of expectation from Job that God points out the need to give and never expect anything in return. Righteousness has to be practiced for righteousness' sake. It is a hard lesson for anyone to learn, but it is a small mustard seed which would grow into a tree and harbors the birds of the air. Not only is God nonretributive, God is also totally benevolent. That is why God gave God's son when humankind least deserved it.

THE SUFFERING SON OF MAN IS THE GLORIFIED SON OF MAN

Before we delve into an attempt to understand the reason why the Son of Man had to suffer as a divine necessity, we should first understand the reason why Jesus chose to designate himself as the Son of Man. He was, in fact, "seed of the woman" which means God had bypassed the male in God's new creation. Therefore, it is rather strange that Jesus should choose to be known as the Son of Man. This designation was chosen as a result of Jesus's desire to convey the meaning that in him, in full measure, the vision of Daniel that one like a son of man would be honored by God (Dan 7:13, 26–27) was to be fulfilled. This vision referred to the Maccabean struggle against the Greek tyrant Antiochus Epiphanies in the second century BC. Those who had become victorious by resisting the tyrant's attempt to corrupt the Jewish faith and desecrate the temple by getting pigs sacrificed were collectively represented in the vision by one like a son of man, that is, a human being. The struggle was not won by male fighters only but also by the resistance offered by women. The story is told in 2 Maccabees 2:1–7 of a brave widow who encouraged seven of her sons to stand firm even as one after the other were killed for refusing to eat the meat of a sacrificed pig. In the end the mother was also tortured and killed. All of them challenged the king, saying that in the resurrection God would deal with him for what he had done.

This indeed was the first open enunciation of the resurrection hope. The people who resisted the tyrant's attempt to make the Jewish people follow Greek gods and adopt Greek cultural practices are referred to as the people of the Most High (Dan 7:26–27). The Son of Man in this vision is the corporate representative of all those who suffered during the Maccabean struggle. This vision of Daniel seems to have been the basic inspiration for Jesus to take the title Son of Man (the human one) to convey his self-understanding as one who collectively gathers together in himself all those who suffer unjustly in human history but remain faithful to God. So when Jesus said that he must suffer at the hands of the imperial rulers to whom the leaders of religion would hand him over, he considered the meaning as dying together in, and along with, the entire collective of humans who suffer tyranny and injustice in the world.

The suffering together in and along with all the victims of injustice and wickedness in the world is the means of redemption by God. Assured of it, Jesus offers a prayer to the Father that all those involved in his crucifixion be forgiven by God. We need to understand that in this prayer are included the entire metaphoric descendants of Cain. They are responsible for the sufferings of the Abel-Hagar community of victims of injustice in human history. This is no fantasy theological imagination running riot. We remember that Abel forgave his murderer brother Cain (see Heb 12:24) and Hagar forgave her spineless husband Abraham who could not stand up to his jealous wife. They were able to so forgive because God inspired them. Forgiveness should therefore be by the offended toward the offender. Jesus's suffering together with the offended establishes his authority to offer forgiveness to the offenders on behalf of the offended. God is co-sufferer with the offended. This is made explicit in the suffering of Jesus, who takes on his lips the cry of despair of the offended.

God is nonretributive. The victims of injustice emulate the same nonretributive nature in offering forgiveness to their oppressors. Such an understanding has far-reaching implications. The demonic realm which held sway over the religious world had deluded the whole world by a false understanding of just retribution as a moral necessity. This religious tenet is common to all religions. Statistics do not bear out that the righteous never suffer and the wicked never escape punishment. Many righteous do suffer and many a wicked tyrant/oppressor/racial supremacist who subjugated and drained the life of those deemed "lesser" escapes punishment. More importantly, such an understanding of the necessity of retribution has resulted in perverting the vision of God. God was understood as one bound by the moral necessity of retribution and therefore provided God's own Son as the substitute to bear the just punishment. Although such an understanding seemed to speak of the great love God had for the sinner, it did not really portray God as fully just, and the victims had been ignored; only those who inflicted pain were reprieved.

Our understanding described above gives credit to the victims as those who share in the redemptive work of Jesus. Worse still is that the victim collective who had been hurt were also deemed as having sinned as much as the wicked. This false understanding arose because it ignored the fact that there are those who sin and those who are sinned against. Simply saying all have sinned is not fair. It is best to understand the human community as made up of the metaphoric descendants of Cain (taking a cue from the story of Lamech's arrogant confidence that though he had murdered someone God would protect him as God protected Cain his forefather), as well as the metaphoric victim collective of Abel and Hagar. Hebrews 12:24 demands we interpret the cry of Abel's blood as pleading for Cain's forgiveness rather than crying out for vengeance as the cry is compared with the plea of the blood of Christ, which of course pleads for all who need forgiveness.

Similarly, Hagar is depicted in a subtle way as one who had forgiven Abraham as Ishmael their son is at the funeral of Abraham
together with Isaac (Gen 25:8). So, both are taken as representative
figures of the victim sector who are ready to forgive those who
hurt them. Jesus also, therefore, speaks of Abel as the first mar-
tyred prophet and the Letter to the Hebrews refers to him as the
first among the believers whose memory should be cherished.

The theory of vicarious atonement, as we know only too
well, envisages Jesus the Son of God as the substitute who bore the
just punishment deserved by every human person. The just God
is portrayed as one who is keen to forgive the descendants of Cain
and ignores the Abel-Hagar victim collective of human history.
His moral anger is appeased; however, all the hurts and losses suffered by the victims are completely ignored. This difficulty is overcome by saying all have sinned, that is, the sinners who hurt and
maul the powerless as well as the sinned-against powerless. The
real problem is that the word "sin" is understood merely as moral
violation. Terrible sins of oppression of all kinds enjoy social, religious, and cultural sanction and endorsement. But, if we choose
to interpret the crucifixion of Jesus the Son of Man by powers
that be of state and religion—taking the cue from his plea for forgiveness of those responsible for his crucifixion, "Father forgive
them . . ."—a very different understanding emerges. Those who
were responsible for the cross of Jesus were the powers of the state
and religion, as well as a maddened crowd. The maddened crowd
acted as it did out of a fundamentalist and narrow nationalist fervor, as happened in Nazareth when Jesus referred to the widow
of Zarephath and Naaman the Syrian as those who had enjoyed
God's favor. So, when he prays for the forgiveness of those who
crucified him he deals a death blow to the demonic realm based
on the fictional retributive justice.

The moral necessity of retribution to fulfill God's supposed inner moral compulsion to punish sin is shown as a false

imagination about God. The victims, following the plea of the blood of Abel for forgiveness of Cain and accepting their representative the Son of Man pleading for forgiveness of the entire metaphoric descendants of Cain of the world (Heb 12:24f.), seem far more in resonance with the true nature of God who is perfect in love and totally nonretributive. Thus, in the lifting up of the Son of Man on the cross, the world of the slaves of the demonic realm stands exposed and they are delivered from the demonic. This results in the coming together of all people at the cross of Jesus. The ransom is paid. Paradoxically, however, the power of evil which claimed the ransom is broken. The power of true love will always vanquish the power of the demonic realm of evil. Thus, justice as well as limitless grace of the nonretributive and nonviolent God stands vindicated. For God was not responsible for all the violence suffered by the Abel-Hagar collective and the suffering inflicted upon Jesus. It is the metaphoric descendants of Cain who are responsible for the through-time cross of the Son of Man.

The book of Revelation depicts God as riding a white horse wearing blood-soaked garments. The perpetrators are forgiven when they realize their atrocity and wickedness was in fact against the benevolent God. It needs to be pointed out that we do not imply that the oppressed are totally sinless. The definition of "sin" here refers only to the sins of attrition and hurt and not just moral violations which do not necessarily cause hurt or harm to anyone. Of course, moral violations are not to be ignored. Often, through them, those who indulge in them mostly hurt themselves and so they need to be dealt with pastorally. There are, however, sins of emulation of the powerful or they are led into this by the powerful, as, for example, in the case of Tamar, when she was denied the legitimate share of her husband's property and falsely labeled with the untrue stigma that she was barren, which caused her to deceive her father-in-law and indulge in seducing him to wipe out her stigma as well as to claim her rights. She was made to stumble.

So compared to her father-in-law, who tried to cheat her, she is less guilty and more just. The sins of the descendants of Cain are, however, major sins of violence, exploitation, degradation, and the denial of opportunities to millions and thus are responsible for the through-time cross of Jesus. And, like Lamech of old (see Gen 4), they claim that God is on their side even while they commit atrocious crimes against vulnerable people. The world, including a large section of the Christian church, has been culpable in closing its eyes to such false claims of God's protection and abetment.

It is preposterous to assume that anyone could exhaustively understand God. But it is undeniable that we humans have been created with a purpose. We are created in God's image according to the first story of creation and God has breathed God's own spirit into us, making us living persons capable of living in fellowship with God. So, we are enabled to know God's purposes and work with, and for, God. But, instead of seeking to understand the ultimate purpose of God in creating us we have dared to go our own way and, in the process, we have created God in our fallen image. Even then, small embers of goodness continue to simmer within us and so the image of God we have received is still feebly alive. Thus, quite a good portion of our moralistic tradition continues to be partially true. God, therefore, continues to strive with us. God who is totally benevolent works to redeem us from this partial state and make us wholly to reflect God's goodness. Hence, M. M. Thomas, former moderator of the World Council of Churches, declared in a CCA Assembly that "humanization is salvation."

GOD IS NON-INTRUSIVE

True to the covenant of handing over responsibility to humans whom God created with free will, God desists from interfering in human affairs. God also does not want us to obey for fear of punishment. God's hope is that humankind will come to reflect God's goodness in full measure. This means we have to be allowed to make mistakes and grow as a result of making them. But it is very costly and painful to those who belong to the vulnerable sections of humankind, who really are God's partners. They are the lambs in the midst of wolves, desisting from turning themselves into wolves but participating in the cross of Christ. Their vocation seems to be to live in the midst of wolves with the purpose of converting them into lambs. In such a situation God also chooses to be vulnerable and bear the burden along with the victims, all the time enabling them to be a challenge to the powerful and the wicked through a life of service, sacrifice, and forgiveness. This way of understanding would be only adding greater pain and a sense of frustration to the victims of wickedness. Advocacy for nonviolence, especially when it is done by those who do not choose to suffer together with the victims, would certainly be hypocritical. Christ made peace through the cross (Eph 2:11–14). Peacemaking has to be accompanied by an insistence on justice. Such a stance would evoke a violent reaction from those who want *status quo* to continue. This would often result in a compromise settlement which would be to their advantage. It is this kind of compromising justice for peace which is in vogue. But Jesus said he came to destroy that sort of peace, even to the point of dividing family unity. Real peacemaking involves costly sacrifice. For it is difficult to gain the trust of the offended, and will incur the wrath of the oppressor who is challenged to give up unjust ways.

How complex it is to ask victimized people to forgive the victimizers can be seen by a number of examples.

When Archbishop Desmond Tutu announced the Truth and Reconciliation Commission which declared amnesty for those who confessed and sought amnesty, many human rights activists criticized him, saying he was interfering in the operation of international jurisprudence and allowing wicked racist criminals to escape. Proving them right were some individuals who had taken up Bishop Tutu's offer of amnesty and later laughed about their crimes, showing no remorse and happy to be very open about their trickery. So also, the Black Conscious Movement was unhappy with Nelson Mandela when he did not take land from the settlers and redistribute it to the landless native population.

In India, there is a flourishing Dalit liberation movement which has taken the name Dalit Panthers, although they do not indulge in violent liberation action. The leaders of this movement feel that the members of this community, who have endured a multitude of violent atrocities, should develop a consciousness about the need to develop resistance. Otherwise they will be considered to be cowards and would continue to be oppressed. Their fear is not altogether wrong. Atrocities against Dalits are on the increase and most caste Hindus show no sign of remorse for their arrogance.

We need to remember, however, that our Lord asked his disciples to pray "forgive us our trespasses [probably best translated "debts"] even as we forgive those who are indebted to us." There have been significant examples to show the power of forgiving love. The mothers of the nearly seven hundred school children from Soweto in South Africa killed during their demonstration against the imposition of Afrikaans language in 1976 exemplified forgiving love in a unique way. When they heard about the announcement of amnesty, they went and met with the mothers and wives of the soldiers involved in the shooting. Though it was a white regime, the soldiers were native people who obeyed the commands of the white officers and fired the shots. The mothers of the child victims told the mothers and the wives of the soldiers that they had forgiven their actions and invited them to a rally, an invitation to which the deeply touched womenfolk of the soldiers responded positively. They brought along the soldiers with them and there was great rejoicing.

Another example is the story of how John Newton, the slave trader, experienced in a vision the forgiveness offered by the many African slaves who had been killed or treated badly by Newton during the voyages on which he had taken them in order to sell them to the plantations of the Americas. It was this experience in the vision that inspired Newton to compose and sing the hymn "Amazing Grace." Notwithstanding the difficulties, and happy stories being so few and far between, we need to get Christian believers to accept that forgiveness should be sought from the offended first, before approaching God. Jesus said that anyone who was going to offer a gift to God in the temple should first effect reconciliation with anyone who the worshipper might have offended. Only then should they dare to attempt to worship God (Matt 5:23–24).

The implication of the story of Bonhoeffer referred to earlier is relevant for our discussion. Just as the white Bonhoeffer underwent a conversion resulting from his immersion in the Black community of Harlem and started speaking about the Black Jesus, so it is important for all Christians who, one way or the other, show supremacist racial/caste/ethnic arrogance to undergo a similar conversion. They need to give up their fascist ways of envisioning God and Christ. So too in India, those people who advocate the caste system should undergo a conversion to accept that God is the God of the Dalits, a Dalit God in fact. It would be appropriate to examine if there are similar stories of reconciliation and mutual acceptance following a history of hostility and atrocity by the deemed "superior" tribe against another tribe in Myanmar.

In order for this to happen, just as Bonhoeffer set an example, first and foremost all Gandhians should accept the concept of annihilation of caste proposed by Dr. Ambedkar and work together with their Dalit comrades for human equality in India. For Christians this means making a serious effort in changing the liturgy to make it possible for people to worship God the God of all grace and inclusive love, giving up all attempts to get a formal absolution after a routine recital of a formal prayer for forgiveness. All ordained pastors should give up their self-understanding that they have been given authority to declare God's forgiveness without leading people into true repentance and without exhorting the offended to be willing to forgive those who had hurt them in some way.

Accepting the validity of the atonement theory has been most difficult to justify, especially as it demanded that the sinners and the sinned against be treated alike. It was a convenient legal fiction that enabled the oppressors to behave like Cain and his descendant Lamech. The questioning of the theory of election and predestination needs clarification. Anyone who has had the experience of actual involvement and has joined in the struggles of the poor, even in token ways, would find it difficult to place the oppressed on a par with the oppressors and their beneficiaries. If God was not on the side of the oppressed but was on the side of those who indulged in oppression, one had to conclude that there is little use for God's existence.

The problem is that God being on the side of the oppressed is not particularly apparent, for their suffering continues, and changes of heart on the part of the oppressors are rather rare. There are not many John Newtons around. In the penultimate realm of God's plan for the new creation, inasmuch as God chooses to be nonintrusive, we have to think about the self-abdication of God and God becoming co-sufferer. The co-sufferer God is clearly portrayed on the cross of Christ when understood as a time event. And if we accept the revelation to John the divine that the Son of God continues as though slain in God's presence and, according to the fourth gospel the lifting up of the Son of Man is a through-time event as the hour that comes is a continuing reality, God suffering together is demonstrated. It is this line of thinking which led to the reinterpretation of atonement as explained above. The following quote from the late James Cone is relevant for all Christians at all times: "The atonement of Jesus Christ represents God taking the place of the oppressed in history so that they might be given the freedom to create a new future as defined by the liberation struggle in history. Instead of black people having to accept the consequences of white oppression Jesus takes our place and undergoes the depth of the pain of being black in a white racist society and thereby transforms the condition of alienation into the possibility and actuality of reconciliation."[1] These words speak for the liberation of the Dalits in India too and for all oppressed peoples the world over. Cone also correctly asserts that "Reconciliation involves tangible reparations."

I have said very little that is new since what Cone said decades ago. In this chapter, I have tried to provide a biblical undergirding for Cone's conclusion, arriving at it from an attempt to spell out the biblical roots of Dalit theology. My question is, Why have the challenges of Martin Luther King Jr. and the theological articulations of Black theologians not produced any great reformation within the church?

REFLECTIONS AHEAD

Just as there was a call for the workers of the world to unite, we need to issue a call for all those who are oppressed—racially, through caste systems, and through all other sociocultural forms of oppression—to unite. There is, in the secular world, a formation called the World Social Forum which affirms, "Another world is possible."

All united forces of the oppressed should join hands with those who are promoting the World Social Forum. So also, our

---

1   James H. Cone, *Black Theology & Black Power* (Maryknoll, NY: Orbis Books, 1969), 237.

sagging hopes are revived by the exciting emergence of the Ambedkar International Mission, which has started to reach out to the continuing leaders of the civil rights movement in the United States and also to other oppressed people's formations like the Burakumin Liberation Front in Japan. In addition, there are movements for the liberation of Palestine and we should be in solidarity with them. And, most importantly, given that the oppressed Dalits are the largest and longest-suffering oppressed group in the world, attempts by Dalit liberation movements should be supported. There is a need for a carefully planned networking and consolidation of forces against all supremacist claims and their power.[2] The good shepherd, however, leads the lambs into the midst of wolves with the words of caution that lambs never turn into wolves but the wolves should be transformed into the guests of lambs.

---

2   Similarly, the stories of socioculturally oppressed groups in Myanmar must be accounted for evolving public theology in the proper context. This part should be done by the Myanmar participants of the ATEM and theologians.

CONTRIBUTORS

Dr. Dhyanchand Carr is professor of New Testament studies, former Principal of Tamil Nadu Theological Seminary, Madurai and former Executive Secretary of Mission and Evangelism in the Christian Conference of Asia.

Lal Tin Hre (MTh, ThD) is a retired pastor of the Presbyterian Church of Myanmar. He was the principal of Tahan Theological College, Kalaymyo, and has served in the office of Association for Theological Education in Myanmar (ATEM) as an executive secretary since 2009.

Naw Amady Htoo teaches at Yangon Kayin Baptist Bible School in Yangon.

K. M. Y. Khawsiama (BTh, MTh, ThD) is an ordained minister of the Methodist Church, Upper Myanmar. He has served as a synod secretary, district chairman, principal of the Tahan Institute of Theology, principal of Myanmar Theological College, adjunct professor at the Union Theological Seminary, New York City, USA (2020), chairman of the education department of the Myanmar Council of Churches, and committee member of the Oxford Institute for Methodist Theological Studies.

Van Lal Thuam Lian (BTh, BA, MA) is a tutor at the Tahan Institute of Theology, Kalaymyo. He is a PhD candidate at Luther King House, University of Manchester, UK.

Rev. Dr. La Rip Marip (PhD) is an associate professor of Old Testament Studies and the dean of students at the Myanmar Institute of Theology (MIT). He has been teaching Old Testament subjects at MIT since 2001, and was ordained by the Lower Myanmar Kachin Baptist Association in 2009. Recently, Yangon Kachin Baptist Church appointed him as one of the advisors to their church council.

Mar Lar Myint (MTh, ThD) is an assistant professor at Tahan Theological College, teaching the New Testament.

Prof. Dr. Lalrindiki Ralte is a former dean of theological education by extension under the Senate of Serampore College/University, India. She is a member of the teaching faculty at Aizawl Theological College, Mizoram.

Van Lal Hming Sangi (MTh) is a lecturer at Tahan Theological College. She became the first Women's Secretary for Presbyterian Women General Conference since 2016.

Rev. David Selvaraj is chairperson of the Anawim Satsang, a network of grassroots community churches. He has served the Church of South India as the founder director of the diaconal ministry and the first national coordinator of HEKS (the relief and development arm of the Swiss Protestant Church) in India.

Ram Lian Thang (BTh, MDiv) is vice-principal and academic dean at Northern Shan State Union Christian College, Lashio.

Min Thang (BTh, BD, MTh) is a research fellow at Chiang Mai University.